OHIO

Cincinnati

CHEAT MT.

Cranberry
Glades
White Sulphur
Springs

W. VA.

KENTUCKY

Ohio

Kanawha

Cheat

ALLEGHENY

SHENANDOAH

BLUE RIDGE

Richmond

Lexington

Lynchburg

VIRGINIA

Raleigh

NORTH CAROLINA

MT. ROGERS

ROAN MT.

Knoxville

Asheville

Gatlinburg

CLINGMANS
DOME

Cumberland

TENNESSEE

Chattanooga

SPRINGER MT.

Tennessee

Atlanta

GEORGIA

Birmingham

ALABAMA

FLORIDA

S.C.

VA.

Holston

TENNESSEE

Knoxville

Great Smoky
Mts. Nat'l
Park
Clingmans Dome
Cades Cove

French   Broad

Mt. Guyot

Mt.
LeConte

NEWFOUND GAP

COWEE
MTS.

UNICOI
MTS.

SNOWBIRD
MTS.

NANTAHALA MTS.

Brasstown Bald

GA.

UNAKA MTS.

Grandfather
Mt.

Roan
Mt.

BLACK MTS.

MT.
MITCHELL

Asheville

N.C.

Richland
Balsam

Black
Mt.

S.C.

0   25   50
STATUTE MILES

N

Southern
Appalachian
Mountains

.... The
Appalachian Trail

.——— BLUE RIDGE PARKWAY

0   50   100   200
STATUTE MILES

THE
APPALACHIANS

THE APPA

The Naturalist's America

‌ACHIANS

BY MAURICE BROOKS

Illustrated with drawings by Lois and
Louis Darling and with photographs

HOUGHTON MIFFLIN COMPANY
BOSTON · *The Riverside Press, Cambridge*

Endpaper map by Samuel H. Bryant

Third Printing R

For Ruth and Fred

Editors' Preface

WE PRESENT HERE the first volume in a new series designed to interest North Americans in the wildlife, plants, and geology of their continent. It is also the purpose of this series, inspired by a similar series in England (*The New Naturalist*), to recapture the inquiring spirit of the old naturalists. In this era of the highly trained biologist there has been a tendency to lose the feeling of wonder and of beauty and to focus, sometimes myopically, on too narrow segments of the natural scene. However, one notes a growing effort to close the gap between science and interpretation, and the doctor of philosophy who writes his papers in the formal clichés of his profession is now finding that he can also express himself gracefully and that it is no disgrace to write well. Few can expect to be Rachel Carsons, but they can try.

The author of this book, Maurice Brooks, was selected for his way with words as well as for his knowledge of the Appalachians. To his friends and students he is, indeed, "Dr. Appalachia." No one knows these mountains more intimately. Although a professor of wildlife management at West Virginia University he is equally knowledgeable about orchids, salamanders, and wood warblers. He is typical of the new breed of all-round naturalists — in other words, an ecologist.

To a European accustomed to the dynamic grandeur of the Alps or to a westerner familiar with the Rockies, the Appalachians may seem unimpressive. However, they are among the oldest mountains on earth, whose parent rocks were first thrust up more than 500 million years ago. During the Paleozoic, when Appalachia was young, its peaks may well have exceeded those of the Alps or the Rockies. Over the ages they have been worn down by weather and erosion to be partially relifted from time to time by the folding of the earth's crust. Thus today we see green mountains, softer in contour than the younger, more rugged ranges. As Henry Sharp the geologist puts it: "The venerable finished beauty of these mountains tells a story beside which that of the Alps is like the raw roughness of a new-quarried block compared to a finished statue."

In Daniel Boone's day the eastern highlands knew the timber wolf, the puma, the eastern bison, and the eastern elk. Two centuries have seen the complete extermination of these lords of the forest with the possible exception of the puma, which is rumored to exist like a ghost in the New Brunswick wilderness. The mountain man was a crack shot, he knew no game laws, and was dead set against "varmints." However, bears still roam the cutover hills, now reclothed in second growth. Beaver dams are again commonplace, and white-tailed deer have actually become abundant, perhaps more so than they were when the red man hunted them; in fact, some of the deer coverts of Pennsylvania and West Virginia are overpopulated. Would that there were a few pumas to cull out the half-starved and runty stock.

Although half the human population of the United States lives but a few hours from the great parkways that thread the Appalachian ridges and the intermountain valleys, only a small percentage has hiked the pathway known as the Appalachian Trail. Marked by white blazes, Appalachian Trail symbols, and rocky cairns, this Olympian trail wanders tortuously through the high country. With a northern anchor on the bleak summit of Mount Katahdin in Maine, not far from the Canadian border, it winds for about 2040 miles to its terminus

on Springer Mountain in Georgia. To climb the high peaks
and dip into the well-farmed valleys is a lesson in vertical distribution, a forceful sermon on the relation of living things
to altitude.

For the well-traveled naturalist the Appalachians hold many
unique facets of interest. To single out three: abundant variety
of deciduous trees, great diversity of salamanders, and the gay
galaxy of wood warblers.

Few places in the world boast a richer, more varied deciduous
forest than that which clothes the southern Appalachians. The
number of native trees in Great Smoky Mountains National
Park alone is greater than that of all Europe. Europe lists 85
native species; the Smokies about 130.

What are the facts behind these figures? Most of our trees and
shrubs assumed their present form some millions of years ago
when the Arctic was warmer and the continents were joined in
the far North. The modern forest which was then evolving was
circumpolar; some plants pushed their domain from Eurasia to
North America, and others, of American origin, pioneered in
the other direction. It was a time of great mingling. The
Arctic was near the center of this circumpolar forest. Then
came a great change in climate. Slowly the "Big Ice" spread out
from the pole; ice thousands of feet thick blotted out the center
of the great forest. Some species of trees certainly disappeared,
others "migrated" southward. The mountain ranges of Europe
— the Alps, Pyrenees, and Carpathians — extending from east
to west, formed impassable walls that blocked retreat. We cannot even guess how many species of European trees perished.
Europe again has a green mantle of trees, but today it is made
up of relatively few species if one does not include the numerous exotics so widely planted.

On the other hand, the North American mountain ranges
extend from north to south; there were no latitudinal walls to
block retreat. Many tree species survived the Ice Age in the

great reservoir of plant life which had its center in the south-eastern part of the continent. When the long period of cold came to an end, some of the hardier trees spread northward again by way of the lowlands. Others withdrew to the cool summits; that is why there are "Canadian" trees such as the red spruce in the Carolinas.

Curiously, a botanist from Appalachia would feel quite at home in parts of China or Japan, 8000 or 9000 miles away. He would find not only trees similar to those at home, but also such "American" spring flowers as Jack-in-the-pulpit, skunk cabbage, mandrake, trailing arbutus, trilliums, Dutchman's breeches, dwarf ginseng, and many others — flowers whose distribution was probably once continuous throughout the circumpolar forest.

The eastern highlands are also the headquarters of North America's newts and salamanders. In the Smokies alone there are about thirty species of salamanders, far more than exist in any other area in the world. Here it was that the plethodont salamanders had their origin, the only family of vertebrates to arise in these ancient hills.

Not to be ignored are the mountain people themselves, descendants of Scotch-Irish or English Presbyterians who long ago found in these unsettled hills the fulfillment of their long-ing for complete freedom — true isolation. But radio, television, the motor car and the tourist, not to mention programs for "depressed areas," are rapidly changing the hill people. Soon their Elizabethan dialect will fade away, but their ballads will be perpetuated by scholars and musicians, as well as by the fake hillbillies of radio and television. The old log cabins, split-rail fences, mills, and other evidences of this fading bit of Americana are still preserved in two of the national parks of the Southern Highlands — Shenandoah and Great Smoky Mountains.

But let Maurice Brooks tell about these things. The exquisite chapter headings are by the Darlings. We defy you to decide who did which drawing, Lois or Louis Darling, so completely compatible is their artistic technique.

ROGER TORY PETERSON
JOHN A. LIVINGSTON

Contents

List of Plates

THE
APPALACHIANS

1. It All Ties Together

DOWN EAST near the tip of Quebec's Gaspé Peninsula the Appalachian Mountains have their continental beginning. Northward and eastward there are isolated peaks that stand as islands in the Gulf of St. Lawrence, and along the western coast of Newfoundland there are low ridges that are part of the Appalachian system. These crests and folds have gone to sea; the Gaspesian highlands, bearing the Indian name of Shickshocks, are firmly anchored to North America.

Nowhere else in the Appalachian system are sea and mountain so closely joined. Along the north shore of the Gaspé, escarpments rise directly from the tidal basin of the St. Lawrence River, in many places with not enough room for the Perron Boulevard, which must dip landward and climb the cliffs. The south shore of the peninsula is gentler, with bold grassy headlands and here and there a broad valley. The littoral is not extensive; always the Shickshock peaks stand on the landward horizon.

Long hours of summer daylight and an abundant rainfall clothe coastal plain and headland with rich and verdant vegetation. Grasses seem to be greener than they ever are southward. Toward the sea there are whole fields of blue and white iris. Cliffsides are covered with masses of primroses and purple-flowered butterworts. And almost everywhere in open country the three-toothed cinquefoil, a modest member of the rose tribe, opens its starry white blossoms to the July sun.

As the short summer ends, cinquefoil petals fade and fall, leaving tiny seed capsules above the wine-red basal foliage. Not all these seeds are to remain where they are borne. Down from the Arctic come flocks of snow buntings, true hyperboreans that have nested as far north as land masses reach poleward. These hardy finches, showing more white plumage than does any other North American songbird, feed eagerly on cinquefoil seeds. Large flocks will cover a headland, the rearward members of the group constantly rising and advancing so that there is a rolling progression, a wave effect, in the flock movement. Cinquefoil seed is, apparently, a preferred food. Snow buntings are birds of open places. As they move southward in search of dependable food supplies, they seek beaches and other open lands, particularly where winds are strong enough to leave areas free of, or thinly covered with, snow. On outer beaches along the Atlantic Coast the birds regularly reach New Jersey, and occasionally they go as far as the North Carolina banks. Away from the sea, however, they are irregular or casual in most places at lower latitudes than 40° N. But a few, it seems, do go down the Appalachians.

The Appalachian Mountains have their northern beginning in the Atlantic Time Zone, the sun striking Peak of Dawn at Percé four hours after it has shone on the Tower of London. Trending southwestward, the Appalachians cut a diagonal across Eastern Time, from Maine to Tennessee. They reach their southern terminus in Georgia and Alabama, having crossed into the Central Time Zone. As the jets would fly, it is about 1600 miles from Gaspé Point to northern Alabama, but any road that one might follow along mountain crests would be half again as long. In latitude the scope is almost exactly 15 degrees, one-sixth the distance from the Equator to the North Pole.

In the Southern Highlands, Appalachian peaks reach skyward to five- and six-thousand-foot elevations. Throughout a good many miles of boundary, one or another high ridge separates North Carolina and Tennessee. Squarely astride this boundary is Roan Mountain, whose complex crest is made up of knobs, the highest being 6313 feet above the sea. Near the summit, and in some of the saddles between crests, are a number of "balds," grassy areas in an otherwise unbroken forest.

Not far from Roan Mountain is Elizabethton, Tennessee, among whose assets is an active chapter of the Tennessee Ornithological Society. One of its members, Fred W. Behrend, has made a study of the birds wintering on Roan Mountain peaks and balds. Throughout several winters he has found his way to these summits, despite heavy snow, strong winds, and, often, intense cold. On an early visit he found one, then two snow buntings, the first, perhaps, ever recorded from mountainous Tennessee and North Carolina. As might have been expected, the birds being there at all, they had unerringly sought the balds, where drifting snow uncovered the tops of low vegetation. On a few occasions Behrend was able to photograph the birds as they picked at exposed seeds. His first thought was that these snow buntings were strays, possibly carried southward by a winter storm. During the years that followed, however, he found them in succeeding winters, the population at one time building to eleven individuals. When severe winter came, the birds somehow found this tiny southern counterpart of a coastal headland.

Through Behrend's kindness I learned of his observations. I asked that he send me samples of the plants on whose seeds the birds were feeding. Presently the plants came, and I had one of the high moments of my nature experience. The first plant I looked at was a three-toothed cinquefoil, my old friend from the moorlands around Percé village. To reach Roan Mountain's balds, the snow buntings fly over hundreds of miles of forested land, with only here and there an opening suitable to their needs. And in many of these openings, all the way down to Georgia, three-toothed cinquefoil grows, its seed capsules offering winter food when the northern finches arrive.

There are many living things that serve to bind the Appalachians into one mountain system — spruce-fir forests, winter wrens, golden-crowned kinglets, and Canada warblers, to name a few. For me at least, no others emphasize the oneness of the mountains so compellingly as do a white bird and a white flower.

2. The Appalachians—
How They Got That Way

DUSK OF A SEPTEMBER DAY was near as the three of us
— Ruth, my wife, Fred, our son, and I — started down the long
metal stairway of the fire tower. We had been aloft for a good
many hours watching the hawk flight along an Appalachian
ridge. As we paused on the lowest landing for a final look, Fred
said, "These mountains — they look pretty small, don't they?" I
was startled, but I knew what he was thinking. He was just back
from his first western camping trip. His eyes and his mind were
still full of the San Francisco Mountains and the Grand Canyon

country; the Indian civilizations at Acoma and the Hopi mesas; the Front Range of the Rockies in Colorado; and the crests of the Tetons above Jackson Hole. I share his enthusiasm for this western country, and I suppose that he was voicing what I had been subconsciously turning over in my own mind.

And yet I resented the remark, even as I was partially agreeing with it. After all, these were my mountains, familiar country in which I had hiked, camped, and hunted plants and animals. My father and his brothers all were naturalists, and I had followed them along a good many miles of Appalachian trails. Familiarity had not dimmed my appreciation for these eastern mountains. I like a land of deciduous forests — the wealth of tree species, the spring wildflowers that open before leafy crowns shut out their sunlight, and the splendors of autumn foliage. It is unfair, I felt, to try a comparison of eastern and western ranges; each creates its own impressions and sets its own values. My job was not so much to defend the country of my nativity as to explain and interpret it.

So we agreed to take a closer look at the mountains near our home. We wanted to know, as intimately as possible, the uplands from Quebec to Georgia. Northern summits above treeline attracted us; so did the "pink beds" of blooming rhododendrons, azaleas, and mountain laurel in highland North Carolina. We sought closer looks at plants that occur only in the Appalachians — rock ferns, flowering species that grow on shale slopes, bog orchids, and those true mountaineers, the heaths. We planned to follow migration flights of wood warblers along the ridges, and watch the southward tide of hawks in autumn. We hoped to see more of Appalachia's own lowly vertebrates, the lungless salamanders. We knew this as a country of rich and varied forests; we felt we should know more about man's adaptations to life in a forested land.

But first of all we had to know the mountains themselves; their peaks and ridges, with the valleys in between; the gaps and notches through which man has pushed his explorations and his commerce; the mineral wealth of ancient strata, sometimes a blessing, but too often bringing disfigurement to the land. We would need a layman's knowledge of the geologic forces that created and carved these ancient highlands. To the lay mind, geologic time is as incomprehensible as is astronomic distance. Geologists, through refined methods and calculations, are constantly pushing their horizons backward; in dating the beginnings of eastern North America, a few hundred millions of years either way are relatively unimportant. There was the sea, and, somewhere above it, the land. Water is the land's enemy; always the forces of erosion work to tear down and level any upstart mass that rises above the ocean's surface. Products of erosion accumulate below the waters. Gradually they become compressed; sandstone, limestone, and shale — all sedimentary rocks — are created.

The earth's interior is ever restless, more so, no doubt, in ancient times than today. Heat and pressure accumulated; where the earth's crust was flawed a volcano might arise, with vast shakings and disruptions of water and land. Some of the sedimentary rocks would be subjected to great pressure and extreme heat. Under such pressures, rocks metamorphosed, becoming crystalline in structure. Sandstones changed to quartzite, limestones became marble, and shales transformed to schist, slate, and like substances. Where volcanic pressures were most active, there were intrusions of lava, much of it derived from sandstone and destined to become granite.

Long before the Appalachians were formed there were land areas in North America — ancient rocks in the Arctic, the Canadian Shield, and others. Where there is land, there is the possibility of life on land. Doubtless primitive plants appeared early, the lichens and fungi much as we see them today. These plants provided a source of food, so in course of time there were animals to feed upon them. There was life in the sea also.

Throughout the long eons, earth's uneasy crust was alternately rising and subsiding. Above water, it offered a refuge to air-dwelling forms, and to sea creatures that could adapt to fresh-water. When it sank beneath the ocean, some of the land forms were caught within the sediment beds, and had their delicate cells transmuted by mineral deposits into fossils. Living things became inorganic, but left the story of their structure so that man might learn to read it.

Refined methods of aging minerals in Appalachia's meta-morphic rock indicate that many of these formations — at New York's Bear Mountain, and in Virginia's Shenandoah National Park, for instance — were laid down about 1100 million years ago. Living things, no doubt, were there, but the great pres-sures and the heat to which these rocks were subjected destroyed all traces of them; we do not look for fossils in the Blue Ridge, or in other portions of what is called "Old" Appalachia.

In some parts of eastern North America, from Quebec's Gaspé Peninsula south, rock formation was following a different pat-tern. There was little vulcanism, and therefore little evidence of lava flows. Undisturbed by great heat and pressure, sediments that were deposited as a result of erosion were stratified and solidified to form the sedimentary rocks that characterize "New" Appalachia. Not that the Appalachian Mountains in any form that we would recognize today had yet appeared. Before they arose there was the vast sweep of geologic time that we call the Paleozoic.

It is impossible, I think, to discuss the Paleozoic without naming the major periods into which it has been divided. Early studies of these periods were made in Great Britain; the more ancient of them bear names that derive from Roman occupation of western England and Wales: Cambrian, Ordovician, Silurian, Devonian. Then the geologists of the New World began to have their say; the next two periods we call Mississippian and Penn-sylvanian, collectively named the Carboniferous, in tribute to the vast quantities of organic fuels — coal, petroleum, and natural gas — which they produced. Paleozoic time ends with the Permian Period. As we shall see, the Paleozoic and its periods span New Appalachia from the Great Valley westward to America's interior lowlands.

Toward the end of the Paleozoic occurred an event that changed the face of eastern North America — the Appalachian Revolution. What the land masses of our region may have been like before mountain folding we shall probably never know; what they have been since that vast upheaval we can tell with greater certainty, since we have the weathered and eroded evidences all about us.

At this point it might be instructive to apply an astronaut's view and a geologist's understanding to eastern North America. Since we must make a selection and have a point of departure, we shall choose the latitude of Washington, D.C. On this parallel all the major topographic provinces have a certain amplitude: their stories can be read, and they have been studied.

First of all, bordering the Atlantic, we have the coastal plain, indented by saltwater estuaries and crossed by slow-moving tidal rivers that bear the runoff from mountains to westward. This is no part of Appalachia, but it is certainly largely composed of eroded materials that have been swept down from distant highlands. Furthermore, as we shall see, much of the coastal plain plant life is curiously similar to that found on Appalachian summits; apparently the mountains have seeded and planted the lowlands.

At some point west from the Atlantic the coastal plain ends, its limits there being determined by outcrops of very hard and resistant crystalline rock over which the eastward-flowing streams tumble in rapids and low falls. This is the "fall line": traditionally a place for settlements along the Eastern seaboard. Fall line marks the head of navigation; to the population centers built just below it, ocean-going vessels may navigate. Furthermore, the falls and rapids furnish power, first for the grist- and sawmills around which early communities were built, then for the factories which use electricity that dropping water helps generate.

West of the fall line the country changes, becoming rolling, with low ridges and broad valleys. At the latitude we are following, hardwood trees begin to replace the conifers that dominate the coastal plain. Animal life, much of it of southern affiliation, changes too; above fall line there are no water moccasins, no green treefrogs, and (this far north) no chuck-will's-widows to call their name during early-summer nights. We have entered the Piedmont, a region preparatory to the mountains that rise beyond it.

The true Appalachians begin tentatively, with broken and isolated masses of ancient metamorphic rock, followed by low but continuous ridges, such as Maryland's Catoctins. Then, with little that is premonitory, soars the Blue Ridge, a real mountain chain which breaks horizons from Pennsylvania to Georgia. In the southern portion of the Appalachian system, the Blue Ridge is the heart of "Old" Appalachia. All its rocks are enduring, resistant to erosion, and therefore bold and steep. Northward they are largely metamorphic, but farther south there are increasing evidences of volcanic activity, in which quartzite is replaced by granite. Most of the strata were laid down prior to Paleozoic times; only occasionally are there early Cambrian outcrops.

Peaks within a hundred miles of Washington rise to elevations above 4000 feet. There are stands of balsam fir and other northern trees whose centers are hundreds of miles toward Canada. Brown creepers, golden-crowned kinglets, red-breasted nuthatches, juncos, and "northern" warblers nest, and forest floors support painted trilliums, wood oxalis, Canada mayflower, and other blossoms of the North Woods. And all of this is found so close to Atlantic tidewater.

We shall return to the Blue Ridge in later chapters, but now we must look westward to the valley below, here called the Shenandoah (farther north known as the Cumberland, to the southwest named the Tennessee, and all constituting the Appalachian valley, the Great Valley of eastern North America). On the traverse we are making, it is about thirty miles wide, its expanse broken by the lower but spectacular Massanutten Ridge, around which Stonewall Jackson played hide-and-seek with Union armies in the Valley Campaign of the Civil War. So forbidding has the Massanutten Ridge proved that even today only one major highway crosses it.

The Shenandoah, which may stand as typical of the entire Great Valley, is a favored land, with good soil and much gracious living. People who dwell there, it has always seemed to me, have been able to combine the finer things of urban and rural life without losing the distinctive qualities of either. There are wide expanses of cropland and orchards; there are also frequent stands of pine, huge oaks, and other forest trees. Not far from our traverse (and within the Shenandoah Valley) the two only known specimens of that will-o'-the-wisp among birds, Sutton's warbler, were collected.

The westward escarpment that defines the Shenandoah Valley is called North Mountain, and with it we may again take up the course of Paleozoic geology. Old Appalachia is to the east; the Great Valley and the ridges beyond are a part of New Appalachia, where rocks are sedimentary, and where the fossil record of ancient life has been preserved. In parts of the valley, and just westward, there are outcrops that date from the first of Paleozoic periods, the Cambrian. Forces of the Appalachian Revolution brought these strata to the surface, and they, with others of their kind, provide us with much of our earliest evidence of life on this earth. Plants, so far as records show, were primitive — algae for the most part. With animals, however, there are evidences of greater specialization. Among fossils which paleontologists prize are trilobites, curious three-lobed

GEOLOGIC TIME SCALE

ERA	SYSTEM AND PERIOD	SERIES AND EPOCH	SOME DISTINCTIVE FEATURES	YEARS BEFORE PRESENT
CENOZOIC	QUATERNARY	RECENT	Modern man	11 thousand
		PLEISTOCENE	Early man; northern glaciation	½ to 2 million
	TERTIARY	PLIOCENE	Large carnivores	13 ± 1 million
		MIOCENE	First abundant grazing mammals	25 ± 1 million
		OLIGOCENE	Large running mammals	36 ± 2 million
		EOCENE	Many modern types of mammals	58 ± 2 million
		PALEOCENE	First placental mammals	63 ± 2 million
MESOZOIC	CRETACEOUS		First flowering plants; climax of dinosaurs and ammonites, followed by extinction	135 ± 5 million
	JURASSIC		First birds, first mammals; dinosaurs and ammonites abundant	181 ± 5 million
	TRIASSIC		First dinosaurs. Abundant cycads and conifers	230 ± 10 million
PALEOZOIC	PERMIAN		Extinction of many kinds of marine animals, including trilobites. Southern glaciation	280 ± 10 million
	CARBONIFEROUS	PENNSYLVANIAN	Great coal forests, conifers. First reptiles	310 ± 10 million
		MISSISSIPPIAN	Sharks and amphibians abundant. Large and numerous scale trees and seed ferns	345 ± 10 million
	DEVONIAN		First amphibians and ammonites; fishes abundant	405 ± 10 million
	SILURIAN		First terrestrial plants and animals	425 ± 10 million
	ORDOVICIAN		First fishes; invertebrates dominant	500 ± 10 million
	CAMBRIAN		First abundant record of marine life; trilobites dominant	600 ± 50 million
	PRECAMBRIAN		Fossils extremely rare, consisting of primitive aquatic plants. Evidence of glaciation. Oldest dated algae, over 2600 million years; oldest dated meteorites 4500 million years	

creatures of the sea that lived during the dawn-age of the Cambrian.

North Mountain (with its counterparts north and south) marks the beginning of a distinctive Appalachian topographic province, the Ridge and Valley Province. Comparatively low but steeply abrupt ridges are arranged parallel to each other on a northeast-southwest axis. Between these ridges are streams, tributaries of the Potomac River, which form a trellised drainage pattern. Occasionally, owing to some accident of mountain folding, one of these streams cuts through a ridge and leaves a spectacular water gap. Thus are crosspieces applied to bind the trellis together.

The Ridge and Valley Province has outcrops of rock from early Paleozoic times, the more ancient ones eastward, and later formations westward toward the main Allegheny axis. Each series of strata presents records, more or less in orderly progression, of increasingly complex plant and animal life. In Ordovician rocks, next above the Cambrian, are evidences that trilobites attained their climax, and began a decline. Of greater interest to man are the hints of a groping toward vertebrates — fishlike creatures with cartilaginous skeletons and heavy external armor.

In that portion of the Ridge and Valley region lying west from Washington, outcrops that date from the Silurian are among the most prominent of landscape features. There are hundreds of miles of stream valleys defined by steep cliffs, many of these of a resistant Silurian stone called white Medina sandstone (in older literature at least). These will catch the eye of any ornithologist. They certainly provide nesting sites for ravens and vultures; here and there are isolated pairs of peregrines, attempting to survive despite the overenthusiastic attentions of falconers, and almost any bird student will speculate as to the possibility of a golden eagle's nest on some inaccessible portion of these cliffs. If these great birds do find homes anywhere in the eastern United States, they are likely to be on Medina sandstone.

During the Silurian Period, the first air-breathing animals (insects and scorpions) appeared, and it is probable that the dominant fish had lungs, just as do some survivors in the Southern Hemisphere. Corals were abundant. It still occasions a start when one comes upon a well-defined fossil coral reef in some Appalachian valley.

So far as man is concerned, the very long Devonian Period which followed the Silurian is of extraordinary significance. Throughout millions of years there were alternating floods and droughts, accompanied by rise and subsidence of land. This was an ideal period for the multiplication of fish types. It also witnessed the appearance of the first land vertebrates, the sala-manders, which are so varied and occur in such numbers in Appalachia. Plants during the Devonian were also progressing toward higher land forms. Primitive relatives of the ferns, with rootlike structures penetrating the soil, gave promise of the vast forests which would burgeon during Carboniferous periods. Toward the close of this period there were seed plants, some-what like ginkgo trees.

The story of flood and drought may be read from vast deposits of Devonian shales which occur in the Ridge and Valley Prov-ince. Farther along, we shall look more closely at endemic plants that find homes in the shale barrens. Fossil remains below the surface are as challenging, and more abundant, than are living things above it. Separate the thin shaly plates almost anywhere; within a few moments you will find evidence of the myriads of sea creatures that were entrapped before these ridges were elevated and folded.

At the close of the Devonian, the stage was set for creation of the coal beds, so much a feature of the Allegheny Mountains. There were incredibly rich forests of plants that would suggest horsetails, clubmosses, and ferns to a modern plant student. In vast swampy areas peat formed, accumulating faster than it could decay. In course of time this wealth of vegetative material was inundated, compressed, and transformed by various processes to coal, petroleum, and gas — representatives of the three physical states of matter — the "fossil" fuels for human occupancy that was still hundreds of million years below the horizon.

Large-scale formation of fossil fuels took place during the first of the Carboniferous periods, the Mississippian. While there are remnant exposures of Mississippian rocks farther east along the latitude we have been following, they become prominent on top of the main axis of the Allegheny ranges, conveniently close to the secondary continental divide that separates waters flowing eastward to the Atlantic from those reaching the Gulf of Mexico through the Mississippi system.

Just over a hundred miles west from Washington, the Alleghenies rise abruptly one or two thousand feet above the Ridge and Valley Province. This escarpment marks the beginning of a new topographic province. On its higher expanses it recaptures much of the northern atmosphere that occurs on Blue Ridge summits, and it introduces many new plants and animals of boreal distribution. To add further to its biological significance, it shelters surprising numbers of plant and animal endemics. Greatest elevations normally occur along the axis ridge known as Allegheny Backbone, but there are also extensive areas above 4000 feet on such westward ridges as Cheat, Gauley, and Back Allegheny.

Along higher Allegheny crests there is a southward extension of the red spruce forest, so typical of Maine and New Brunswick. Here hermit and Swainson's thrushes nest, red crossbills occur at all seasons, and varying hares, brown in summer and white in winter, reach their farthest southward limits. Visitors will soon come to recognize the loosely cemented sand and coarse gravel, geologically Pottsville conglomerate, which outcrops on many of the higher Allegheny peaks. Another characteristic

Mississippian formation is Greenbrier limestone, holding within its depths many of the caves which we shall be discussing in a later chapter. Some of Appalachia's finest ferns are at home on these limestone ledges.

Between high Allegheny ridges and the prairies of interior America is a region of eroded hills, which are dissected by streams that flow in almost every possible direction and then are finally drawn to the Ohio River. So broken and irregular is the topography that it takes close looking to see this area as a plateau, but actually the hilltops maintain remarkably even elevations. This is the Appalachian Plateau, with outcrops that date from the Pennsylvanian Period to the east and from the Permian to the west, where hills run out and the level lands begin.

Within Pennsylvanian formations are some of the richest coal beds the world holds. The Pittsburgh coal seam has often been called, and with justification, "the world's most valuable mineral deposit." This and other coal seams have profoundly affected the habitance and economy of the region, since the mining of coal is ever an ugly and destructive process. Still, there are forests in the coves, remarkably rich and varied ones, with trees that suggest regions farther north or farther south.

During the Carboniferous Age, ancestral forms of fish and amphibians flourished, and somewhere and somehow there appeared the forerunners of reptiles, birds, and mammals. Seed plants also developed; life on the land began to take on forms we would recognize today. And, climactically, toward the end of the Paleozoic, mountain folding in eastern North America produced the heights which, modified as they have been, constitute today's Appalachians. During the vast ages since the Permian drew a curtain on ancient life forms, the Appalachians have stood, eroded, leveled, faulted, and dissected, but always above the sea, always a haven for air-breathing creatures, and for those which must dwell in freshwater.

It isn't far that we have traveled, from the coastal plain to the

prairies — three hundred miles or so — but we have bridged
space and time from Precambrian ages of no recognizable life
upon earth to the abundant flora and fauna of the Paleozoic's
close. This is the story of a thousand million years, and more.
This is the account, recorded in the rocks and at the surface, of
one of the world's great experiment stations, dealing with
emergence and development of life on land and in freshwater
streams. Best of all, one need not be a geologist or a paleontol-
ogist to appreciate the story; many of its major features are
written so that all may read.

Not all portions of Appalachia show their geology so clearly;
sometimes the topography is more crowded and the account condensed. But in general this is the pattern, from Quebec to
Georgia. The Appalachian Revolution was a Paleozoic phenom-
enon; eastern mountains were formed before the Mesozoic age
of the great reptiles. In our region all the rocks we see, at the
surface or below it, are very old.

For a better understanding of all that Appalachia includes,
there must be mention of its principal mountains. Some, the
low ranges of western Newfoundland and the Shickshocks in
the Gaspé, for instance, have been noted. South of the Shickshocks are Quebec hills that rise above the St. Lawrence plain,
the Notre Dame range attaining respectable heights.

In Maine there is the great monadnock of Katahdin, and
farther west in that state lower Appalachian ridges. New Hampshire's White Mountains are splendid, one of Appalachia's finest
features. The Green Mountains of Vermont extend from
Quebec to Massachusetts, and southward in the latter state they
are named the Berkshires, whose hills enter Connecticut and
eastern New York.

New York's second mountains, the Catskills, are a part of
Appalachia; its most extensive and elevated range, the Adirondacks, are not. These bold peaks, between the Hudson and
the St. Lawrence, are a southward extension of the great

Canadian Shield, most of which is in Canada but which again enters the United States in the highlands just south of Lake Superior. The Appalachians cannot claim the Adirondacks, and so they lose some of the finest of eastern peaks.

South of the Catskills, across northern New Jersey and eastern Pennsylvania, there are many Appalachian ridges, none of them high but making rugged country nevertheless. Scarcely noticeable among other ridges, the great Blue Ridge begins to rise south of Harrisburg, Pennsylvania, and it continues — sometimes as one main axis, sometimes as divided ranges — south to South Carolina, Georgia, and Alabama. In southwestern New York the Alleghenies begin, covering much of western Pennsylvania, western Maryland, eastern Ohio, West Virginia, and Virginia. The Great Smokies (actually a portion of one of the Blue Ridge divisions) lie farther west, and farther still, in eastern Kentucky, southwestern Virginia, and Tennessee, are the irregular masses of the Cumberlands. There are, of course, local divisions of all these ranges, and many of them will be mentioned in the proper context. Here we are concerned only with primary features.

Living things are best studied, and best understood, in the environments which support them. This chapter, a layman's approach to geology and topography, will, I hope, set the stage for forests, birds, heaths, ferns, orchids, salamanders, and other groups that have attained prominent places in the Appalachian landscape.

3. Trails and Parkways

THERE ARE TWO WAYS to look at mountains — from the lowlands below and from the heights themselves. The first has many advantages, of course. It is less taxing, and there is special appeal in a view that lifts our eyes skyward. Even such modest mountains as we find in much of Appalachia can loom large on the horizon.

Those who stay in the lowland, however, can have no real idea of the different world on the summits. On any summer day, many thousands of visitors drive around the foothills of New Hampshire's White Mountains. They move through dense woods, enjoying warmth and sunshine, and at vantage points they will look up, in wonder, to the peaks of the Presidential Range. A few will leave the valley highways and make the drive to Mount Washington's summit. Still fewer will take one of the hiking trails to the heights. These will see the subarctic plants above treeline, will brace themselves against piercing winds, and will not be surprised if snow falls during a July storm. For these lucky few, mountains take on new meanings.

When Ruth, Fred, and I started our planned exploration of Appalachia, we studied the best ways to see these mountains. No person may know all of them — they are too extensive, too numerous, and too diverse. We did have certain advantages. We lived among them, and some of their manifestations were just a step from home. The three of us are campers; and Fred found congenial souls among his friends, so that we often had four or five pairs of eyes with us. But our West Virginia mountains are not like the Appalachians in Quebec, nor yet in Georgia. Somehow we must find a way to sample the ranges and their peaks — not just some of them, but representatives of all of them.

This in essence has been our technique. We drive, as circumstances permit, to some desirable locality. As will be seen, such driving may be rewarding; there are roads to many of the finest of Appalachia's peaks, and the Skyline Drive of Virginia's Shenandoah National Park, together with its great southward extension the Blue Ridge Parkway, is what I consider to be one of America's greatest recreation attractions. At some place along the way, we make headquarters, and from these we do our travel afoot. There are always trails, and along them the hiker has time to pause, and to enjoy. He sets his own goals and his own pace; he can diverge to see an unfamiliar wildflower, to follow an inviting stream, or to search for an endemic salamander that might be under some decaying log just off the pathway. If camp is made early, there are the evening hours, sometimes the best of the day, for walking.

There are always trails — and there are some great ones in Appalachia too inviting to be missed. The Long Trail of the Green Mountains, from Quebec to Massachusetts, is a Vermont feature, enjoyed by hikers numbering in the thousands. There are splendid and challenging trails in the White Mountains; enthusiasts keep detailed maps of them, carefully marking in red those which they have covered. At almost every stop in the Shenandoah National Park and in the Great Smokies there are inviting trails, some to nearby attractions, others perhaps to the summit of Mount Le Conte.

There is one above all others — the Appalachian Trail, which leads without a break from Mount Katahdin, Maine, to Springer Mountain, Georgia, a way of travel through 2050 miles of Appalachia. Its northward beginning is above treeline, and where it can it keeps to the crests, descending only to cross rivers or the valleys which separate mountain masses. The Appalachian Trail has been a major axis for our exploration; we have sampled it in many places, sometimes for an hour but frequently for a day or longer. It is often rugged, sometimes it is obscure; it always is wonderful.

The story of the Appalachian Trail has been many times told; it cannot be told too often. Benton MacKaye, of Shirley, Massachusetts, whose voice is still raised in support of wilderness preservation and recreation planning, was first to propose the Trail, his earliest published expression dating from 1921. Outdoor people were quick to grasp the idea and give it support; a portion in the Bear Mountain region of New York was completed in 1922. The plan had enthusiastic help from New England's Appalachian Mountain Club, the energetic and imaginative Dartmouth Outing Club, and from other hiking groups along its route. People in surprising numbers came to local meetings to hear of the concept, make plans, and carry them to execution. The undertaking seemed tremendous; some of its backers were firm in their faith that the Trail could and would be built.

Early planning for the Trail coincided with a rapid expansion of national forests and national parks in eastern North America.

State park systems were also growing, and Trail planners took full advantage of recreation values in these publicly held lands. When, a few years later, the Civilian Conservation Corps was organized, some thousands of men were put to work in the outdoors, and many took a hand in building the Trail. In 1947, years earlier than many an enthusiast had hoped, the last gap was closed; the Trail was a continuous 2000-mile reality.

The hiker who begins his journey on Katahdin in June will be surrounded by arctic blossoms, the only woody vegetation being prostrate shrubs and willows so dwarfed as to be unrecognizable as trees. If he completes the passage to Georgia in October perhaps, he will end his travels in a bewilderingly rich Appalachian forest, its trees dressed in the full glory of autumnal color. His sojourn will have taken him into fourteen states, and from the Bear Mountain crossing of the Hudson River, the Trail's lowest descent, to the summit of Clingmans Dome, 6642 feet high in the Great Smokies. His longest stay will have been in Virginia; 461 miles of the Trail are within that Commonwealth. He will have passed through eight national forests from New Hampshire to Georgia, and through the Shenandoah and the Great Smoky Mountains National Parks.

In the White Mountains he will face one continuous stretch of almost twenty miles during which he is above treeline, the only possible shelters being the hospitable huts of the Appalachian Mountain Club. Appropriately enough, he will pass through the campus of Dartmouth College, where so much early impetus was given to the Trail. He will use a portion of the older Long Trail in Vermont, and he will come to realize that even thickly populated southern New England has rugged country.

As the hiker progresses southward he will continue to find, on higher peaks at least, many of the plants and animals that were characteristic farther north; but when he descends into the valleys he will note the appearance of a greater variety of living things — rosebay rhododendron, flowering dogwood, redbud among woody plants, and such wood warblers as the hooded, Kentucky, and the yellow-breasted chat. This is genuine transition country; species whose centers of abundance are northward meet and mingle with those from farther south. Each sharp change of elevation is a living lesson in the biotic zonation on mountain slopes.

The changing nature of forests, particularly at high elevations, will be apparent to any observer. On New England heights just below treeline, the forests are predominantly coniferous — spruces and fir toward the summits, pines and hemlock farther downslope. In the Catskills and south across Pennsylvania, deciduous trees cover most ridges and summits; there may be pines, but these are not often dominant. Only at the highest points from Virginia southward into Tennessee do spruces and firs occur; broad-leaved trees in ever-increasing variety compose the forests.

Partly by good luck and also partly by design, the Trail throughout states of the near-South passes through and over a number of the featured attractions of southern Appalachia. The summit of Roan Mountain, at the Tennessee–North Carolina line, is a vast garden of Catawba rhododendron, with hundreds of acres of this free-blooming heath, and the Trail traverses the length of it. Nearby are several of the largest and most characteristic of Appalachian "grass balds," those curious high-country openings which so excite the speculation of ecologists. Farther southward, in the Great Smokies, the Nantahalas, and other ranges, there are more of these balds along the Trail, some of them sheltering their own specialties in the form of endemic races of salamanders.

The unspoiled character of the country through which the Trail passes is made possible through a master stroke in recreation planning, the creation of the Appalachian Parkway. By agreement between the Trail's governing body, the Appalachian Trail Conference, and the national parks and forests through which the Trail passes (some 900 miles of its length are thus covered), an area of one-mile extent on either side of the path is set aside as the Trailway. Along it no paralleling roads are to be constructed. Man's interference with the landscape is to be kept at a minimum. States through which the Trail passes have compacted to leave undisturbed a quarter-mile strip on either side, and many private landowners have voluntarily joined the pact.

What sort of pathway is this that unites our eastern mountain ranges? The answer is, of course, every sort. In some of the national parks and forests, Civilian Conservation Corps workers graded the path, placing stone steps at steep points, building culverts and bridges, and making a forest way along which horseback riders may pass. In other sections the Trail has only been cleared and marked; hikers must find their way over stones and through ravines by the strength of their own bodies. Where long, smooth mountain ridges provide the route, grades are gentle and travel is easy. In country of violently broken terrain (White Mountains notches, for example), there is hard, steep climbing and descent. Of necessity there are stretches (usually short) through open country. There are special difficulties of trail marking here; hikers must watch carefully and pay particular attention to their Trail guidebooks.

For each of five major sections of the Trail there are guidebooks, wonderfully detailed and helpful. These have mileage figures, data on safe water and on food supplies near the Trail, directions for desirable side trips, and the maps to orient the traveler. There are chapters on characteristic wildflowers and trees, geologic formations, first aid, and other such useful matters.

Sleeping accommodations for hikers vary as widely as do Trail conditions. There are the famous White Mountains huts of the Appalachian Mountain Club; there are lodges open only to bona fide members of the Appalachian Trail Conference;

there are Adirondack-type shelters open to all comers on a first-arrival basis; there are long stretches without shelters of any kind. Save in a few concentrated recreation areas, national parks and forests usually offer more in the way of shelter than do sections of pathway through private lands. Experienced hikers, who have learned that the easiest way is usually the best way on a long trip, will own and use the guidebook appropriate to the Trail section along which they are hiking.

Each portion of the Trail has its special character and local features. In the splendidly developed Great Smokies section, for example, at major forkings and intersections there are plastic tablets conspicuously attached to trees. On these one is invited to write messages for companions or friends; one reads that Bill "left for Fontana Dam on Thursday; will meet Carl at Icewater Spring Shelter on Monday, June 6." At some of the shelters there is emergency food — coffee and tea, a few cans of soup, or some dehydrated vegetables. You are invited to use it if you need it; you are also invited to leave any unneeded food for the next fellow. Should you use dry firewood you are asked to chop up a replacement supply. If you find the shelters already fully occupied, you must expect to spread your blankets outside. Hikers are traditionally good-natured and mannerly, and a sheltered spot will usually be found for you; if not, you make the best of things.

Trail traffic affords a living museum of outdoor costumes and packing and camping gear. The cost and the elaborateness of clothing and equipment will tell nothing about the owner's financial and social status; in general, however, the more experienced the hiker, the simpler and more "shaken down" will be his gear. Packs are of every type: knapsacks, Adirondack baskets, bedrolls reminiscent of those carried by Civil War veterans, Yukon packs for heavy loads. Just about everything the trade or man's ingenuity can devise is in use. Trail clothing is a special problem; flies can be pretty fierce, and, especially in the New

England mountains, anything from shorts and halter to red woolens may be appropriate in a single day. The mark of the veteran is to have enough, but not too much.

Maintenance and marking of the Trail is under the direction of a local unit of the Appalachian Trail Conference. On public lands much of the labor may be done by forest and park employees, but on many sections of the Trail this work is done by Club members, persons of energy, enthusiasm, and goodwill. Members of an affiliate of the Trail Conference are notified, by postcard perhaps, that a work session is scheduled at a given time and place. The member is invited to bring his own tools and food, his camping equipment should he wish to spend the night, and to contribute his time and energy to grading, brush removal, cleanup, remarking, and other necessary jobs. The marvel of all this is that the system works; people come, and the jobs get done.

There are special problems for campers and hikers in two of the most popular sections of the Trail — those traversing the Shenandoah and the Great Smoky Mountains National Parks. In national parks nature is not to be disturbed; one does not chop down for firewood the nearest convenient tree, even though the tree be dead. The wildflower lover does not indulge his (or her) passion by picking blossoms, or by digging up plants for beautification of the home garden. Even the rock-picker is discouraged; a few thousand of these with their efficient little hammers could alter the landscape considerably over the years. Firewood is usually provided at marked shelters and camping areas by the National Park Service employees; you can only hope that the last group of campers had good manners, and left some for you. Should a park ranger find you in violation of plainly posted rules, you may have some serious talking to do. Some state parks operate under strict regulations. It is well to know the ground rules at all times. Most important, be careful with fire; you won't like the burn scars you see along the Trail.

I make mention of hazards along the Trail with considerable

hesitancy; it is so easy to blow these up out of proportion. But they do exist, and they must be faced. People who have been indoors all winter are usually not in physical condition to attempt the steeper slopes and trails in Appalachia; take it easy until your body is accustomed to climbing. There are miles of ungraded, rocky trails, and it is easy to slip on these. A heavy person with a broken leg in an out-of-the way area is a problem to everyone.

You will have adequate warning, but until you are experienced you still may not believe it: above treeline in New England every day of the year may have dangerous weather, and it can come with amazing speed. Freezing rain, icy clothes, heavy wind, and dense fog may have to be faced, and climbing over steep rocks under such conditions is no endeavor for an amateur. The last time I was in the White Mountains a hiker who didn't believe this was carried, dead of exposure, off Mount Clay. It was June, and the weather had been warm, too.

Blackflies and mosquitoes pick the days when hiking is hardest — the times when humidity is high, temperatures warmish, and there is no breeze. They are not so troublesome on the heights, but the Trail does go downward along streams, and it must pass by lakes and over swampy areas. All of these can be bad. Just about the time you are settling around your evening campfire, particularly in spruce and balsam forests, the gnats — no-see-ums — take over, and during their shift of duty life may not be beautiful. Farther south there are such things as chiggers and ticks, both spoken of with respect by those who know.

I shall be expected to mention venomous snakes, and so I mention them. In all my hiking along the Appalachian Trail, I have never seen one. Other people have; they exist, and they must be taken into consideration. If I am going on a long hike away from my car, I take one of the light snakebite kits along and read the directions before starting off. If you aspire to become an experienced hiker and camper, you will know of these and other possible dangers in the woods. You will do what you can to protect yourself from them and to ameliorate the discomforts against which there is no protection. Above all, you won't let them keep you out of the woods.

It is not my purpose to recruit members for any of the affiliated outdoor groups that make up the Appalachian Trail Conference. If you are interested, you may secure information on the entire project, or on the portion of it closest to you, by writing the Appalachian Trail Conference, 1916 Sunderland Place, N.W., Washington, D.C. 20036.

Were all persons hikers the chapter might end here, but they are not, and those who travel by other means should still have a chance to savor the Appalachians. They do, and in magnificent fashion too, by way of the Skyline Drive in the Shenandoah National Park and the Blue Ridge Parkway, its southward extension across Virginia and a good portion of mountainous western North Carolina. This is a continuous highway, with brief gaps which are soon to be closed, and when the project is completed, eastern North America will have a scenic drive, more than 500 miles in length, following the crests of Old Appalachia from Shenandoah National Park to Great Smoky Mountains National Park.

On either side of the Blue Ridge there are arterial highways designed to carry the mass migrations of Florida winterers, and to bring north the products of southern gardens and orchards. These are fast, crowded commercial routes, giving no hint of the motoring tranquility afforded by Skyline Drive and the Parkway. One has only to climb until he sees the blue and white signs — each bearing the figure of a mountain to the left and a lone pine tree on the right — which introduce and mark a great recreation area.

The transition from valley highway to scenic parkway is astounding. On the summit road, the way is bordered by trees, flowering shrubs, and wildflowers. No billboards admonish one to drink this or smoke that. There are no trucks, and drivers of passenger cars lose their sense of urgency. Travel pace slows to thirty or forty miles per hour, and there is time to turn out at scenic spots. Air is cool, the road smooth, and the views magnificent. Suddenly, motoring is again recreation.

During earlier decades of this century two eastern national parks, the Shenandoah and the Great Smoky Mountains, came into being. They were separated by almost 500 miles, but the long range of the Blue Ridge came near bridging the gap between them. As national parks developed, so did national forests. Appalachian crests and slopes were of prime importance in watershed protection, in timber production, and as recreation resources for an exploding population. The George Washington, the Jefferson, and the Pisgah National Forests soon occupied most of the mountain land between Shenandoah and the Great Smokies. Park and forest planners began to look with thoughtful eyes at the Blue Ridge and its possibilities.

The master plan first took shape as park engineers carved a 97-mile scenic road along the Blue Ridge crest from Front Royal, Virginia, at the north, almost to Staunton, Virginia, on the south. This highway was like nothing else in the East; it skirted the summits, curving now to the east where it could overlook Piedmont country, then to the west for vistas of the Shenandoah Valley. Commercial traffic was barred; nature was disturbed as little as possible; park regulations protected plants and wildlife; the only developments were under park planning and franchise.

This is the famed Skyline Drive, a highway which set new standards and established recreation as a major objective in road-building. So attractive has it become that the annual visitors number in millions. With its success, a logical question arose: Why stop at the park's southern border, since the Blue Ridge continues southward for many miles? So the Blue Ridge Parkway was planned as an extension of the Skyline Drive; save for three gaps which are rapidly being closed, it is now a continuous mountain road to the east slopes of the Great Smoky Mountains above the Indian village of Cherokee.

Because the Blue Ridge consists of very old, and very hard, rocks, this range's topography is more rugged than are many of the other eastern mountains. Metamorphic and igneous rocks, uplifted in the Appalachian Revolution, are resistant to the erosive forces of wind, water, and ice; slopes remain steep, peaks are sharp, there are many bold cliffs, and where streams have been able to cut through the mountains there are deep and spectacular gaps.

This is well-watered country: waterfalls are frequent, and tumbling trout brooks, sparkling and unpolluted, are a pleasant feature. Trees, both deciduous and conifers, are in great variety, but even more outstanding is the wealth of flowering shrubs — rhododendrons, azaleas, mountain laurel, dogwoods, and many others — which make natural gardens of the slopes and summits. Throughout the growing season, but particularly in spring before forest leaves appear, there are displays of wildflowers, which reach the peak of their abundance, perhaps, in the Great Smokies, where the park's Wildflower Pilgrimage is an annual feature.

From the beginning it has been an important part of planning that the Parkway and its environs should be a living museum of mountain plants and animals, of pioneer living, and of the Appalachian arts and crafts that were so necessary to life in remote mountains. Simply, and quite unobtrusively, these objectives have been reached. So skillful has the planting been along the highway that travelers can scarcely decide where nature has been assisted by man. Occasionally there are pioneer cabins, built of squared logs, roofed with white oak shingles rived from wooden blocks, and with outside fieldstone chimneys. In some of these, weaving is still carried on, much as it was in pioneer lands two hundred years ago.

The Mabry Mill, in southwestern Virginia, is a museum in its own right, an operating water-powered gristmill which still produces buhr-ground cornmeal and buckwheat flour. Nearby is the essential blacksmith shop, where mill parts were fashioned and repaired, and where hardware needs of a mountain community were met. Flumes carry water from three mountain springs to turn the overshot mill wheel. And, for the satisfaction of mankind, there is a nearby restaurant which specializes in corn and buckwheat cakes, accompanied by sugar-cured ham or bacon, the cakes sweetened with maple syrup, mountain honey, or blackberry preserves.

At franchised restaurants and stopping places along the Parkway, native food products and craft articles, many of them made under the supervision of the Southern Highlands Handicraft Guild, are offered for sale. Near Blowing Rock, North Carolina, is a major unit in the guild's marketing and display system, the Parkway Craft Center, where every crafted article must meet high standards of authenticity and workmanship.

There are other living museum features — a display of North Carolina minerals just off the Parkway, marked self-guiding nature trails at many stops, and park ranger naturalists who give scheduled lectures, conduct tours, and are generally helpful to those who would know and appreciate this mountain land. At Boone, North Carolina, just a short distance off the Parkway, is enacted one of the successful historical dramas which have developed in southern states, this one called *Horn in the West.* Another such drama-pageant, the Cherokee Indians' *Unto These Hills,* is given near the Parkway's southwestern terminus.

Short side trips off the Parkway take the motorist to Roan Mountain's summit, where each June there is a rhododendron festival, to a North Carolina state park which includes the summit of Mount Mitchell, highest point east of the Mississippi, and to the famous suspension bridge near the top of Grandfather Mountain, near Linville, North Carolina. In the Craggy Mountains, where there is a Parkway information center, the highway climbs almost to the 6000-foot contour (passing through fine stands of spruce-fir forest) , skirts a curious growth of low trees called *Krummholz* in the Alps but in southern mountain parlance known as an "orchard," and traverses one of the finest of Catawba rhododendron slicks.

Parkway travelers will find a serious lack: there are few places to spend the night, unless one takes a side road. Camping places are fairly adequate, but motorists not equipped for camping will usually have to leave the Parkway. There is one special exception — Doughton Park, just south of the Virginia–North Carolina border. This is an area of broad, sweeping mountain meadows, here and there interspersed with groves of trees. Around these, and clinging to the many rock ledges, are masses of Catawba rhododendron and flame azaleas, both at their best in early June. Well away from the highway is a lodge with standards of fine hotels and with superlative surroundings. A nearby restaurant specializes in native mountain foods and is so mindful of man's happiness and physical well-being that it provides hot biscuits for breakfast.

One of the Parkway's great charms is that the traveler is constantly changing elevation. Particularly in spring this produces interesting successions of blossoming which would never be apparent in lands with more even terrain. In early May one drops into the valleys where dogwood is in flower; a climb of a thousand feet leaves it behind, then a drop again finds it in profusion. Two or three weeks later the aspect is reversed; dogwood will be gone in the valleys but fully open on the heights. There are many flowering trees and shrubs that have extensive altitudinal ranges; these have a prolonged blooming season at different levels, and a curious and interesting lengthening of spring, summer, and autumn is the result.

Rosebay and Catawba rhododendron, mountain laurel, and azaleas all have wide altitudinal tolerances, and they exhibit this extended period of blooming to a remarkable degree. No other showy plant, I think, displays it so fully as does black locust (*Robinia pseudo-acacia*). This native tree grows at all save the very highest elevations. It is usually abundant where it occurs, and habitually produces a heavy bloom of fragrant, white, clustered flowers. In the lower river valleys black locust often opens in April; on the heights it will be fully out in mid-June. Its season may well be seven weeks in length; during this time it will be at its prime somewhere along the way.

The many bold cliffs of the Blue Ridge afford nesting sites for ravens and occasional pairs of peregrine falcons. Ravens are most likely to be seen coursing above the highway, alternately flapping and soaring as they search for animals killed by cars. In early spring it is worth something to watch their courtship flights; they often turn complete somersaults, an aerial maneuver presumably designed to impress a prospective mate. Peregrines are more frequently seen in glimpses, their extraordinary flight soon carrying them out of view.

There always are birds along the Parkway, but spring and fall bring heavy migrations of warblers, thrushes, tanagers, grosbeaks, blue jays, and occasionally hawks. Ruffed grouse and wild turkeys are resident, most frequently to be seen in early morning or late evening. There are black bears and some deer. In places the population of bobcats — bay lynxes — is surprisingly high. These wild cats can be found by the lights of a car as they crouch along the highway. Where mature oaks and hickories grow, there are many gray squirrels. On a few occasions I have seen mass movements of these animals, and I suspect that in few other areas are squirrels sufficiently abundant to appear in heavy migrations, such as are recorded in older literature.

When should you visit the Skyline Drive and the Blue Ridge Parkway? I am sure that you can guess my answer: as often as you can and as long as you can. There are some choices, however, and I shall offer a few suggestions. Most facilities along the Parkway are open from May through October. A few do not open until June; a few close in September. Make inquiry at the information centers along the route. During May and early June, use is comparatively light, and restaurants, lodges, picnic spots, and campsites are uncrowded. This is the season of some of the finest flowering along the way — shadbush, redbud, dogwood, buckeye, viburnums, to mention a few. Late May and June find azaleas and purple rhododendron at their best. I have already mentioned the black locust season. Workers in the park facilities and in the museums, craft centers, and information offices will have time to talk with you, and will be glad to see you.

At this season, also, visitors from the North are likely to make a great discovery, sensed subconsciously at first, then becoming a matter for congratulation and rejoicing. Late May and June are pretty fierce fly months in northern woods. Slowly it will dawn on travelers that along the Skyline Drive and the Parkway blackflies are absent and mosquitoes few and far between. The family may gather around a picnic table, even on a motionless, cloudy day, with no thought of bug "dope." It won't be needed. A walk through the woods does not require feverish application of a repellant, nor does it develop into a swatting contest. This country just doesn't have many biting insects. Take notice that I haven't mentioned gnats; morning and evening they are sometimes troublesome, but usually their shifts are short ones. In the open they won't bother you at all.

After schools are out traffic picks up, and it reaches a peak during the best of the rhododendron season, particularly around Craggy Gardens, on nearby Roan Mountain, and in the Great Smokies. If you expect to use camping sites, try to make it in the middle of the week, and even then plan to stop early, before evening.

July and August are crowded, of course. There still are flowers to see — sourwood with its lily-of-the-valley bells in July and Hercules-club in August — but the season of berries has come also. Red-berried elder matures its glowing, scarlet fruits.

Small red fire cherries are sought by birds. Serviceberry, or shadbush ("sarvice" to the local people) , ripens its edible pomes in midseason.

September is less crowded, and it brings two of the mountains' finest displays. Toward the middle of this month, alderleaved viburnum — hobblebush or wayfarer's bush, call it what you will — is ripening its fruit clusters, and its broad leaves turn soft rosy pink. For many persons this is one of the region's most appealing shows.

The second September highlight is furnished by another viburnum, the wild raisin. Its leaves, too, turn pink or red, but the fruits overshadow them. Flat clusters of berries may include some still greenish white, some bright pink, and others maturing to a deep purple-blue. Every swampy area has these shrubs, and every visitor is likely to marvel at the color harmonies.

October brings the full range of autumnal foliage coloration, here especially rich because of the wide variety of woody plant species, the clear air, and abundant sunshine. During fall weekends traffic on the Parkway is heavy; between times it is much lighter. The last of the season's flowers — asters, goldenrods, gentians, and autumn ladies-tresses — are yet on display, but forest foliage is the prime attraction.

Thus is the long growing season rounded out. It is good at all times, it is superlative at some. Appalachia has poured out her gifts here. The Parkway is a road to dream about — and to dream along. Speed ceases to be an objective and time stands still. There are no clocks; human activity is not bound by schedule. You set your own pace, and you are comforted in knowing that many miles, all good, stretch before you. After a while it seems that there is no end, but when it comes you are privileged to turn about, retrace your way, and see it once again in new aspect and perspective.

4. Gaspesia

FOR MOST OF US, I suppose, the Appalachian Mountains are in the United States, and in the English language. Our books encourage us in this; they take us to New England borders, and stop there, just as though plants and animals were also controlled by artificial boundaries. Neither the mountains nor the living things inhabiting them are so controlled; they cross over into Quebec and become French. In the Gaspé Peninsula, conditions are alpine. Mountains rise abruptly 4000 feet above the Gulf of St. Lawrence, summits are above treeline, and plants and animals have a distinct subarctic character.

I reached the Gaspé's Shickshock range by indirection; the gulf islands with their seafowl were the magnet, but the mountains I had to discover for myself. Like most persons who acquired a bird interest in the early years of this century, I started out with Chester A. Reed's handy pocket guide to eastern land birds. This book did wonders. It had illustrations in color, ranges, and notes on song, nesting, and habitat. It accomplished its purpose, but it couldn't do what I wanted most, which was to learn more about individual birds — where they occurred, what the country was like, particularly in far places, and how, if it ever became possible, I might get there to see them. There were too many unsatisfied longings.

By good luck I got hold of one of the few books of its time that told *about* birds and didn't just describe them, Frank M. Chapman's *Bird Studies with a Camera*. I know the perils of retrospection, but I will say that few, if any, who begin their bird study in this day of rich and varied literature will ever understand the impact that this and others of Chapman's works made on my generation. They were, almost literally, manna in a hungry land. Chapman's purpose was to use the developing techniques of photography as a means of recording bird life histories. This was a new and revolutionary concept in field science. To develop and perfect his methods, he needed birds that were approachable, that had little innate fear of man. Insular populations seemed to be the answer, since many island-dwelling birds are colonial, have relatively few natural predators, and are sometimes so isolated as to have been little disturbed by humans.

Certain rocky islands in the Gulf of St. Lawrence, particularly Bonaventure and Bird Rock, seemed to meet his requirements and to offer large and conspicuous bird populations that could be photographed. So he went to the Gaspé, made headquarters at Percé village, and took photographs of gannets on their ledges, just as some thousands of his followers have done. Chapman's visit was in 1898; he took pictures of nesting ledges at one of the few places where an approach from above is possible. I snapped pictures there in 1930, and again in the 1950's. To all appearances, we photographed the same birds.

My first approach to the Gaspé was anything but a calm and dispassionate one; I had been romanticizing the place for twenty years. I was prepared to be impressed with the gannets and other seafowl. But I wasn't prepared for the beauty of the region, nor for its rich and varied plant and animal life. Blessed is the land whose fulfillment is greater than its promise.

This is scenic country. The Shickshocks rise abruptly from sea level. Lower slopes are covered with a dense stand of low spruces and firs. Treeline is well below the summits; above it are fell-fields, wet moorland much like the western Scottish Highlands. High cliffs break the slopes, and down the steeps come many rushing streams with constant rapids and frequent falls. Along the north shore of the peninsula every height gives a different view of the St. Lawrence, here a majestic sunken river thirty or forty miles across. Basic colors of the landscape are stratified: blue of the river, dark green of the slopes, red of the sandstone cliffs, gray-green of the fell-fields, and often in June lingering snowdrifts on higher peaks.

At the mouth of each stream, or wherever a tiny excuse for a harbor allows, there is a village, its horizon dominated by the spire of its church. These *Canadiens* are a gregarious people; they prefer a communal life, and isolated homesteads are infrequent. Often lacking color in their homesteads, they lavish it on their churches. The pattern of land ownership is an interesting one; tillable lands were once held in common, but when these commons were divided each family received a holding in the form of a narrow strip. Long wooden fences separate these strips, the resulting quadrilateral designs being especially noticeable upriver from the Gaspé.

Beyond Matane there is no railroad around the north shore; all traffic is on the river or along the Perron Boulevard, a scenic highway that constantly drops to river level, then climbs the ridges in this dissected topography. Some grades are very steep; the road cannot avoid them, so it makes its way over them. In the early years of the highway, before guardrails had been placed, driving down these slopes was an experience. The first time I saw a sign warning drivers to descend in *low* gear I thought it was a joke; I soon learned better. There are still sudden drops where the highway has about the same pitch as does many a house roof.

The Gaspé is in the same latitude as Normandy, and, like northern France, it is a well-watered land. Summer days are long in this comparatively high latitude; it is only dusk at ten o'clock in the evening, and I have watched the sun rise from the Gulf at three-fifty in the morning. Plants have many hours of daylight; diurnal animals can be active during most of the twenty-four hours. Climate in summer is very like that of northern France or southern England.

During the remainder of the year, however, climate on the two sides of the Atlantic is a matter of contrast, not comparison. Down between Labrador and Newfoundland, through the Strait of Belle Isle, flows a branch of the Labrador Current. Its cold waters bathe Gaspé Point, the result being short summers, a restricted growing season, and severe maritime-climate winters. On any summer day a shift of the breeze will bring dense fog off the current. There may be a number of alternations between clear skies and heavy clouds in any twenty-four-hour period. Cold water from Labrador, not warm water from the Gulf of Mexico, sets the climatic pattern.

For some reason little understood by climatologists and geologists, the Shickshock Mountains and certain other ranges of northern Appalachia seem to have escaped heavy glaciation. In his extensive studies of Gaspesian plant life, Merritt Lyndon Fernald found striking similarities between floras here in the New World and those in northwestern Europe. He concluded that both areas shared a preglacial vegetation which, through some cause, was not destroyed by advancing ice sheets. Studies by geologists have tended to support Fernald's conclusions.

The botanist interested in arctic and subarctic plants can do about as well on the Gaspé as in Scandinavia or on the Scottish bens. Many species are identical; others are only racially separated. This is true not only of the plants but of animals as well. Most seafowl that nest on the Gaspé are also resident in northern Europe. Both areas have many land birds in common, and mammals show a similar correspondence. Even the butterflies of the two regions are much alike.

The Shickshocks become lower as one travels eastward, until they are only high hills, steep cliffs, and rocky headlands. Gaspé Point, the peninsula's extremity, looks toward Anticosti Island

and Newfoundland, and it offers a biological preview of these two islands. On its shores and moors are plants typical of more boreal lands, some of them not found on higher Shickshock summits. Several species of eyebright (*Euphrasia*) are typical, and this is a southern station for velvet-bells (*Bartsia*), a handsome purple-flowered species which is at home along the coasts of Labrador and Greenland.

Birds breeding in Labrador and northward use Anticosti and Cape Gaspé as steppingstones in migration, much as others make use of Point Pelee and the chain of islands in western Lake Erie. Stanley Ball, who has been privileged to study autumnal migration at the point and on the cape, has observed remarkable flights. One of his observations sticks in my mind. He watched goshawks attacking and killing broad-winged hawks as these buteos were in passage toward Gaspé's mainland.

Many travelers along the peninsula's north shore rush eastward, lured by Percé Rock and Bonaventure with its gannets. These attractions will wait; take time to explore this country too. There are side roads which enter Gaspesia Provincial Park, and some of these make high Shickshock peaks accessible. Common eiders nest on islands in the great river, and flocks of hundreds are often feeding near shore. Every cliff has the possibility of some wildflower gem, or some fern which would be rare in any other portion of its range. Each stream calls for exploration of its banks.

My favorite among Gaspesian plants grows along some of these rushing waters. It is the little Swedish dogwood (*Cornus suecica*), found at a number of stations along the north shore. In form and growth habits it is similar to its close relative dwarf dogwood (or bunchberry), an abundant plant in northern forests across the continent. Like the commoner species, Swedish dogwood opens its flowers between white petal-like floral bracts. Dwarf dogwood has rather inconspicuous greenish-white flowers; in the Swedish species these are deep violet. A massed ground cover of these purple-centered blossoms is one of Gaspesia's finest sights.

On my first trip to the Gaspé I was lucky enough to have the guidance of Lewis M. Terrill, of Montreal. This naturalist is a true amateur of the outdoors, a type the British Commonwealth seems to produce by spontaneous generation. When I wanted to see a particular plant he could lead me to it, or tell me how to find it. He knew where yellow rails were nesting at Corner of the Beach, and which pieces of woodland were likely to have brown-capped boreal chickadees rather than the familiar black-capped species. His ability to find birds' nests was uncanny; he would pass a thousand young spruces or balsams, any one of which looked all right to me, and then say, "This looks like a good place for blackpoll warblers to nest." Often enough, when he shook the sapling out flew a blackpoll. I accused him of having scouted every tree in the area, but he denied it.

Outdoor enthusiasts tend to create cults in their admiration for some particular group of living things. Among plant lovers there is a fern cult, an orchid cult, an alpine plant cult, even a saxifrage cult. Terrill, so far as I could tell, was a thirty-third-degree member of each of these, and what escaped him was found by his wife Betty. They would have traveled far to find a better place than the Gaspé for indulging such enthusiasms.

Huge limestone cliffs tower in many parts of the Gaspé, and each is worth exploring. Where moisture seeps from crevices and plants can find a foothold, there are often beautiful things to see. We enjoyed little bird's-eye primroses, looking like the decoration on an old English china pattern. Their flowers were varicolored and their scent fragrant. Another plant of the crevices is butterwort, a close relative of the aquatic animal-trapping bladderworts. Fleshy leaves, slick to the touch, give this plant its name, and it bears showy purple blossoms that suggest violets without being at all like them. Incidentally, there is a sur-

prising wealth of plants with blue or purple blossoms in the
Gaspé — irises, gentians, and violets, in addition to those already mentioned.

In the proper places I shall have more to say of ferns and
orchids in this particular outpost of the Appalachians. A few
matters must be mentioned here. Some orchids, which farther
south keep to dense woods or shaded bogs, grow in open country,
often in roadside ditches. A prize for fern hunters is moonwort
(*Botrychium lunaria*), often sought after, usually missed. It is
superstition-laden, as are many ferns out of Old England; it is
purported, once it is stepped upon, to pull from horses' hoofs
shoes that are new-set. Fleshy-leaved moonworts grow freely on
many Laurentian headlands; on Mont-Ste-Anne, above Percé
village, there are thousands of these ferns. On a steep cliff of the
same mountain I have found three of the alpine saxifrages, here
"rock breakers" in a literal sense.

Because spring and summer come almost together, blooming
seasons on the Gaspé are telescoped. Plants that farther south
blossom weeks apart open together here in what amounts to a
floral explosion. This effect is particularly noticeable in garden
plantings of perennials, vines, and shrubs. Flowering that
bridges the weeks from March to May in West Virginia occurs
in Gaspesia in one riotous summer period. Lilacs are often at
their best for Dominion Day, or the Fourth of July. With them
will be the flowers of midsummer, all come in unison.

Sooner or later the north shore is behind you, the corner
turned at Gaspé village. This busy small town is appropriately
named and placed; *Gaspé* is a Micmac Indian word meaning
"end of the land." Gaspé Point is only a short distance beyond
the village. The town is on a huge inlet that indents the coast;
in the fine harborage provided, convoys made up during two
world wars for the Great Circle course across the Atlantic. Many
a sailor who had never heard of the Gaspé found himself in
Gaspé Basin. Miles away to the southward, Percé Rock is in

view, but the highway runs around the basin, and there are still a good many miles to travel. Finally, however, you climb a steep headland, pause for the view, then pitch down the Pic-de-l'Aurore, and you are in Percé. All this long way you have been wondering if the place can be as spectacular as you remember it, or as you have been told it is. Never worry; it is even better than you thought.

The philosopher who said that wise travelers go not from place to place but from person to person must have had Percé in mind. So much is here, both to landward and to seaward, that a visitor, no matter how eager and observing, will miss many things that expert guidance would reveal. I have made mention of Lewis Terrill; I must add my thanks to Captain Biard, members of the Bisson family, and especially to Willie Duvall. May I advise you, when you visit Percé, to inquire for members of these families; they are of the aristocracy of Gaspesia.

Bonaventure Island, where the gannet ledges are, in part has been owned by the Duvall family for many generations. An ancestor, Peter Duvall, carried letters of marque as a privateer from King George, and he warred against the French, earning the title of "pirate." A price on his head was never collected, so he and his family were rewarded with Bonaventure.

Willie is a student of local history, a field naturalist, a conservationist, and a gentleman. If he takes you "around the Island" in his stout Nova Scotia-built boat, you will see birds, and learn things about them, which will make the trip even more rewarding than it otherwise is. One of Willie's sons is carrying on the good work. The gannet cliffs, and the sanctuary of which they are a part, are named for Willie; he has — and has a right to — patronymic interest in them.

Captain Biard took us on our first trip around Bonaventure, telling us about local history as we went. His daughter and son-in-law, the Bissons, managed a local hotel; they introduced us to people whom we would not otherwise have met. Willie landed us on the island, and was our guide there. He showed us where the orchids were at their best back in the forest, and where we could hear (and dimly see) the partner exchange of the Leach's petrels as they came in from sea to relieve their mates in the nesting burrows.

Of course I wanted Ruth and Fred also to see the Gaspé, since this portion of Appalachia is much too good to miss. We went in mid-June when the season was lingering briefly between spring and summer, when the fields were clothed in living green of the North Country, and when birds were at the height of their activity. Again Willie Duvall was the guide, and I was happy that Fred could look and listen as he directed us.

We started at South Inlet, working along the flanks of Percé Rock. Of course the herring gulls and double-crested cormorants were in evidence at all times. From close in to the rock we could see guillemots displaying their vivid red feet as they rested on the ledges. Kittiwakes, most appealing of gulls, were on many of the shelves. Out in the channel we began to find other water birds — a red-throated loon in summer plumage, many black-backed gulls, a few brant lingering into June, a surf scoter, and a scattering of the alcids. On crags at the north end of Bonaventure, a few common cormorants were resting, and as we moved nearer we saw a wonderfully colored male harlequin duck standing on a rock.

As we rounded the point to the seaward side of the island, the real ornithological display began. There were the razor-billed auks, murres, and puffins, some resting, some breaking from the water in front of the boat, some flying to and from the cliff. Handsome birds were in movement everywhere we looked. Over all else were the gannets.

When I first visited Bonaventure in 1930, only a single gannet pair was nesting on top of the cliffs; the others were on shelves below. I suppose that these venturesome birds were among the most photographed living things in North America; certainly

I have been looking at pictures of them ever since. By 1950 gannets in hundreds were nesting on the clifftops, and their activities were clearing the soil of grass, herbs, and even low trees. It is conceivable that they may in time take over all open land on the seaward side of the island; I hope, however, that they never destroy the wonderful fields of blue and white iris which greet the visitor as he emerges from the forest. I have one picture that lingers — a mass of close-nesting gannets in constant movement, behind them a rippling border of iris, and in the low balsams just beyond a flock of white-winged crossbills.

Those who desire it may find overnight accommodations on Bonaventure Island. Bird students, if they are properly guided, will find the nesting colony of Leach's petrels toward the north end of the island. Those who make a night visit to the colony are not likely to forget the experience. Save for burrows, which presumably shelter petrel nests and incubating birds, there is no diurnal evidence of life in the chosen area of the petrels. Not until the light has faded will the birds arrive, and twilight is very long in these northern lands.

Finally darkness comes, and with it the first petrels, mothlike in fluttering flight, begin to arrive from their feeding grounds far out to sea. They announce their coming by a variety of notes, some rather harsh, but others soft and musical. If your visit is timed to bright moonlight, you will observe that the arriving birds seem to orient themselves while still in flight. Then they drop to the ground near a burrow entrance, move to an opening which they somehow determine is the proper one, and, with vocal greetings to the other member of the pair, begin the exchange of duties. Members relieved from incubation cares emerge presently from the burrows, move about on land for a few moments, and then, finding some nearby elevated point, launch themselves for the long flight seaward.

Not all the birds in the colony arrive at one time; there is activity almost throughout darkness. Some visitors have noted an increase in movement and vocalization after midnight, others have found the peak during the first hour after full darkness. Petrels are so much creatures of the open ocean that they seem reluctant to come to land. But come they must. Like Antaeus, they must touch the earth to be renewed.

Certain visitors to Gaspesia have objected (I think rightly) that Percé Rock has been so much pictured as to hold a distorted place in the entire composition. It is only a part of the scene: just to landward is Mont-Joli and its cross, towering above is forested Mont-Ste-Anne, and northeastward rise the Three Sisters and the Peak of Dawn. Seaward are Bonaventure Island and the Gulf of St. Lawrence. It would be a real loss to miss any of them.

As with the Percé Rock, so with the birds. The lure of gannets, alcids, and other water birds, all so easily approached and observed, has lessened anticipation of the land birds which nest in field, swamp, forest, and mountain land around Percé. A walk along the forest roads and trails can be very rewarding; the road to the top of Mont-Ste-Anne has particularly rich ornithological possibilities.

I have mentioned one of my special favorites, the white-winged crossbills. After the manner of their kind, these northern finches are common as sparrows one year and unaccountably absent the next. They are always to be found in Gaspesia, but, after all, that is an area of about 9000 square miles. Red crossbills also occur, although they are much less common than their pink and white relatives.

In spruce and balsam forests, boreal chickadees are often more abundant than are the black-capped species. Wood warblers that prefer the North seem exceptionally abundant — blackpolls in the low balsams, baybreasts nearer the coast, Tennessees in shade trees about the villages, yellow palms in sphagnum bogs, and Wilson's in willow and alder thickets. Farther south in the Appalachians, black-throated green warblers sing two common songs; on the Gaspé some individuals have a third song that I have not heard elsewhere in which the next-to-last note is higher than the others.

Just uphill from the Anglican church is an area of small bogs, thickets, open areas, and dense forest. All the spotted-breast thrushes of the region find nesting places here, and the evening chorus of the gray-cheeked species is especially fine.

Six miles or so north of Percé is the village of Corner of the Beach — Coin-du-Banc. Here the railway which skirts the coast is carried across a large marshy area on a trestle. This marsh is a prime place for rails and other wetlands birds, and the trestle affords a good observation and listening post. Of evenings the yellow rails, seemingly abundant here, give their metallic *tic-tic-tic* call. I have aroused them to voice and activity during the day by striking a pebble against a steel rail in the same rhythmic pattern.

Most of Gaspesia is forested, the low spruces and balsams predominating, and willows, aspens, and birches finding places along the streams and shores. There are few roads to penetrate these forests, although pulp cutters are opening trails into new areas. One graveled road crosses the peninsula, another is projected. These will make accessible some of the fine high country in the Shickshocks.

On the south shore of the peninsula, toward Baie des Chaleurs, coastal plain and foreland are gentler; there is much grassland, and potatoes and dairy products are important in the local economy. Here, too, the Micmac Indians, still a numerous tribe, have their reserved lands, and along the highway they offer for sale beautifully made baskets which bear their trade mark in a diamond-shaped woven pattern where handles are attached to basket.

These, along with other Gaspesian crafts, are among the best that Canada produces. I shall pay my respects to them later on.

There is a fine blending of the talent of different races and ethnic groups — basketry of the Indians, wood carving of the French-speaking *Canadiens,* and weaving by both French- and English-speaking groups. By the way, do not be mislead by some of the French names around Percé and Gaspé; many of these families came from the Channel Islands, and they are as English as Yorkshire.

Gaspesian forests do not support large populations of game animals. There is considerable black bear hunting, and deer increase following pulpwood operations and the sprouting attendant on forest fires. Back in the Shickshocks are some woodland caribou, but they are hard to find. Although ruffed grouse and spruce grouse occur, they are seldom in large numbers. The more sought-after furbearers — mink, marten, fisher, otter, beaver, and lynx — are present, but not so abundantly as to enrich trappers.

With game fish, however, it is a different story. Brook trout, as well as introduced trout species, are in all streams pouring down from the Shickshocks. Atlantic salmon ascend most of the peninsula's rivers, some of which are fabled among anglers. The Province of Quebec asserts ownership to fish and fishing waters; these are leased to sportsmen who cherish their rights and defend them fiercely. Most larger streams, however, have open areas where any fisherman with the proper licenses may try his luck.

In the Gaspé, all rivers quickly run to the sea, and all roads along the coast lead back to Percé. This is hallowed ground — to the biologist, the geologist, the painter, the collector of landscapes. It is one of the crowning glories of Appalachia.

Facing the North Inlet at Percé are the Three Sisters, bold cliffs rising hundreds of feet above the water. On a shelf of one of these a pair of peregrines — noble falcons of romance and history — make their nest. Often enough, one of the pair sits at the top of the cliff. He can look down on Percé Rock, and across the channel to Bonaventure. Far to the northeast he sees Gaspé Point, with the waters of the gulf surrounding it. Below is the village, and beyond that the fields, the forest, and the rising mountains. All the life and color, the form and beauty of Gaspesia are round about him. If you like, you may join him there and see for yourself.

5. Alpine Summits

TREELINE ON A MOUNTAIN is exciting, especially to one who lives in forested country. Here is a denial of the usual state of things, a place where timber struggles to maintain itself. It barely succeeds here; it loses the battle a few feet above. There are evidences of temporary successes, then of retreats as less favorable conditions develop. Farther downslope, trees grow easily and naturally, covering every available bit of the land. Warfare against the elements and the eventual loss of the battle seem unnatural. That, of course, is the forest man's point of view; I suppose trees are strange to an Eskimo.

There are two ways to reach timberline. One involves a long journey for most of us — say, to Fort Churchill on Hudson Bay. The other way is to climb a mountain, in one of a few possible places in the East; or to climb one of the many ranges and peaks in the West. Strictly speaking, there are timberlines wherever forest gives way to grassland or desert, but these changes usually come about by slow transition rather than with dramatic suddenness. Our concern is with Appalachian peaks high enough to approach or tower above the places where tree growth must give way to other plant life.

Not too many Appalachian summits meet these terms. In the Gaspé's Shickshocks, there are sizable areas above the trees, and even larger stands of alpine and subalpine timber lower down. Mount Katahdin in Maine has an extensive treeless summit. The Presidential Range in New Hampshire has the East's most lengthy crest above treeline, a continuous ridge almost twenty miles in extent. Vermont's Mount Mansfield has a rocky crest that gives the effect of treeline. In the Adirondacks, Mount Marcy and Mount McIntyre go beyond timber; others in that range approach the limits of trees. As we have noted, however, the Adirondacks are not a part of Appalachia, and so do not come within the scope of this volume.

The ecologists (who are admirable when they use English) have a term for places such as treeline. They refer to these as tension zones, and nothing could be more expressive. Tension is evident in the slow growth of trees, the tortuous twisting of their branches and the horizontal position they assume to take full advantage of sunlight. When a shoot does attempt vertical growth, its twigs on the windward side will be shortened or absent. Some woody plants support and protect themselves by becoming compacted, so much so that they appear to have been severely pruned. Of course they have been, although it is nature, not man, that has done the pruning.

Tension is apparent in the advantage that trees take of every small depression, every ravine, every sheltered spot, to push their branches a few inches farther up the mountain. It shows in the dead tips of plants that have ventured too far. It can be seen in the limited number of species which even attempt growth under such circumstances; less hardy kinds have dropped out farther downslope.

In the preceding chapter I referred to the fact that parts, at least, of the Shickshocks escaped glaciation — why, no one knows. Some of New Hampshire's higher peaks achieve the same effect, not because glacial ice was absent, but because the summits towered above any ice sheet that formed. The result of this freedom from ice has been the preservation of elements in an ancient circumpolar flora, plant species that grow in alpine or subarctic situations in Europe and Asia as well as in North America.

Butterfly populations, too, responded to a lack of complete glaciation. The arctics, medium-sized smoky or yellowish-brown butterflies, are widely distributed in boreal situations. One species, the melissa arctic *(Oeneis melissa)*, is better known as the "White Mountain butterfly." Near and above treeline in the Presidential Range, these butterflies occur, here much farther south than in any other part of their range. Their larvae feed on grasses, and the adults may be seen along highways and trails, most frequently in early July. Apparently some of these northern insects were pushed southward by advancing ice sheets; they found sanctuary on Mount Washington's summit, survived glaciation, and have not been able to adapt to lower elevations. A similar situation, involving a different species, is found on Mount Katahdin. One of the arctics of wide distribution *(O. polixenes)* has an isolated population on this Maine peak. In the Shickshocks there are at least two other arctics that persist on treeless peaks. These remnant colonies tie Appalachian summits to true polar regions.

If you are a sturdy and determined hiker, you can visit every peak in the northeastern United States which transcends treeline; you can also visit many of the Shickshocks peaks, although that will take more doing. Unless you are a confirmed walker, however, you will visit Mount Washington and consider that you have done your duty by timberline. That you can visit Mount Washington's summit so comfortably is due to happy circumstances. You can walk up, of course; there are a number of practical trails. You can drive your car to the top over the hundred-year-old highway that started as a carriage road and evolved into a motor road. You can ride up the famous cog railway, also nearly a hundred years old. By any of these means of travel you will pass treeline, and will experience the alpine region above it.

Easy access to Mount Washington is a fortunate thing for other reasons also. It is the highest of northeastern peaks, it has the most extensive area above timberline, and it is connected above treeline with other nearby mountain crests. You can live in luxury at the Summit House, waiting for better weather, should things be inclement, or you can find more modest shelter in the Appalachian Mountain Club's Lakes of the Clouds hut perched along the Appalachian Trail two miles west of the highway terminus.

Most people with nature interests will, I presume, want to drive to the summit. This has many advantages; you set your own pace, you stop as you wish along the way, and you have quick and ready shelter should weather become threatening. Fortunately for the motorist, there are turnouts and parking places along the highway. If I may offer a suggestion: it is much easier to keep going to the top as you ascend; plan your stops for the drive down the mountain. Cars driven up steep grades in low gear get hot; vapor locks develop in stopped motors, and starting again may be a problem. This will be avoided if you make your pauses as you descend.

Driving (and hiking too, of course) allows observation of the forest types which clothe lower reaches of the mountain, closeup views of the wildflowers that grow beneath the trees, and opportunities to see and listen to birds along the way. The extraordinary transition at timberline is more readily seen, and more likely to be understood.

Of course, the cog railway is fun, too. If you are hesitant

about driving a steep, curving mountain road, leave it either to one of those powerful little steam engines to get you safely to the top, and back again or to one of the station wagons in which you can be driven to the summit.

The Mount Washington toll road (and most of the hiking trails as well) begins the ascent in northern hardwood forest — birch and maple trees predominating. This is familiar woodland to anyone who knows the Appalachians, even as far south as Georgia. Wood thrushes, veeries, and rose-breasted grosbeaks sing, and redstarts constantly display their bright colors. Wildflowers in early June will include Canada violets, foam flower, red trilliums, and Solomon's seal. There is a variety of wild food, and deer like to browse around the openings.

The first noticeable forest change comes as coniferous trees — chiefly hemlock, white pine, and red spruce — begin to mingle with the hardwoods. In this woodland cover, northern warblers (black-throated blues, Canadas, magnolias, and black-throated greens) are more in evidence. Juncos become common, their tails suggesting animated pairs of scissors as they show, then cover the white feathers at their margins. New wildflowers appear, too. Northern clintonia grows in beds; dwarf dogwood (bunchberry) covers roadbanks; painted trilliums replace the red species.

This is good habitat for pink lady's-slippers; they seem to thrive in mixtures of decaying hardwood leaves and conifer needles. Near the base of the cog railway, Ruth spotted three of these flowers which were pure-white, strikingly beautiful orchids. I have seen the same variant along the Millinocket Tote Road leading to Mount Katahdin.

Somewhere near this level, the hobblebush, a shrub already mentioned as a major autumnal attraction in the Great Smokies, becomes common, and it will be with us almost to treeline. Its blossoms are surely among the whitest known in nature, and they are at their best in early June. I have not seen the fall foliage display here, but the handsome fruits are often photographed, and I can imagine that this is one of the region's finest September features.

Next above this mixed forest is a dense stand of almost pure conifers, largely spruce and balsam fir. Forest floors are carpeted with oxalis, whose three-part leaves may have been the original Irish shamrocks. Goldthread, so named because of its vivid yellow rootlets, provides delicate white flowers on mossy logs or roadbanks. Dwarf dogwood is still with us, perhaps even more abundant here than at lower elevations.

Winter wrens like the dark tangles of spruce as nesting sites and singing perches. Swainson's thrushes and hermit thrushes as well (at least until the latter became unaccountably scarce) are at home here, as are myrtle warblers and most of the species listed for the mixed forest just below this one. Kinglets call from the treetops, and yellow-bellied sapsuckers are much in evidence.

In the last forest below timberline, balsam firs are dominant, and often these trees occur in pure stands. Progressive dwarfing occurs as treeline is neared, and most trees will show the effects of wind, snow, and ice. There still are flowers in the ground cover — dwarf dogwood, Canada mayflower, oxalis, and goldthread. Logs may be overgrown with delicate, small, vining twinflower (*Linnaea borealis*).

For the first time in the ascent, there are now present a number of bird species that would not occur in the Appalachians considerably farther south, say in Pennsylvania or West Virginia. The gray-cheeked thrush lives in these stunted balsams and selects the topmost twig of one of them for its evening song-perch. Boreal chickadees are here, as are gray jays. There is a chance of finding three-toed woodpeckers, and pine grosbeaks sometimes remain to nest. Spruce grouse occur, but the observer who sees one of these elusive birds is lucky indeed.

One of the most common summer residents is the blackpoll warbler, larger than many of its relatives, and somewhat slower in movement than most. These birds sing everywhere in the low balsams and spruces, but it is often amazingly difficult to see the author of this *tsi-tsi-tsi-tsi-tsi-tsi* song. Just under the thickest cluster of needles the males take their perches, and it may take a lot of looking to find this black and white bird.

As the tension zone is neared, balsams and spruce become more compacted, more dwarfed, and more nearly horizontal, until finally the trees are prostrate, only a few inches above the ground, and one walks on top of the forest. To this point changes have come gradually, in slow transition that makes it difficult to draw exact boundaries. Not so at treeline: growth stops abruptly, there are trees here, there are none a foot above, and if arborescent vegetation creeps slightly higher in sheltered places, the line of demarcation is still dramatic.

It is to emphasize this climactic boundary that I have traced biotic changes up the mountainside. We may understand better what is above if we know what is below.

One bird species, the white-throated sparrow, was with us as we started, and another, the slate-colored junco, joined us soon after we began the climb. These will be the only two that regularly accompany us into the treeless zone; all the remainder of the mountain's rich avifauna is below us. Of course there are ravens, hawks, and other birds flying over at times; these do not count because they do not nest above treeline. We shall not be much aware of birds at the heights.

Among the flowering plants, only a few species can make the transition. Most of the herbs we have seen below drop out; those that occur above timberline seldom penetrate far below it. We leave the trees and enter a new botanical world. Those who have not seen a natural alpine garden will be amazed at the richness, variety, and color that June's warm weather brings.

It is good to take a closer look at a few of these alpines, particularly those with showy blossoms. As a start, there is diapensia (*Diapensia lapponica*), a low evergreen herb, distantly related to galax, so prominent on southern Appalachian slopes (how these mountain plants do show similarities!). When we look at the bell-shaped white flowers of diapensia, another relationship is suggested: these alpine flowers resemble those of Oconee-bells (*Shortia galacifolia*), a classic among "lost" plants of the Southern Highlands. The resemblance is a natural one; the two plants are related. Diapensia is one of the circumpolar plants, widespread in true arctic regions, and found on isolated mountain summits in Eurasia and North America. As far south as Newfoundland it blooms on exposed beaches; farther south it is found in the Shickshocks, on Mount Katahdin, in the White Mountains, and on a few Adirondack summits. On the upper slopes of Mount Washington it is common, growing in tufted whirls or in masses, often with bright-flowered arctic azalea and Lapland rhododendron. It begins to open its buds in early June; by the middle of that month it is in full display.

Lapland rosebay (*Rhododendron lapponicum*) has a range matching diapensia's, and the two grow and bloom together. This dwarf heath has leaves of fingernail size, and its royal-purple flowers are larger than the leaves. A free bloomer, it is among the showiest of the alpines. Between it and the treelike rhododendrons farther south there are many similarities, but the dimension of flower parts and leaves is certainly different.

Third member of this closely associated trio is arctic azalea (*Loiseleuria procumbens*), whose hemispheric range is similar except that it apparently misses Adirondack peaks. It reappears in the Canadian Rockies. The matted leaves of this alpine gem are oval and only a quarter of an inch long. So closely does it hug the earth that when its lovely rose-colored flowers are open they are scarcely an inch aboveground.

It would be hard to find more pleasing gardens than these three make. Fortunately for the car driver or the hiker, they are not shy and hidden — they are in full view along the automobile road and the trails. Down to treeline they extend, and there they stop.

Here may be as good a place as any to offer a special word for

Mount Washington travelers. The mountain's peak is not the place to look for these arctic plants; slopes are too steep and too rocky, and wind is too severe even for them. The alpine gardens are down below, in the saddles that join Washington to other peaks in the range, or on benches that relieve the steep pitch of the terrain. A famous place to look for flowers is along the Appalachian Trail as it skirts around the head of Tuckerman Ravine on the route to Lakes of the Clouds hut. There are fine displays at many of the parking places along the motor road. Those who ride the cog railway, however, will have to descend a bit to see many flowers. I have found cranberry plants within a short distance of the summit, but most other flowering plants that grow there are inconspicuous grasses and rushes.

Toward the end of June, when Lapland rosebay is near the end of its flowering, two other heather-like plants come into bloom. They also are of hemispheric distribution in arctic and alpine situations. In the western mountains of North America they are simply called "heathers." There are no appropriate English names; we shall have to call them *Phyllodoce* and *Cassiope*. The first has white flowers that turn blue as they age; the second bears white or rose-colored bells. Both plants are low matted evergreens, and both are true alpines.

Another handsome heath that grows at treeline, and sometimes above it, but is not at all restricted to this zone is rhodora (*Rhododendron canadense*). There are plants of this heath on Mount Washington, but it is particularly abundant near the top of Cannon Mountain, where an aerial tramway serves visitors to the Franconia Notch region.

It would not do to omit the little three-toothed cinquefoil, which we met in the first chapter. It begins in the Arctic and follows the Appalachians to the balds in Georgia. On all the White Mountain summits it is common. I know of no other plant that so favors the heights, and dwells on so many of them.

Willows and birches are not stopped by treeline, although

as they extend beyond it they become low shrubs, often with creeping, vinelike habits. Botanists have a field day with the very difficult dwarf species on Mount Katahdin and in the Shickshocks. They are so near to each other in many characters and yet so tantalizingly different. Are they good species, hybrids, strongly marked races, or just what? In any event, it is strange to see a prostrate willow creeping over a low boulder, opening its catkins where the sun strikes most directly.

Ferns and their allies are poorly represented in alpine regions, although a few of the clubmosses (*Lycopodium*) grew above treeline. On Mount Washington and other northeastern summits there is a stiff, bristly species which has been called *Lycopodium selago*. In the Shickshocks, on the fell-fields above treeline is alpine clubmoss (*L. alpinum*), a more truly arctic species.

It should be understood that the treeless portions of the Shickshocks are farther north — more extensive, more varied (there are many peaty areas), and richer in arctic and subarctic plants. Many of these spill off the summits in rocky gorges and along streams, and treeline (for them) is not so clearly a range limit. The plants mentioned above, however, are easily seen; most of them are common on New England's treeless summits.

Save for insects, animal life above treeline in the Appalachians is disappointing. Those who know the western mountains above timberline will miss the constant movement of conies, marmots, chipmunks, and golden-mantled ground squirrels. I have seen groundhogs in the East at or near treeline on grassed ski slopes, but no other larger mammals so high.

In the Appalachian hills of western Newfoundland, the rock ptarmigan is common and, seemingly, is pretty well restricted to this upland region. There are no ptarmigans in eastern mountains south of Newfoundland. That other delightful tribe of high alpine western birds, the rosy finches, is missing in the Appalachians.

I have mentioned juncos and white-throated sparrows above treeline on Mount Washington. On Mount Katahdin and in the Shickshocks another bird of high latitudes or mountain summits, the water pipit, joins them. This adds up to a scanty avifauna; students will not flock to treeless Appalachian peaks for bird study. Both plants and animals on higher Appalachian summits illustrate the biological principle that northward we find many individuals of only a relatively few species. Southward, the reverse is true: in the southern Appalachians at lower elevations there is a tremendous diversity of species. Note again the very wide distribution of most of the arctic-alpine plants we have discussed; the same thing holds for the water pipit. Balsam fir is continental in its extent, and many of the herbs just below treeline are found in suitable places throughout northern portions of this hemisphere.

On treeless Appalachian summits there is little or no true endemism — these mountain peaks have not produced plants and animals of sharply restricted distribution. The arctic butterflies previously mentioned might be listed as exceptions, but they are generally regarded as races of otherwise wide-ranging species. From Pennsylvania southward in the Appalachian ranges, endemism is common; many plants and animals have restricted ranges, some of them confined to relatively small mountain areas. And yet, with all these differences, how much alike the northern and the southern peaks are! The balsam forest on top of Mount Mitchell is remarkably similar to the forest just below treeline on Mount Washington. Juncos and winter wrens, kinglets and crossbills, wood oxalis and Canada mayflower, all are found in both situations.

Because it may easily be reached, the numbers of those who visit Mount Washington's summit as compared to those who reach any of the other eastern alpine peaks may well be of the order of one hundred to one. Some rugged hiking is required to ascend above treeline elsewhere in the Appalachians. And

Mount Marcy, climbed by many hikers over an elaborate series of trails, cannot be counted as a part of Appalachia.

The Adirondacks, so geologists tell us, are a part of the Canadian Shield, and the story of their rocks is a different one. Those who know Algonquin Provincial Park in Ontario will be impressed with the similarities between that area and the lower, western portions of the Adirondacks. Here are the same unyielding rocks, frequent lakes, conifer-clad swampy areas, and hills forested in sugar maple. To me it is a matter of regret that I cannot treat more fully these fine New York mountains. One of the best trails in the East leaves Keene Four Corners, goes up John's Brook, and in about ten miles reaches Marcy's summit. The active Adirondack Mountain Club does a fine job in marking and maintaining this and other trails in the region.

I have vivid memories of one climb up the John's Brook trail. Bill Webb, a moss collector from the University of Georgia, and I started from Keene one June afternoon expecting to spend the night in the rock shelter near Marcy's top. What neither of us had counted on was that my hiking shoes would act up; in an hour I had bad blisters on both heels. We kept on climbing, he carrying most of the load and I limping along, until evening found us near treeline, unable to reach the shelter. It wasn't much of a place for camping, but we spread our blankets under the low balsams, ate some cold food, and made the best of it. I was afraid to take off shoes and socks, and since sleep was out of the question I listened to the birds until late dusk, then heard the chorus that began at early dawn. Even the discomforts could not spoil the singing of Swainson's, gray-cheeked, and hermit thrushes. As I recall it, the first morning thrush notes began at 3:10. It helped, too, to have a black-backed three-toed woodpecker, my first, feeding at a dead balsam only a few feet away. And, by the way, we did go on to the top. It was a suitable prelude to the Shickshocks, which we reached a few days later.

The towering mass of Katahdin has always held special interest

for me, and of course we return to Appalachia on this mountain.
I know why it has so attracted me, and perhaps the circumstances
will cause some nostalgia in others of my generation. I am about
to date myself.

Our home in West Virginia enjoyed three generations of
The Youth's Companion, and its weekly arrival was an event:
Homer Greene, James Willard Schultz — there were many stars
among its contributors, but none so bright as C. A. Stephens.
His stories of Maine — the Old Squire's farm, the winter frolics,
the Big Woods — were unforgettable. In some of his early fiction
(I never knew where fiction began and biography ended) four
boys, Kit, Wash, Wade, and Raed, cast their vote for an education less formal than one they might receive in college. They
planned a camping trip to Mount Katahdin, hoping that there
they might find some mineral deposit which would finance their
education by travel. The resident Indian devil of the mountain,
Pamola, did his best to stop or hinder them; but right prevailed,
and persistence paid off. They found a vein of graphite, sold it
for fifteen thousand dollars, and were off to Labrador, Iceland,
and the Amazon. Each trip inevitably resulted in a book, and
I had them all.

This was my first contact with Katahdin. Maine was far
away, but I knew I would get there some day, and, like my
heroes, visit the peak. I have — several times — but I have yet
to see the view from Katahdin's summit. Each time I have tried
to, Pamola has spread a veil of clouds to keep his kingdom
inviolate.

6. Fire Tower

A FIRE TOWER is a comforting sight, in settled country or in the wilderness. It stands as evidence that someone cares about the forest, and has made plans to keep it growing — green and productive. When fires start, and they will, the lookout in his tower sets in motion a chain of action, a planned attack that sooner or later will lead to the control of any blaze. This is a welcome thought to conservationists.

I invite your attention to Gaudineer Knob in southeastern West Virginia, and to the tower the United States Forest Service has erected on its summit. Don Gaudineer, for whom the peak was named, was a ranger on the Greenbrier district of the Monongahela National Forest. When fire threatened his family he gave his life to save them, and so a fine mountain bears his name.

The tower area is about thirty minutes in latitude south of Washington, a strange place for the red spruce forest that covers slope and crest. Elevation, however, tells the story. At the base of the tower Gaudineer Knob is 4445 feet above sea level. In average temperature and length of growing season this mountaintop is climatically a part of northern New England or eastern Canada. Plants and animals respond to these conditions; many of those present would be at home in New Brunswick, or north of Lake Superior. Here is a precious bit of Canada which spills southward along Appalachian ridges.

Cheat Mountain range, of which Gaudineer is a part, is well watered, and so for most of the year fire danger is minimal or nonexistent. During spring and fall, however, things are different, and there is the ever-present threat of a blaze that runs wild. From March to May and from October to December the tower will be manned, a lookout in the glass-walled cabin that stands above a young spruce forest.

From his platform above the trees a lookout approaches the condition of the cliché: he comes near to being master of all he surveys. He is higher than any other nearby object, and so for long distances his view is unobstructed. The safety and welfare of thousands of acres are in his keeping; he knows his job and accepts his responsibility. By the way, the gender of my pronouns would often be wrong; a good many girls and women serve the Forest Service and the states as lookouts.

Gaudineer Tower is strategically located. It stands on three divides, one political, two topographic. A portion of the tower is in Randolph County, the remainder in Pocahontas County. Westward Shavers Fork of the Cheat River gathers its waters for a journey northward to the Monongahela, and to Pittsburgh's Golden Triangle, where the Ohio is born. East of the tower is

the Greenbrier, whose waters, before they too eventually join
the Ohio, will have become a part of the New River, a stream
that flows northwestward from Ashe County, North Carolina.
To the west of the tower, mountain peaks are jumbled and
mountain ridges deeply dissected. This land is a portion of the
Allegheny Plateau, the topography of which is broken and
unsystematic. To the east, however, the ridges are long and
remarkably smooth. They form a part of the Ridge and Valley
Province where streams in the valleys have a trellised pattern,
and mountain folds are oriented to a northeast-southwest axis.

In the panoramic sweep from Gaudineer there are few cleared
areas. A short distance away is the small opening of White Top,
where, during the Civil War, Union forces built Fort Milroy to
guard the Staunton-Parkersburg Turnpike, thus establishing the
highest permanently occupied army camp that the long war
knew. Toward the Greenbrier there are some glady areas, a
few of which are flooded by beaver dams. Most of the landscape
is forested, though, with second-growth spruce on the heights,
and northern hardwoods — beech, birch, and maple — on the
lower slopes.

Two miles south of the tower a paved highway, U.S. 250,
crosses the mountains, but the road is out of sight. Beyond it is
an authentic wilderness, a ridge known locally as Back Allegheny, with an elevation always above 4000 feet. In almost
twenty miles no road nor trail follows its crest, and none crosses
it except one lumber railroad. The original spruce forest was
cut in the early 1900's, and a second harvest is being taken after
fifty years.

A mile or so north of the tower is West Virginia's one remnant
of original spruce forest, a 130-acre tract purchased at the insistence of Arthur Wood, who believed that future generations
should know what an Appalachian spruce stand was like. Wood
served as Supervisor of the Monongahela National Forest, and
he left his imprint on many good things. In striking contrast to

the ancient forest, one of man's newer ventures in space probing is nearby. At Greenbank is one of the world's great radio astronomy stations, and here the astrophysicists have been swinging the huge disk of their receiver to intercept possible signals from other sentient beings in outer space.

The lookout in his tower is not completely isolated. At hand is a telephone, and its ringing is an incongruous sound in a wild area. He also has companionship of a sort in other lookout stations. To the west he can see the tower on Barton Knob. Its management and ownership are different, since it is state-owned, but its purpose is the same. Farther north and west on clear days he may just make out Bickels Knob Tower, and to the east Smokecamp Tower is within easy sighting. Any of these may be helpful when there is a fire to locate.

Ordinarily the lookout is no Saint Simeon Stylites on a pedestal. He goes to ground level for water and to meet his body's needs. On days and nights of blessed rain he checks out with the ranger and returns to his own home. There are many times of low fire danger, and during these his vigilance is relaxed. Should conditions become threatening and high-class fire days develop, he is on the job with little respite. He knows, and disregards, the regular sources of smoke: portable sawmills here and there along a stream, the waste dump at Durbin, and the tannery at Frank. But let a strange smoke appear, particularly if it has the characteristic light color imparted by burning wood, and things begin to happen. On a platform in his cubicle is a circular map, oriented as to direction and with his own tower at its center. Above the map is mounted an alidade which swings throughout the great circle of 360 degrees. He moves the alidade, sighting along its top, until a cross-hair squarely covers the smoke. Then he reads the bearing in degrees shown by the graduated margin of his map-holder. Next he estimates the distance from his tower to the smoke, not always an exact process, but helpful. Then and not until then, he telephones headquarters. He has done his job, and the responsibility passes to other hands.

In the meantime, if the smoke is a sizable one, lookouts on one or more neighboring towers will have sighted it and will be reporting their data. Soon headquarters can do some triangulating, establish the approximate location of the fire, and dispatch a crew to investigate and begin suppression if that is necessary. It's a good system and it works. In an area that suffers from frequent fires, the Monongahela National Forest is justly proud of its record. The average yearly burn is less than 3/10 of 1 percent — about three acres in each thousand.

The Forest Service welcomes visitors to Gaudineer Knob. For business uses, and for the public's convenience, their engineers have built a gravel-surfaced road to its summit. Here there are picnic areas beautifully screened by dense spruce hedges, and in these are tables and outdoor grills. Near the base of the tower a well provides cold water. And, *mirabile dictu,* there are few biting flies, even on a warm June day.

Visitors may climb to a platform surrounding the glassed-in cubicle on top of the tower, even when the tower is not manned. When the lookout is on duty it is good forest manners to ask his permission before climbing. No salutes of the quarter-deck are necessary, but the visitor is coming aboard what is temporarily the lookout's home craft. The similarity of a fire tower to a crow's nest will not escape old navy hands.

There is an interesting layering of living things apparent in the sixty-foot climb. At ground level the characteristic Gaudineer birds in summer are juncos and winter wrens. A dozen feet from the ground magnolia warblers are abundant. Redbreasted nuthatches search along the higher branches, and golden-crowned kinglets hunt tiny insects in outer twigs. The thirty-foot level is a good place for Blackburnian warblers; I found my only nest of these birds by looking squarely into it from halfway up the tower. The tallest of young spruces bear cones, these nearly always near treetop. When red crossbills are abundant, as they are some years, they feast on spruce seeds, using their crossed mandibles as chisel-like tools to open cone scales. The fortunate climber may watch them at their own level.

Above treetop, the view is likely to claim first attention, but a visitor might do well to take a long look at the young spruce forest below him, and to reflect on the cause of its being there. It is the result of one of those conjunctions of time and chance that have always fascinated the thoughtful.

Harvesting a spruce forest presents special difficulties to lumbermen. Spruce is a shallow-rooted tree, and it needs the support of nearby trees if it is to resist severe wind. When selection cutting is attempted, residual trees in the stand often blow down, a waste of wood and a major fire hazard. Clear-cutting seems to be the only feasible lumbering procedure; but this cutting of all trees in a stand leaves none to produce seed. Much too often a fine spruce stand is followed in succession by ferns, briers, and such low-grade woody plants as aspens, fire cherry, and other species which foresters call "weed" trees. That this type of succession did not occur on Gaudineer is due to a narrow belt of tall spruces growing on the Greenbrier side of the mountain, just below the break of the first steep slope.

Some years before the Civil War a speculating land company bought a tract of 69,000 acres on the slope of Shavers Mountain. Their tract fronted for about seven miles along the eastern side of the mountain. To survey and mark their holdings the company hired a crew of men who must have found rough going in this wilderness. The crew did a good job, but its chief forgot one thing — the fact that a compass needle points to magnetic, not true north. In this area the angle of declination is about four degrees, a significant source of error on a seven-mile front.

An experienced Virginia surveyor, in checking the data, discovered the error but said nothing about it. Presently, however, when the sale was being concluded and the deeds recorded, he brought the error to light, and under a sort of "doctrine of vacancy" claimed the wedge of land left by a corrected survey. His title was established, and he and his heirs found themselves owner of a seven-mile strip of forest, aggregating almost 900 acres. While timber above and below the wedge was cut, this narrow holding was undisturbed. Its thickest end, a fringe of tall spruces on the near horizon, is just east of Gaudineer Tower. From these trees came seed to produce a new forest, a happy result of a hundred-year-old mistake. Northern birds, mammals, and plants are here because the young spruces, hundreds of acres of them, provide food and shelter.

Some of West Virginia's finest mountain country surrounds Gaudineer Tower. Just eastward is the long range of Middle Mountain, and along its crest the Forest Service maintains a road, forty miles through high country, most of it wooded and all a delight to the biologist. There is no better place in the state to look for wild turkeys, particularly in early morning of a late-summer day. Large areas on this mountain ridge were planted by Civilian Conservation Corps workers; new forests of spruce and pine are in being.

Beyond Middle Mountain, a distant, smooth line on the horizon is the Allegheny Backbone, here a secondary continental divide separating waters that flow down through the Potomac to Chesapeake Bay from those which join the New, the Great Kanawha, the Ohio, and the Mississippi on their way to the Gulf of Mexico. Spruce Knob, only a little higher than the remainder of the ridge around it, but still West Virginia's highest point at 4860 feet, is just visible on clear days.

To the south, Gaudineer Tower overlooks the upper reaches of the Greenbrier River, rich in the lore of logger and woodsman. Down through a valley sheltered by high mountains on either side, the Greenbrier flows through a southern extension of the great white pine forest. Thousands of acres of fine timber were here, and this was not long in coming to the attention of lumbermen. And then came an interesting discovery. The timber was here, with the water to carry it to mill, but mountain people were entirely without experience in log-driving. They could fell the trees and skid them to streambanks, but they could not ride them down the flood.

So here began one of the gaudy periods in mountain logging. Rivermen from northern streams, Maine and New Brunswick woodsmen, were imported to do the job, and for some years they labored, cutting timber and building splash-dams in winter, then awaiting the spring thaw and flood to carry their cargo to the mill. These men did not know Paul Bunyan (he was a Great Lakes creation, after all), but they had their own Bull of the Woods, Tony Beaver, whose exploits were limited only by the imagination of the storyteller. Lower Greenbrier towns saw lively days when the log-drivers arrived. And many a "Mc" or "Mac" on a valley name is evidence that some of these New Brunswick Scotsmen chose to settle along the river.

To the north and west, Gaudineer looks down on Cheat River country, a land of heavy second-growth forest, all of it high, and much of it roadless. So abundant is precipitation that vegetation from ground cover to forest crown grows in layers, each of which shelters its appropriate animal species. This makes for richness and variety in populations of living things.

The Gaudineer region is climactic in the mid-Appalachians, at the center of the highest and most extensive mountain mass between the White Mountains and the southern Blue Ridge in Virginia, North Carolina, and Tennessee. To a remarkable degree, it combines the qualities and characteristics of these widely separated ranges. It partakes of both North and South, and therein lies much of its attraction for naturalists. At times all the bird voices seem to be those of the North Woods, but suddenly one also hears a yellow-breasted chat, a hooded warbler, or a blue-gray gnatcatcher. The whole effect is delightfully confusing.

This mountain area is fast becoming something of a center for biologists and other outdoors people. The list of visitors is impressive — some of our foremost scientists, authors, and artists have known and enjoyed Gaudineer and its environs. Unlike so many of these wild areas, Gaudineer had its own resident observer, on the ground here for almost fifty years. His name was Harvey Cromer, and he began his working career as a lumberman, first in West Virginia, then in the Great Smokies. Still a young man, he returned to West Virginia, settled at Cheat Bridge, became a scout for a pulp and paper company, and, as the years passed, a mentor of the outdoors for all who would listen.

Harvey Cromer was never a scientist, and he would have shunned the name naturalist, but those living things around him which he hadn't seen and didn't know about were few indeed. I liked to visit him, and to ask all sorts of questions. If he didn't know he was quick to say so, but he usually came up with information, some of it astonishingly perceptive and accurate. He told me more about varying hares (he called them "snowshoe rabbits") and the mysterious disease which periodically strikes these mammals than I ever learned from any other field observer. He showed me a Bonaparte's gull which he had shot, identified, and had mounted — a strange bird to appear in this forested region. He was a calendar of outdoor events; he knew when and where things happened on the mountain. Some of his observations puzzled me as he told me about them, and they still do. I don't know what to say about his story of panther tracks in the snow on Gaudineer's slopes. He was usually careful and accurate, but if these big cats still occur, even casually, in West Virginia, why has no wildlife biologist been able to find trace of them?

I derive a certain comfort and satisfaction in thinking that these mountains still hold their secrets — not all the discoveries have yet been made. One summer a warbler (even that is an assumption) sang in the big spruces near Gaudineer's top. I heard it many times, I looked for it, unsuccessfully, I never have heard, there or elsewhere, another one like it. Some day I might know — but not yet.

Leaving the unknowns, it remains abundantly evident that, no matter what the season, there is always something worth seeing round and about Gaudineer. In autumn the lookout is on duty in his tower, and the foreground of his view is a sea of young spruce tops. In nice counterpoint to this dark green is the blaze of color on maple, birch, beech, and basswood just downslope. On fair days monarch butterflies — hundreds of them — drift southward, perhaps to winter in the Everglades. Occasional hawks pass over, although the tower is not on the side of the mountain most favored by migrating raptors.

Fall warblers, just as confusing as they are supposed to be, find much food in aphids that infest spruce twigs. There is constant scurrying among the chipmunks, and red squirrels are busy cutting and piling cones which will be their winter's food supply. Wild turkeys, safe enough from the hunter so long as they stay in rhododendron tangles, gobble at dawn and dusk.

This is a season of bright fruits, much of the color being supplied by deciduous hollies. Many people who admire evergreen American holly, with its Christmas associations, neglect the hollies which shed their leaves but leave a harvest of red fruits. There are three such species in the Gaudineer area, two of them widely distributed and well known. These are mountain holly (*Ilex montana*), the opalescent red fruits of which are at their best against the blue October skies, and winterberry (*I. verticillata*), a scarlet-berried shrub with fruits persisting into late winter. The third member of the holly group is long-stalked holly (*I. longipes*), a plant of limited distribution from West Virginia southward. It bears tremendous crops of large cerise fruits, each on a pedicel that holds it well away from the twig. It prefers to have its roots in water; in the Blister Swamp just below Gaudineer's summit there are thousands of these shrubs, and they provide one of autumn's most colorful effects. Like some other hollies, this one has a yellow-fruited form, the only known station being near White Top, about three miles from Gaudineer Tower.

Winter is a silent season on the heights. Few birds can find food under heavy snow and ice, and few care to weather arctic storms that sweep the crests. Every spruce needle acquires a coating of frost crystals, sparkling decorations that may last for weeks. Varying hares, now in spotless white pelage, search for the highbush cranberries, a favorite food at all seasons. A few ravens live on discards that other creatures overlook or reject.

Snow often piles deep, drifted by driving winds. This, too, has produced its story. Before the Civil War, mail was carried along the old Staunton-Parkersburg Turnpike from the upper Shenandoah Valley to Ohio River settlements. Along the way were taverns and coach houses, a famous one, Traveler's Repose by name, a few miles from Gaudineer. One fall a new carrier took over the job, stopped at Traveler's Repose, liked the hospitality there, and stayed for the winter. After a while the people in Parkersburg, becoming impatient, managed to get word to Pittsburgh, thence to Washington, and a tracer was sent out to locate the missing carrier and his mail. Thereupon, he penned a famous letter, addressed to the Postmaster General. It concluded, "If the floodgates of hell were to open, and it were to rain fire and brimstone for six straight weeks, it wouldn't melt all the snow on Cheat Mountain, so if the people in Parkersburg want their damned old mail, let them come and get it!"

Spring comes slowly, and with many false starts. Along the south foot of Gaudineer Knob is a narrow swampy area, the Blister Swamp already mentioned. Here northern balsam fir grows, exudations on its trunk causing blisters, and accounting for the local name of the area. On warm nights, perhaps in April, spotted salamanders emerge from hibernation, seek forest pools for their mating, and deposit there the cottony egg masses that perpetuate their kind. As frost leaves the ground, earthworms become active, and woodcocks arrive to probe for them. Early nests of these birds will be built while there still is danger that snow will cover the eggs.

Farther up the slopes, where snow lingers, it will be May before spring wildflowers open under bare branches of northern hardwoods. Toward the last of that month, painted trilliums and pink lady's-slippers blossom just as leaves are opening on the trees. Among the spruces, flowers are few: oxalis and Canada mayflower are most common, and here and there heartleaf twayblades, tiny orchids of the north country, show their cleft-lipped blooms in early June.

Birds, too, are slow in reaching the high places. Until insects hatch, there is little for birds to eat in a spruce forest. Juncos need make only a short altitudinal migration; they arrive with the first snowless days. Hermit thrushes also are hardy, and they are often scratching for food in early April, a month before the other nesting brown-backed thrushes — wood, veery, and Swainson's — appear. Northern waterthrushes begin singing in April, at home here on the heights well away from water. Most other summer residents are on their breeding grounds by mid-May. Frost or even snow may yet come, but the birds are ready to set up housekeeping.

The summer visitor to Gaudineer must divide his time. He cannot afford to miss the massed beds of mountain laurel and rhododendron, these at their best as June turns to July. He must allow enough hours for wood warblers: from foot of mountain to its summit twenty-two warbler species are summer residents, more kinds than are known to nest on any other Appalachian peak. If he has an interest in the cold-blooded vertebrates, he will want to see the little gold-flecked Cheat

Mountain salamander, a creature not known to occur outside this mountain range.

Just at dusk varying hares, now in summer brown and white, come out to eat grass beneath the fire tower. The platform above affords good views of their feeding and playing. Forest Service men like to see them, and try to encourage their presence. Ephe Olliver, Supervisor of the Monongahela National Forest, carries a sack of fertilizer in the back of his car, and when he visits a tower he scatters handfuls to promote grass growth.

Dusk also brings out the flying squirrels, here the larger northern species, near the southern limits of its range. Sometimes one will pause for a moment on an exposed snag near the tower. Winter wrens will still be singing, juncos chirping, and magnolia warblers giving querulous notes as though they were scolding the children.

But the dusk really belongs to the thrushes. Their full chorus begins earlier; at first most of the birds are well downhill, where wood thrushes will remain. As shadows creep upward, veeries and hermit thrushes seek the light toward the summit. Veeries usually keep to the undergrowth, but hermits like to sing from the highest tip of a spruce. Closest of all in approach to the tower are Swainson's thrushes. They seem reluctant to miss one daylight moment, one ray from the summer sunset. As the tower is on the highest point, so are the birds drawn to it in the dusk. Finally, singing must stop, there are a few sleepy chirps — then silence. The June day has ended.

This is fine country, and I keep returning to it. I am happy that it is protected — the tower is a symbol and a promise. This bit of the northland is a rare thing. It enables me to visit Canada or New England without leaving the boundaries of my native state. Strongly as one may feel the north-country atmosphere at Gaudineer, it is pleasant to have confirmation from others. When one of the international ornithological societies met in West Virginia, we arranged a field trip to the Cheat Mountain range. I walked along a trail with friends from Ontario, Doris and Murray Speirs. They looked at the spruce forest and the plants growing within its shade. They listened to the birds and watched the butterflies. They absorbed the atmosphere of the region, and reacted to its charm. Finally Doris turned to her husband and said, "Why, Murray, we're back home."

7. Four Peaks South

HOW MUCH HIGHER would Mount Mitchell have to be to reach treeline? This intriguing question has confronted ecologists who visit the Appalachians' highest peak, 6684 feet above the Atlantic. Like other southern peaks in the 6000-foot range, all of them in North Carolina and neighboring Tennessee, Mount Mitchell's summit is clothed in spruce and fir forest, in appearance almost identical with the one on Mount Washington just below the 5000-foot contour. The New Hampshire peak rises upward above the trees; those of higher elevations in the southern Appalachians don't make it. The Appalachian Revolution, it would appear, made two climactic efforts, one in New England and the other far southward. In between it eased up;

highest points in Massachusetts, Pennsylvania, and Maryland are in the 3000-foot range, and New York's Catskills are only somewhat higher. In southwestern Virginia, peaks begin to soar — above 5500 feet at White Top and Mount Rogers — and, as North Carolina and Tennessee are reached, 6000-foot elevations become commonplace. Heights such as these are the rule in the Unakas, the Blacks, the Balsams, and the Great Smokies.

A mountain is impressive in proportion to its rise above the base. If the highest point is only moderately above surrounding peaks and ridges, and if the enclosing valleys are themselves elevated, dramatic effect is lost. This is a weakness of West Virginia's Cheat range; valleys on either side often lie at 3000 feet or more.

Southern Appalachian peaks, many of them at least, stand 4000, or even 5000 feet above their valleys. Take Mount Le Conte in the Smokies as an example. The viewer standing in the streets of Gatlinburg is about 1400 feet above sea level. He looks upward along an unbroken slope to the summit at 6593 feet, more than 5100 feet above him. This is comparable, so far as rise is concerned, to standing in Estes Park and looking toward the Rockies' Front Range.

Four of southern Appalachia's highest peaks may be reached, or approached, by automobile highways. These are Grandfather Mountain and Mount Mitchell in North Carolina, and Roan Mountain and Clingmans Dome, both of which lie athwart the North Carolina–Tennessee border. Determined hikers will seek and conquer other summits; these four may be visited and ascended (to points that have commanding views at least) by anyone who can ride in a car. Because of their accessibility, and also because they include some of the finest of Appalachian features, I have chosen to call special attention to them.

Northernmost of the four is Grandfather Mountain, breaking the skyline above Blowing Rock, Boone, Linville, Banner Elk, and other summer gathering points in western North Carolina's resort country. Travelers going southward along the Blue Ridge Parkway will begin to see Grandfather's two-pronged peak while they are still forty or fifty miles distant from it. It has the virtue of standing alone, higher than any nearby terrain. The view is challenging, the climb rewarding. For many reasons it seems desirable to go directly to Grandfather's summit, at least to the end of the toll road, which climbs to 5000 feet. There is a strong temptation to linger around the base. The Blowing Rock itself, the Parkway Craft Center, Linville Gorge and Falls, summer theater at Boone, and many other attractions are also distractions. Above them all towers the mountain. The visitor will have more appreciation for details if he has seen the whole area in panorama.

Just off the Blue Ridge Parkway, on U.S. 221 toward Linville, the toll road begins a relatively short, steep ascent. At convenient places along it are picnic tables and camping areas, and it leads to a parking area at about the 5000-foot elevation. For most persons this will be the end of the trail; the view embraces high country to south and west, Roan Mountain and Mount Mitchell dominating. A swinging bridge spans a chasm, and the trail beyond leads to bold overlooks. This bridge, and the people who cross it, are, I suppose, among the most photographed objects in all Appalachia.

Above the bridge and parking area stands Grandfather's rocky summit. It is almost a thousand feet higher, and there is a trail toward it from the parking area. Some few visitors to the mountain will use that trail, leaving their cars and going on afoot. Now a word of caution: mountaineers will make light of this climb, but it will not be without excitement for less experienced hikers. Before Grandfather's nose, on Calloway Peak, is reached at 5938 feet, the climber will have used ten ladders, some of them scaling sheer cliffs. This trail is not for weaklings or for those in poor physical condition. Anyone who attempts it should have shoes with soles that cling to smooth quartzite rock. A slip in the wrong place could be costly.

Fire swept around the slopes of Grandfather Mountain many years ago, and vegetation has been slow in reclothing areas of thin soil and bare rock. Fire cherry, yellow birch, highbush blueberry, mountain ash, and various deciduous hollies, along with Catawba rhododendron and other heaths, have found footholds, nevertheless, and the first portion of the climb leads through this growth. On exposed headlands the rhododendron has been shaped and compacted by wind, as on other summits. It has the appearance of having been planted here, each bush professionally pruned to fit the niche in which it is growing.

About halfway up the slope the trail makes a short but rough descent into a saddle. Clambering up and down over these stones will afford a taste of what is to come, and the hiker may now decide whether or not he wants to tackle the ladders just ahead. If he goes on he will use the first of these to get over a shelving rock with a steep (and close) overhang, a formation that has been named the Attic Window. And having come this far, he finds himself in a different plant community. He has left the old fire scars below him — from here to the summit his way is through low fir forest, amazingly like that on top of Wildcat or Cannon Mountain in New Hampshire.

If he has an interest in plants, the climber will know, though, that he is not in New England. All about him are plants peculiar to the southern Appalachians — galax, various saxifrages, some of the primitive lilies, and a tall shrubby cranberry (*Vaccinium erythrocarpum*) that is so different from the trailing bog varieties of commerce as scarcely to be recognizable. Most noticeable of all, especially if in flower, will be low masses of Appalachian sand-myrtle (*Leiophyllum*) clinging in rock crevices and on exposed places, a handsome and interesting alpine plant. Sand-myrtle has small evergreen leaves and clusters of white blossoms, the red stamens giving a color note. In appearance, it is remarkably like its close relative, alpine azalea, a heath that we found above treeline in the White Mountains. Here is another correspondence — plants of different species resembling each other and occupying corresponding niches in separated mountain masses.

This species, along with many others, tells a story of Appalachian botany. For years plant students puzzled over the fact that so many instances were known in which a plant was found thriving on the coastal plain and also in isolated situations at the top of one or more Appalachian peak. Finally it became clear that the mountains, rising above the sea and beyond the reach of glacial ice, served as conservators and distribution points for these plants. Their seeds were carried to the lowlands; where they found congenial conditions, they established themselves. It is not surprising, then, that sand-myrtle clings to sandy crevices on Appalachian peaks and also occurs in sandy pine barrens along the Atlantic Coast from New Jersey southward.

Although the fir which makes up a major portion of the forest looks like northern balsam fir, it is actually a southern endemic species, Fraser's fir (*Abies fraseri*). The red spruce is, however, identical with trees in more northerly stands, as is much of the herbaceous understory — such as Canada mayflower, wood oxalis, and northern Clinton's lily. Here, too, are the fine growths of hobblebush which are so prominent along roads and trails up Mount Washington.

If plants impart an air of the north country, so do the birds. Canada, black-throated blue, black-throated green, and Blackburnian warblers, juncos, winter wrens, brown creepers, red-breasted nuthatches, golden-crowned kinglets, and veeries all occur. Ravens alternately flap and soar and there are occasional peregrines. With all of these there are more austral species as well — the situation a confusing one for those who like living things to fit into convenient slots.

At the end of that ten-ladder climb is a view of the southern

mountain country that is limited only by atmospheric conditions. Clumps of sand-myrtle seem to increase in vigor and
saxifrages grow and bloom more freely toward the summit.
Above all, there is a sense of accomplishment. You appreciate
those ladders, and you view with approval the improvised pitons
(actually railway spikes) which hold them in place. If you are
very lucky, you may find a gold-spotted Weller's salamander at
the place of its discovery.

When we look at lungless salamanders in Chapter 17, I shall
have more to say about the Grandfather Mountain region. It
has a history among herpetologists that runs parallel to that of
Kate's Mountain among botanists. Not so many years ago students of the cold-blooded vertebrates discovered the summer
attractions at Blowing Rock. Using that resort as a center, they
walked or drove a buggy out on the roads around Grandfather's
base, and few of them returned empty-handed. As a collecting
area it may be second only to the Smokies.

Other scientists, some of them among the pioneers, have
worked the area, always with appreciation. In August 1794,
André Michaux climbed the mountain, and with understandable (if mistaken) enthusiasm wrote, "Climbed to the summit
of the highest mountain of all North America, and with my
companion and guide, sang the Marseilles Hymn, and cried,
'Long live America and the French Republic! Long live Liberty!'" Asa Gray also explored in the area when he was pre-
paring his celebrated *Manual of Botany*. The State of North
Carolina has commemorated both of these visits with suitable
historical markers. It has done a like thing at the base of Roan
Mountain, since both scientists explored that peak as well.

Sometimes scientists (and scientists-to-be) came to Blowing
Rock for other reasons. From the Carolina Low Country,
Charles G. Vardell, founder of Flora Macdonald College, came
to western North Carolina to establish a summer home. He was
a tall Scot with five daughters. In his new house he built a

hatrack high on the wall, then spoke to the girls somewhat as follows: "Pretty soon you will be bringing boys in here courting, and I expect you to. I want all of you to get married, but I don't want any short men in my family. If your beaus can't hang their hats on that rack, don't bring them back." All of the girls did marry, and all had tall husbands. One was Ellison Smyth, of Virginia Polytechnic Institute; another was James J. Murray, foremost Virginia ornithologist; a third, standing an even six feet and the shortest of the lot, was Alexander Sprunt, Jr., known to bird students for his lectures and his books.

From the rock-capped peak of Grandfather Mountain, if the air is clear, two others of the four chosen mountains can be seen — Roan Mountain to the west and Mount Mitchell to the south-west. Unless one knows where to look he might not pick them out. Both stand among other peaks almost as high; neither has the individuality of Grandfather, although both are higher. But if they lack boldness of outline, they make up for it in the interest they hold for biologists, wildflower enthusiasts, and out-doors people generally.

Roan Mountain shares fame with Grandfather as a collecting ground, largely because it too has long been accessible. The toll road that once reached its summit has passed into public owner-ship, and today there is a continuous paved highway joining North Carolina and Tennessee across the saddle near Roan High Knob. High point is at 6313 feet, but there is a complex of peaks nearly as high, these joined by saddles on which are some of the finest of Appalachian balds.

The contrast between Roan Mountain and Grandfather could scarcely be more striking. In place of sheer cliffs and rocky peaks, the condition on Grandfather, Roan has wide mountain meadows, open grasslands interspersed with dense groves of firs, and a natural garden, 1200 acres in extent, of Catawba rhodo-dendrons. If we like legends, there is an explanation for this garden. Once the Catawba Indians, a strong and numerous people, challenged all the nations of the earth to a great battle on Roan Mountain. Days passed before the Catawbas were victorious, but in the fighting they shed much precious blood, and ever since the rhododendrons have bloomed red in mute tribute to their sacrifice.

Whatever the reason may be, the rhododendrons are there, thousands of them, rounded and compacted by mountain winds. So patterned is their arrangement that one might think this a portion of some great estate, a detached portion, perhaps, of the fabled Vanderbilt holdings near Asheville. Between the shrubs are natural openings, walkways that lead to new vistas, and on and on until it seems there is no end to the blooming. To see this display, visitors come by thousands. Both states have cooperated in building parking areas, picnic sites, branch roads and trails, and other facilities for the public on holiday. Blooming reaches its height past mid-June, the 20th of that month being a good average date. Avoid weekends near that time if you can; other days are much less likely to find the mountain roads crowded. If only Saturday and Sunday are available to you, see the show anyway. It will repay you for slow driving on long mountain grades.

With an amateur's enthusiasm and a professional's skill, Fred Behrend (he of the snow bunting studies already mentioned) has opened up for us the possibilities of winter birding on Roan High Knob and the other peaks and balds associated with it. These mountains may be in the near-South, but their climate is Canadian. Heavy snows, dense fogs, ice-crystal formations on every spruce and fir needle, subzero temperatures, and howling winds — these are things of Boreas and not of some kindlier spirit.

Almost every weekend during several winters, Behrend made his way to the heights, driving as far as he could, walking when he could no longer drive. His major discovery, of course, was the presence, year after year, of scattered individuals or small flocks of snow buntings; but he also had records of evening and pine grosbeaks when these were scarce in Tennessee, or even new for the state. He found cardinals, towhees, fox and white-throated sparrows, and robins above 5000 feet, all in midwinter, and sometimes during very cold periods. No one previously had suspected that these birds wintered so high in the southern Appalachians.

As spring came on and snows melted, bird populations increased. Surprising numbers of grassland dwellers found their way to the balds. Apparently there is a great crossover of species that nest in the lowlands. Many birds which do not nest there are on the heights in spring and fall. I shall not forget my own surprise at seeing numbers of meadowlarks one April on Charlies Bunion, a most unlikely-looking knife-edge ridge in the Great Smokies. Behrend's observations opened up new vistas as to transmontane migration.

It is a fine thing to see these mountain masses from their summits, but one has a greater appreciation of the heights if he descends to some of the valleys which separate them. Between Grandfather and Roan there is a maze of roads, some modern, many decidedly not. It is an experience to drop two thousand, three thousand, even four thousand feet into a narrow valley and to reflect on the isolation of those who lived there before the automobile and the radio. Mountains and the problems they present always look larger when we view them from below. It is not to be wondered at that cove and valley dwellers made long climbs to the balds; a more extensive landscape must often have seemed a necessity to shut-ins such as these.

The road from Roan Mountain to Mount Mitchell passes near Penland School, where Miss Lucy Morgan and her disciples have worked sheer magic among mountain people. Color and beauty have always been there, a sense of design is latent in an occasional natural artist, and Miss Lucy has taught her people to see their world and to use the talents with which they have been endowed. We shall return to Penland when we visit other craft centers, but you might drive through these valleys without knowing that the school is there, and that would be a pity.

Down through Spruce Pine, North Carolina Route 26 leads to the Blue Ridge Parkway, natural approach to Appalachia's highest peak. Low gaps along the Parkway are behind us, and farmlands are in far-off valleys. This is high and rugged country, forested for the most part and too steep for agriculture. The highway climbs from 3000 feet to 4000 feet, and it will go considerably higher. It is building up to the Craggies, and it has the Blacks to westward. Mount Mitchell is the climax of this range, most elevated land mass east of the Mississippi.

For Carolinians who live in the bright-leaf tobacco belt of the coastal plain, it must come as something of a shock to hear weather reports and temperature data from Mount Mitchell. Spring may be over and summer come to the lowlands, but snow drifts linger under the firs near Mitchell's peak. Frosts may occur during any summer month, and every night is cool. And this happens within the state, not in some far-off land to the north.

Near Milepost 355 on the Parkway, a side road, North Carolina 128, leads westward for five miles to a parking area near Mitchell's summit. From the car park a quarter-mile trail leads through the firs to a tower on the high point. The Black Mountains and the Craggies are nearby, the Balsams are to the southwest, the Smokies dimly beyond them, and on the northern horizon are Roan and its peaks and the familiar twin points of Grandfather. This is the top of eastern North America.

The Mitchell area is preserved as a North Carolina state park, some 1200 acres in extent. Most of this country was lumbered years ago; in fact, the present auto highway follows closely the grade of the old log road. Despite the logging, virgin stands of spruce and fir are to be found, and trails from the summit area lead to these.

Just downslope from the parking area is a lodge and restaurant maintained by the state. Visitors in its dining room have a tremendous view of the Craggies, and of Black Mountain Gap, which lies in the foreground. The state park also has campgrounds, picnic sites, and staff naturalists who interpret local geology and biology and conduct trips to special features of the area. Visitors who follow the park's trails and avail themselves of the guidance offered should have a basis for appreciating all that Mitchell holds.

Mount Mitchell takes its name from Elisha Mitchell, a devoted scholar-explorer of the company of William Bartram, Henry Schoolcraft, and others who made known to us the wild places of eastern North America. On one of his solitary exploration trips, Mitchell lost his footing, tumbled over a waterfall, and lay for more than a week before searchers found his body. Appropriately enough, he was buried near the mountain's summit, under a marker inscribed:

> Here lies in the hope of a blessed resurrection the body of Rev. Elisha Mitchell, D.D., who, after being for 39 years a professor in the University of North Carolina, lost his life in the scientific exploration of this mountain in the sixty-fourth year of his age, June 27th, 1857.

Mitchell's rival explorer was Thomas L. Clingman, also a scholar and writer. Between these two arose one of the disputes that have enlivened scientific exploration from time to time. After some rather acrid exchanges, both agreed on the highest point; the question was as to which one of them had first explored and measured it. Sentiment that arose after Mitchell's death may have been the deciding factor. In any event, Mitchell's name was given to the topmost peak, and Clingman is commemorated in the second-highest of the Blacks.

Plants and animals on Mount Mitchell are largely those we

have already seen on Grandfather and Roan. A surprising number of them were first discovered here, the mountain standing as the type locality for species or race. Older scientific literature would indicate that some forms are endemic to the Black Mountains, but further exploration, as roads and trails have been opened, has usually shown that living things are not so restricted in distribution as was once believed. It has already been made clear, I hope, that a visitor to any Appalachian peak, north or south, will see many species common to all the ranges from Canada to Alabama.

So we have reached three of our four high points, all three close together in miles, but each with an individuality and character to mark it. Grandfather is topped by bold rock cliffs, bare save for such vegetation as may cling in its quartzite crevices; Roan has its high grasslands and open rhododendron gardens; Mitchell is highest, with a forest of low, wind-shaped firs on its summit. The fourth peak, Clingmans Dome, is barely on the

---

Scenery and Vegetation. Appalachian peaks, ridges, and

valleys extend from Quebec to Georgia. They hold varied and beautiful scenery — northern summits reaching above treeline, the mountains farther south being clothed with coniferous and broad-leaved forests. In southern portions of the range, rhododendrons, azaleas, and mountain laurel compose the famous "pink beds." Rocky crevices hold ferns of many species, and shale slopes and orchid bogs may be nearby. Deciduous woodlands with their wealth of spring wildflowers, meadow and streambanks lush with summer blooms, and the splendor of Appalachian autumn are succeeded by snowy winters, when the country is still colorful because of many evergreen plants and brightly tinted fruits.

Opposite: In May and June massed displays of rhododendrons emblazon rocky summits and balds of the Appalachian highlands. From Lapland rosebay to the purple Catawba species, all have bright flowers and evergreen foliage.

Though split-rail fences bound the Great Smokies, much of this land is only recently explored and, because it lies within a national park, will remain unspoiled. Wildflower Week in the Smokies is a national institution.

The elaborate structure and upright growth of coral mushrooms (*Clavaria*) are diagnostic. Fleshy fungi abound where soils are deep, fertile, and well-watered.

Cantharellus floccosus, the vase-shaped chanterelle of coniferous forests, is among the more beautiful mushrooms. In late summer it is abundant some years, unaccountably scarce in others.

Luray Caverns in Virginia, just west of the Blue Ridge, are representative of developed limestone caves in Appalachia. Water-worn tunnels, sometimes miles in extent, challenge professional speleologist and amateur "spelunker" alike. Most cave animal life concentrates in twilight zones where some light penetrates.

Flowering dogwood, the state flower of Virginia, blooms in white profusion from April to June throughout much of Appalachia. It is almost the perfect small tree: the winter buds and twigs are attractive, the blossoms are classic in form, the autumn fruits colorful. Wildlife feeds on these red fruits, and when they are abundant robins often stay far north of their usual winter range.

Opposite: Morning sun pours through a leafy canopy onto a quiet stream. Though fire, lumbering, air pollution, and strip mining have all affected native forests of Appalachia, nature is quick to heal scars, and millions of acres are protected.

Spring suns bring out Dutchman's breeches (above) in rich deciduous woodland. Its fragrant blossoms nod above delicate fernlike leaves. Ground pine
(below, left) is a *Lycopodium* clubmoss, a relative of the ferns. It and its
relatives give winter color to mountain regions throughout the world. Lacking
chlorophyll, the waxy-white Indian pipe (below, right) cannot manufacture
food. This curious seed plant depends on decaying organic matter for its
subsistence.

Streams cut easily through shale beds, falling over more resistant strata. The many exposed crevices offer footholds to Appalachian spleenworts and other ferns and flowering plants, some of them endemic in such situations. Fossil hunters find these areas rewarding.

Sunlight through tall trees outlines the forms of deciduous woodland in the Massachusetts Berkshires.

Opposite, above: The monadnock of Mount Katahdin, Maine. Here above treeline the Appalachian Trail begins its 2040-mile course to Springer Mountain in Georgia. Below: Clouds hang low over a northern mountain lake, where balsam firs mix with hardwoods.

Heart of Gaspesia is the picturesque fishing village of Percé. The jagged heights of Percé Rock (left) provide vantage points for nesting gulls, guillemots, and cormorants. Bonaventure Island (background) has a great gannet colony, together with a wealth of other animal and plantlife.

Opposite: Rose pogonia is a beautiful bog orchid found rather generally throughout Appalachia. It opens its fragrant blossoms from May to August. In late summer, white boneset, purple Joe-pyeweed, and the brilliant cardinal lobelia clothe open streambanks.

Farmland in Vermont. Vermont's maple sugar country has the reputation, but fine syrup and sugar are produced commercially as far south as the Virginias. No odor is more enticing than that of slowly evaporating maple sap.

The blaze of autumn foliage reaches its greatest intensity in maple and birch forests around mountain lakes. Almost always there are somber evergreen conifers for background. Fall color is a long season in Appalachia, beginning in late September and still displayed by oaks and sweetgum in November.

Among "confusing fall warblers" the bay-breasted warbler has few peers: it is distressingly like a blackpoll. This autumn migrant resting in a Virginia creeper shows its characteristic wingbars and a remnant of spring color along its sides. It will winter from Panama to northern South America.

horizon, but if you have seen the three you will continue on to the last of the quartet.

It is not possible, I believe, for one who has visited the Great Smokies to revisit them without an upsurge of emotion. They soar, lifting the eye skyward as do no mountains south of the Presidential Range. They are wild, only recently explored, and, one suspects, still holding surprises. Many of their coves and slopes stand virgin, a forest as rich as our planet in its mid-latitude regions has to offer. Above all, they are likely to endure unspoiled: the National Park Service has spread its beneficent protection over them.

If one is driven by geometric logic, the shortest way to the Smokies from Mount Mitchell is through Asheville (remember, the Blue Ridge Parkway is not yet completed), across the Balsams, and in through the Cherokee Indian Reservation to U.S. 441, the only paved highway which spans the range from east to west. But the shortest distance isn't always best. Particularly if this is your first visit to the Smokies, let me suggest that you cross over to the Appalachian Valley in Tennessee, and so approach the mountains on their western slope.

There is reason in this. The North Carolina approach is through one spectacular mountain mass after another, each one holding peaks as rugged (and about as high) as any the Smokies have to offer. The Great Smokies, when one reaches them, are splendid, but still just one more mountain range.

An approach from the Tennessee portion of the Great Valley is entirely different. The valley is comparatively low, and distant Cumberland hills to the west serve merely to break the horizon. In full sweep the Smokies rise to the east, Le Conte, Kephart, Collins, Clingmans Dome, and other peaks as far as the eye can reach. The detour is justified; this is the way to see the Smokies for the first time. Assuming that this approach has been used, the visitor will pass through Gatlinburg (a mountain village transformed in one short generation into a busy and sophisticated tourist center), and will enter the Great Smoky Mountains National Park at the eastern edge of the village.

Just inside the park boundary are headquarters buildings housing offices, displays, maps and charts, and a museum devoted to local geology, topography, and biology. Here, if you are lucky, you may find Arthur Stupka, senior park naturalist, who has been with the Great Smokies park almost since its inception. He knows the park in all its facets and at all its seasons as does no other person. Other ranger naturalists on his staff will be glad to help you, and to answer your questions. A national park, after all, is an educational institution.

Following up the Little Pigeon River, first through gently sloping Sugarlands Cove, then onto steeper slopes, the transpark highway climbs in fifteen miles or so to Newfound Gap, on the Tennessee–North Carolina line. Here you are about 3600 feet above your starting point, and you have passed through oak-pine forest, cove hardwoods, northern hardwoods, dense stands of hemlock along the streams, and have entered a spruce-fir forest. Barring certain subtle differences, you are once again in New England.

At Newfound Gap the side road to Forney Ridge overlook, at the foot of the last climb to Clingmans Dome, turns south (more nearly west actually, in terms of the Great Smokies' orientation). At Indian Gap, where once a road across the mountains was constructed by Cherokees in an abortive attempt to supply Confederate armies under siege in eastern Virginia, the road (and the Appalachian Trail which here closely parallels it) is almost exactly a mile above sea level. A few miles beyond is the dip of Collins Gap, where birders sometimes come in spring to hear the calling of saw-whet owls. Rising from the gap, the paved highway ends at a parking area and turnaround 6300 feet up on Clingmans slope. Trails that lead from this spot to Andrews Bald, Fontana Dam, and other interesting spots have already been mentioned; we shall follow the short one to the

second-highest of eastern summits, the 6642-foot elevation of
Clingmans Dome. This, by the way, is the highest point on the
Appalachian Trail.

The ascent by foot is an easy one, through spruces, firs, and
scattered hardwoods. Like so many other Appalachian peaks,
this one has its special botanical feature, a dense stand of shrubby
mountain cranberry (already noted on Grandfather Mountain).
In June these shrubs are covered with the pink shooting-star
blossoms that characterize plants of this group; in autumn the
small red fruits ripen. I have not seen this southern endemic so
abundant elsewhere.

Visitors who reach the summit without previous warning are
in for a surprise. Above the wooded peak is a highly modern
observation tower which looks as if it might have been designed
by some not-quite-jelled student of Frank Lloyd Wright. A
curved and gently sloping ramp leads to the observation platform at the top of the tower. There is no doubt about it, an
invalid's wheelchair can be pushed to the top. It has been done,
and this is a talking point for the structure's defenders. Once at
the top, there is again no doubt that the view is magnificent.
The Smokies, the Balsams, the Nantahalas, the Unicois, and
Fontana Lake are all within the vista. No one will deny the need
for an observation tower on Clingmans summit. I have visited
it when none was there; you reached the peak but you were so
shut in by trees that you had little sense of accomplishment.
Whether the particular style that was finally adopted was justified must be left to each user. It is now possible to enjoy the
view above the trees, and that will be enough for many who
climb to the top of Old Smoky.

Curiously enough, the century-old rivalry between Mitchell
and Clingman has not quite disappeared. The observation platform on Clingmans is perhaps a few feet higher than the tower
on Mitchell; I have heard visitors to the former gloating in the
fact that they were the highest earthbound individuals in

eastern North America. It takes a very little to make some of us happy.

A climactic point like Clingmans Dome creates its own traditions and gathers its own legendry. Sometimes the fact is strange enough. In the park's early days, two visiting birders found their way to Clingmans and used an old wooden tower there as a vantage point for watching migration. Their reward was the passing of two white pelicans, about as unlikely a pair of vagrants as anyone might imagine.

Once we have reached southern Appalachia, this journey to four peaks is not a long one. It could be made, if necessity demanded, in a summer day. Done so hastily it would be a stunt, and not much more. There should be recreation in the experience, and that requires time for contemplation and for understanding. Mountains reveal themselves slowly. One needs to see these heights in all kinds of weather. From any one of them it is a marvelous thing to see the formation of showers on a summer afternoon. Sunlight may bathe the summit but down in the coves clouds are thickening, lightning is playing, and there may be two, three, or four local storms in action at one time. I remember flying out of Knoxville one winter morning. Haze was heavy above us, and for a time I could not see through it. Then as we climbed we broke into sunshine and I looked over to see the Smokies, only their summits above the clouds. There they stood — Clingman, Collins, Le Conte, Kephart, Guyot, and other heights stretching away northeastward. I had found a new dimension for viewing them.

Summer storms often break up at sunset, and level rays of light must pass through scattering clouds. At such times the peaks may be at their finest. Light lingers on the high places and there is depth of color and expanse of sky that lowlands can never see. Darkness, when it comes, is only another form of beauty. These are subjective matters, and it is not given the viewer to share his experiences. But we opened this chapter with a question, still unanswered and likely to remain so. It is a fair one for all that, and deserves full consideration. In seeking an answer one reasons only by analogy. At what point would the plants and animals at the top of Mount Mitchell be at home on the slopes of Mount Washington? How much extra must be allowed for the several degrees of latitude which separate these peaks? I have tried to see both mountains and I have made my guess. If fifteen hundred feet were added to Mitchell's summit, the new mountain would, I believe, reach treeline. Did such a mountain exist in North Carolina, we might find Appalachian sand-myrtle meeting its close relative, arctic azalea, in the tension zone where life is never static, always in advance or in retreat.

8. From Cove to Bald

THE SOUTHERN APPALACHIANS mean many things to many people. For some who have not been there, this is a land of primitive customs and primitive people, an "out-back" area that preserves the tools, the language, the ballads, and the attitudes of Elizabethan times. Outlanders who know these mountains will think of their scenery, their magnificent forests and wild-flower displays, their national parks, and, most of all, of the quiet, independent, friendly people who make their homes there. If you ask the residents themselves, they are likely to speak in terms of natural features — woodlands that provide game and building materials, gaps which allow passage by road or trail, coves where soil is good and water abundant, and balds on the mountains where cattle and sheep may find summer pasture.

It took European settlers many years to get away from the Atlantic seaboard and the piedmont. As population slowly increased, however, new lands had to be found and cleared. Once these were under cultivation, the results too often came in quick and disastrous order. Crops best suited to producing wealth had to be planted in rows and to be kept free of weeds. Corn, tobacco, and cotton were the staples, and northwestern Europeans had no tradition and experience of such crops. Neither could they foresee the effects of a summer deluge on steep slopes, once the soil had been broken.

In a colonial economy, land was wealth. Where the law of primogeniture was observed, younger sons who desired social advance or political preferment had no recourse but to seek new lands to westward. Good land in Pennsylvania and Maryland was soon taken; surpluses among Penn's German families, and land-hungry Ulster Scots, driven to the New World by famine that accompanied the appearance of potato blight, followed the valleys and ridges southwestward. The Great Valley was their highway, and they found homes on either side of it. By such racial stocks were the southern Appalachians settled.

Land use in a mountain country always develops by trial and error. Germans from the Rhine Valley had lived on steep slopes. They knew about terracing and other hillside soil and water conservation practices. These thrifty farmers, however, usually found valley lands or rolling plateaus; they had no need of mountainsides, so these were avoided. Scots, whether from the homeland or from Ulster, were more often animal husbandrymen. They required cropland for grains and grasslands for pasture. The first they found in mountain coves, the second were often supplied by balds — those yet unexplained grassy openings toward the summits of southern Appalachian peaks.

The coves could not furnish fertile soil for as many settlers as wished to build homes. Some were driven to the hills, forced to clear and plow slopes that should never have been disturbed. From the beginning theirs has been a losing cause. Many have given up and moved to the cities or lowlands; a few remain, according to their natures living either in fiercely proud independence or on government subsidies. At their best, they preserve some of the finest traditions of past times; at their worst, they help to make Appalachia and its people a problem for the nation.

It is appropriate, I suppose, to define the term "cove." In hilly or mountainous country, rainfall and melted snow pour down the slopes in torrents, these carrying soil, gravel, and other products of erosion. As slopes become more gentle and water is slowed in its course, some of this debris is deposited, the larger elements first and then finally smaller soil particles. The result of such deposition is a fan delta, a common land form in the Southwest at the mouths of arroyos. In older mountain areas these fan deltas become stabilized by vegetation, and time softens their outlines. Each year there is an accretion of eroded material from above, and each year growing plants and animals contribute to soil formation. After enough millennia have passed the result is a cove, a naturally terraced valley near the foot of a mountain slope. Such areas are likely to be well watered, and to have deep and fertile soils. They are protected by heights to the rear and by flanking ridges on either side. They are good places for human habitation.

As we have seen, westward slopes of the Appalachians face into the prevailing wind, and as a consequence receive heavier precipitation. This results in more erosion and more deposition; western slopes are likely to have the most extensive coves. When mountains are both ancient and massive, as is true of the Great

Smokies, cove development is at its best. There are, of course, fine coves on the North Carolina side of the range, but the largest and most famous are on the Tennessee slopes.

Parenthetically, I may as well admit here to some inaccuracy when I speak of eastern and western slopes of the Smokies. One becomes used to thinking of all Appalachian ridges as having a northeast-southwest orientation, but the Great Smokies are an exception: their main axis lies almost east-west. This is true of few mountain ranges in North America; the Uintas come to mind as having this orientation, but they, too, are exceptional in the Rockies system.

As a further complication, national parks people often divide the Smokies at Newfound Gap; when the visitor stands there facing into Tennessee, the portion on his right will be the "East Smokies," and to his left will be the "West Smokies." It would be more accurate therefore to refer to the Tennessee side as the northern slope, and to the North Carolina side as the southern slope. This comes awkwardly for me, and would, I believe, lead to confusion. It is easier, even if not quite correct, to refer to eastern (North Carolina) and western (Tennessee) slopes. In so doing I find a greater comfort, and I hope the reader will share my feelings. Having made this digression to show respect for the magnetic compass, I return to the coves.

Everyone who drives across the Smokies travels through Sugarlands Cove. Gatlinburg is at the edge of it. Sugarlands Cove narrows as the highway enters the park, but it extends to the first really steep slope, where the road begins to make sharp curves and bends. Sugar maple is perhaps the most abundant tree growing in this cove; hence the name. There are trees and shrubs of many other species, of course; hardwoods seldom grow in pure stands of any one species, and a solid forest of maples would be an anomaly. Through Sugarlands Cove passes the Little Pigeon River, the stream that helped create it. Smaller tributaries enter it from both sides, and there are frequent springs at the cove's margins.

If a visit is made during the growing season, particularly in April or May, one aspect of Appalachian coves soon becomes apparent. These are natural gardens of wildflowers; blossoms are both profuse in numbers and varied in species. Rich woods soil, abundant moisture, and shelter from unfavorable weather all contribute to a floral display which attracts pilgrims from near and far. Wildflower Week in the Great Smokies is a national institution.

North of Sugarlands Cove (east, if you insist) is Greenbrier Cove, holding some of the finest hardwood timber stands in the world. There are record holders among these trees, the best examples, so far as is known, of their kinds. Greenbrier Cove is not much touched by roads; this is hiking or horseback country, but every forester who visits the Smokies wants to spend some time there.

A few miles in the opposite direction from Gatlinburg is Cades Cove, largest and most famous of its kind. I have some Canadian friends who are connoisseurs of wildflowers; they have time and funds for travel, and they go about the land seeking areas especially favored. Each has his own favorite spots, but on one thing they are agreed — no other place that they have explored can match Cades Cove in the Smokies. They visit it and its neighboring coves when they can, and they tell of its charms to any who will listen. For them this is the best of all wildflower gardens. Several square miles in extent, the whole mountain valley is a museum — of trees and shrubs, of wild-flowers, of game and fish, and of pioneer life. This is the Appalachian cove *par excellence;* in its composition are all the proper elements. And, to the enjoyment of the visitor, it is accessible.

In Chapter 12 I shall have more to say about Appalachian forests, but a few notes must be entered here. First of all, these coves have been so important in eastern forest development that they have produced a major timber type. Lumbermen, foresters, and ecologists will know what you mean when you speak of "cove hardwoods." No other stands of deciduous trees in any midlatitude region (save, perhaps, in central China) are so rich and complex in woody species. Trees in these coves have been gathered from north and south; they are an assemblage of broad-leaved species from eastern North America. In Cades Cove, for example, is a stand of sweet gum (*Liquidambar styraciflua*), a southern coastal plains species important as a timber tree in South Carolina and Georgia. Nearby are northern hardwoods that would be at home around Lake Superior.

Mention (and only that) must be made here of such cove specialties as yellowwood (*Cladrastis*) and silverbell (*Halesia*). They, along with others, are to receive the attention they deserve. One plant at its best in deep moist cove soils is ginseng (*Panax quinquefolia*). "Sang," the mountain people call it, and it holds a very special place in their traditions and their hearts. In an economy that was largely conducted by barter and trade, and in which hard money was a rarity, ginseng could be sold at all times for cash. When taxes had to be paid, a few days of sang digging would raise the necessary funds. Fall was a good time to go sanging, since each mature plant held a cluster of bright red fruit, and since its leaves turned a shade of golden yellow which could be recognized at considerable distance. Cove woodland floors held a multitude of herbs, and any short-cuts to finding this one were welcomed.

Added to the economic importance of ginseng was a touch of romance: its roots, properly dried and handled, would be sent to faraway China. Cove people had few ties to foreign lands, but this was an authentic bond between unlike people. What these unseen Chinese did with the roots, once they were transported, was a mystery, but since all things must have an answer, the sang diggers dismissed the matter by saying that Orientals used the plant as a medicine. And, if one stretches a definition, they were right. Medicines are supposed to restore health and happiness in their users, and ginseng must certainly have fulfilled these functions. The Chinese held to the doctrine of signatures: if a plant resembled an animal, or a portion of one, that plant must be beneficial to the animal or the organ. This was sound reasoning, backed up by logic and experience. It happens that some ginseng roots simulate the human form, in that they are forked below a root portion which might represent trunk and head. This was man's form; therefore here was man's medicine. Medicine, that is, of a very special and precious kind. Fortunate Chinese who possessed such a treasure used it as an aphrodisiac. It made them irresistible to their lady friends; they knew it, the ladies knew it, and it worked.

I have often wondered what some of my stern and highly moral sang-digging ancestors would have done had they known the ultimate use to which their finds were put. On careful consideration, I believe they would have gone right on selling sang. That plant had special qualities even here at home — it transcended the moral law. Stealing was a sin, a mortal one since it was covered by the Ten Commandments, but the definition of stealing had some elasticity. If you found a patch of ginseng on a neighbor's land, you observed no formalities and asked no questions. You dug the sang, and you carefully replaced the soil so that he might not detect the removal. There was sense to that, too. Around the plants you dug were seedlings — one- and two-prongers, which if not disturbed would soon be good commercial three-, four-, and five-prongers, money in any man's pocket. If you were of a religious turn, you prayed that the landowner would not discover these promising seedlings.

I have been writing this in the past tense, but I needn't have done so. Sang is still being dug, and it commands a ready sale. It is shipped to Taiwan and to Hong Kong. From that latter port, some most certainly works through the Bamboo Curtain. We may not approve a tie between Appalachian coves and Red Chinese, but there quite likely is one.

In the West Virginia community where I was born, ginseng was held in special esteem, but not, I hasten to say, for the same reasons as apply in China. In the early years of the last century some of my ancestors left Vermont and Massachusetts hills and moved to what was then western Virginia. They brought some things that were new to the land — a maple sugar tradition, a strong Abolition sentiment, and a belief in public education. More specifically, they brought their own preacher, a man nurtured in Puritan tradition, but, unfortunately, of advanced years. It was obvious that he would not last long on this rough frontier. Before he departed a successor must be found.

It was no small task that faced the community in sending one of its sons to college. Fortunately there were appropriate candidates, too many, in fact. Finally, two of the most promising were chosen, then, after prayer, lots were cast (there is Old Testament precedent for this), and the choice fell on Loyal Young. Once the decision was made, the community went to work.

Women relatives and friends agreed to make his clothing. The local cobbler donated a pair of shoes. And each able-bodied male in the church pledged a few days of sang hunting. At the end of the summer, those men had dug, dried, and sold two hundred dollars' worth of ginseng, and this was the cash that educated the young ministerial student. Canonsburg, Pennsylvania, had the nearest suitable college, so, walking barefoot to save his one pair of shoes, Loyal Young traveled the nearly two hundred miles to college. He graduated in due time, and became something of a figure in church circles in western Pennsylvania and West Virginia. He was often called the "sang" preacher, and with good reason.

Southern coves and mountain slopes have another plant that has loomed large in the economy of pioneers. It is a member of the onion group, and it is named ramp, or wild leek (*Allium tricoccum*). My friends and neighbors would not appreciate it if I left this one out; it is important, and it deserves mention.

Many forget that canning and preserving foods is a relatively recent development. Settlers who cleared lands in Appalachian coves had no means of preserving fresh fruits or vegetables for winter. A few they could dry; some could be pickled; but for the most part such crops were seasonal, not to be found during the cold months. Staple foods were cornmeal and salt pork — dried fruits were precious and were used only on special occasions.

The result of this limited and monotonous diet was a great craving for green vegetables as spring approached. And there were the ramps to oblige. They showed their lily-like leaves on warm slopes almost as soon as snow departed, and beneath each pair of leaves was a succulent small onion. The plant was a life-saver, it brought needed food elements just in time to prevent scurvy. Ramps are not biting to the tongue, but they contain a garlic essence — allyl sulphate — in what must be its most persistent form. Even the rabid ramp-eater will admit, if pressed, that he grows a little tired of the taste about three days after he has feasted. Ramps, in other words, are not for the weak.

From West Virginia to Tennessee, there continue to be annual ramp festivals and suppers. The vegetable probably will be served both raw and cooked, so diners will have a choice, or may sample both delicacies. To give outland subscribers a deeper sense of and sharper nostalgia for a mountain spring, one weekly newspaper in the hills mixed ramp oil into its printer's ink, and sent that edition to bed in a fragrance that was distinctive, to say the least. Rumor has it that mail clerks and post offices called upon to handle this paper in transit made unkind remarks about the practice; in any event, it has not been repeated.

I have dealt with ginseng and ramps at some length to bring out the point that settlers in these once remote mountain coves used what they found at hand. To a remarkable degree they lived on local products, buying little and importing less. Some foods were excellent, some were not, but they had no other choice than to take what nature provided.

Cove soils, as we have seen, are often fertile and productive. They produce crops, and the best of them are much too valuable to be left as grazing lands. So graziers in these valleys faced a problem, once settlements became populous. Where would they find grass for cattle, sheep, and horses during the summer months? It seemed in many cases that a beneficent providence had foreseen just such a need, and had provided for it. High up in the saddles between Appalachian peaks were the balds — grassy openings that no ax had cleared, capable of supporting livestock during the growing season of young animals. People in Tennessee's Cades Cove who needed pasturage built a trail, a long and steep one, up to Gregory Bald, almost three thousand feet higher than their valley floor. Here dense clouds and fog, frequent showers, and heavy dews kept forage plants succulent. On such food sheep could flourish; during the summer, spring-born lambs reached full size. Cove and bald complemented each other; the result was a fuller life for man and his animals.

So now we come to one of the great mysteries of southern Appalachia. What causes brought about these grassy islands in a sea of forest, and what forces are preserving them? Their presence is a challenge to the ecologist; they refute or contravene his laws of plant succession. This is wooded country, the forest is the climax vegetative cover, end product of a progression that began with bare rock and waste places. Why has normal development toward a forest been checked in these grass balds? Many persons have wondered.

First of all, a few of the facts. There are eighty or more of these grassy openings in the southern Appalachians. They begin in Virginia and extend to Georgia. In no place do they approach treeline; mountains this far south are not high enough. Most often, they do not occur at mountain summits, but rather in the saddles connecting higher peaks. Forested country may be found both above and below them. Seldom or never do they occur below the 4000-foot contour, and many are above 5000 feet. They are not restricted to a single mountain range, but are found in all of the higher southern mountain masses. Finally, some of them at least were in existence when the first white explorers reached this land.

Students of plant life in extraordinary numbers have studied and explored in the Southern Highlands — first the pioneers such as Michaux, Pursh, and Rafinesque; then systematists like Asa Gray; and last the flood of ecologists, as roads were opened, parks were developed, and remote places became accessible. A goodly number of these have tried their hand at explaining balds. Some have sought first causes; others have been concerned with forces that arrest normal plant succession.

Since a good many balds face the east, it has been suggested that Indians cleared these highlands as places of worship, preserving the opening by use of fire. Some have thought that lightning-set fires on particular ridges have created and kept the openings. Early graziers have been credited with creating some of them. Periodic attacks of insects on certain tree species and at certain altitudinal levels have been offered in explanation. There have been many other theories and more variants on those listed above.

At this point I have decided to reveal a trade secret. All the world of ecology comes to the Great Smokies, and all who come walk the trails, and perhaps visit Andrews Bald in company with park naturalists. These professionals who have spent years in the park have a highly pragmatic system for evaluating visiting ecologists. It works in inverse ratio to the visitor's positiveness and assurance in explaining bald creation and continuance. Just possibly a knowledge of this grading system might save someone a bit of embarrassment. The truth is, of course, that no one explanation will meet all known conditions. There may be an element of truth in all, or most, of the causes which have been suggested. Bald formation, then, is like bird migration, in that no one pat theory will fit all the facts.

Some local observers who have watched shrubs and trees invading these grasslands feel that all such areas which are protected from grazing will disappear within a century or less. Others are not so sure; certain balds are a part of the Indian's tradition, and they seem to have been here for a long time. Perhaps they will continue as openings even under complete protection.

Forest Service roads have been built to some of the more extensive Appalachian balds, and state highways reach a few. Others must be reached by trail, and a few are still in trailless areas. There is a fine bald, with a road to it, in the saddle between Mount Rogers and White Top, Virginia's highest points. In the complex of Roan Mountain are several balds, some alongside highways that come up through both North Carolina and Tennessee. Some of the largest and finest are in the Nantahalas, south and east from the Smokies. Any visitor who drives or hikes may see what such areas look like.

Because it is a star tourist attraction, I shall describe Andrews Bald in the Great Smokies. As many, or more, people visit Roan Mountain each year as go to Andrews Bald, but Roan Mountain has other attractions, and most who go there are not primarily interested in grassy openings. Those who hike the two miles to Andrews Bald are probably interested in what such a detached and unexplained bit of grassland is like.

At Newfound Gap, traffic center of the high Smokies, a surfaced side road leads past Indian Gap to the Forney Ridge parking area just below Clingmans Dome. Leading from the parking area is a complex system of trails. This is a way station on the Appalachian Trail, and it may, of course, be followed in either direction. An easy half-mile trail leads to the observation tower on Clingmans Dome, second highest Appalachian peak. A third trail leads southward two miles to Andrews Bald.

Even though we have a principal objective, approaches too may hold their charms. This trail, all near or above the 6000-foot line, is one of the park's best places for finding northern birds and seeing boreal plants. Spruces and balsams predominate in the forest cover, and under these are many of the flowers we first met on Mount Washington's slopes. Olive-sided flycatchers, here at the southern extremity of their range, call from exposed spruce snags. There are many warblers which are also common breeders in the Shickshocks, and in the evenings there is a veery chorus such as might be heard around a Vermont lake.

Should the hiker be interested in cold-blooded vertebrates, this trail and its environs will afford a wealth of salamander species which could not be matched if populations on all northern Appalachian peaks were brought together. Nearest to a Smoky Mountains endemic is the striking red-cheeked salamander (of which more later), but there are others, some of them near their type localities. It is exciting to move a fallen spruce log and find these specialized amphibians underneath.

Andrews Bald, once the hiker reaches it, is not dramatic or strange. It looks like any bit of cleared land in a mountain forest, with some shrubs appearing at forest edges, and grasses and weeds elsewhere. It would be easy to forget that this area represents an ecological puzzle if it stood alone. When we recall that there are some eighty other such openings, the questions which surround them grow more insistent. Like so many others, Andrews Bald faces southeast. If Indians did come here to worship the rising sun, they picked a commanding spot. The view is tremendous, with the long line of the Smokies to the

west, the Balsams to the north and east, and the Nantahalas to
the south. Far down the slopes is the valley of the Little
Tennessee River, and parts of the deep lake created by Fontana
Dam show through forest openings.

Many of the invading shrubs are azaleas, among the most
decorative of mountain heaths. Near one margin of the opening
is a special feature of Andrews Bald, a small "hanging bog" on
a hill slope. Bogs of this nature occur where water seeps from
the ground, and because of some combination of circumstances
is spread out and retained on the slope. There are mosses here,
and other wetlands plants. One does not expect a bog on sloping
land, hence the term used to describe this and others of its kind.
Arthur Stupka, park naturalist, once told me that this was the
only one in the higher Great Smokies.

Before the park was established, Andrews Bald was used as
grazing ground by settlers down in the coves. They climbed
the mountain periodically to salt their livestock, and in this
connection they made an interesting natural history observation.
When Art Stupka questioned old settlers in the area he asked
about red crossbills, among many other things — birds that
occur in the conifers and might possibly be nesting within the
park. By that name the birds were unknown, but when he
described them more fully a light broke. In hopeful recognition,
some grazier asked, "You mean those salt-birds, don't you?"
And, sure enough, he did. Observers in western mountains have
learned to look for crossbills and other wandering finches at
places where salt is made available to cattle. The birds feed on
ground where salt has been scattered, and when a salt brick has
been placed they will cut at its edges with their crossed
mandibles. Old-timers in the Smokies had observed this habit
and had named the birds accordingly.

Grass balds are fine places for observing the "edge effect" on
wildlife, a concept Aldo Leopold did so much to bring to
common understanding. He, and others, observed that animals

like to live in places where they can change their environment
quickly. A forest margin has higher populations, normally, than
does the interior of a woodland. At edges, whether adjoining
fields, along roads, or bordering streams, there is a greater variety
of food, different types of cover, different light values, and other
things, perhaps, of value in the animal's struggle to survive and
to reproduce its kind.

Wild turkeys come out into Andrews Bald to sun and dust
themselves, catch grasshoppers, and find seeds of legumes which
are lacking in the forest. Ruffed grouse also feed around its
margins. Deer are not abundant in such heavily forested areas
as the Smokies, but those present undoubtedly use the balds.

There are peregrines and ravens within the park; the balds
are points of vantage from which to observe them. Although I
have not been present at the proper seasons, I can imagine that
during migration wood warblers, which swarm throughout
southern Appalachian ranges, must be especially numerous
around these grassy openings.

Had it not been for the balds with their forage for domestic
animals, dwellers in the coves might have been different people.
They could have stayed on their fertile lands, planting a little
corn, raising a few vegetables, content to forget the mountain
wilderness which rose around them. But the demands of growing herds and flocks were exigent; grass was available if they
could reach it, so they went exploring for the easiest trails, and
they found their way to the summits. By so doing they became
men of the forest as well as farmers. Coves and balds were for
husbandry, but woodlands and game were in between. From
valley to peak, the mountain was a good place in which to live.

And so we see a pattern in Appalachia from north to south.
In Newfoundland, in the Gaspé, and in New England there are
treeless areas, kept that way by climate. From the White Mountains southward for hundreds of miles, woodlands are all but
universal. Then as we reach White Top in Virginia and on to

Brasstown Bald in Georgia there are once again treeless areas.
No matter if causes and circumstances are different, these open
areas a thousand miles apart are curiously alike. Juncos seem to
find it so, since they nest on Shickshock summits and on Blue
Ridge balds. Even the snow buntings venture down in winter
to see what southern mountain grasslands hold for them.

9. The Southern Muskegs

WE WERE CAMPED at Cranberry Glades, in Pocahontas County, West Virginia, and my father caught a mouse that looked strange to him. He walked sixteen miles (each way) into Seebert to send it to the United States Biological Survey. When we came out for supplies a few days later, there was a telegram, signed by Edward A. Preble, asking if we could take him to the place where that mouse was caught. We could, and did.

This was pretty heady medicine, even for one too young to appreciate all of it. Preble was just back from the Arctic, after a two years' study of the muskox. His companion on this trip was Ernest Thompson Seton, and I had read Seton's book about it, *The Arctic Prairie*. For my generation, at least, Seton was the last word on the outdoors, and I was privileged to camp with one who had traveled with him.

Preble was not a man who talked very much unless there was occasion for it, and we were silent as we entered the glades area, worked our way through Flag Glade, stumbled through the alder thicket beyond, and entered Big Glade. Preble took a look at its mile-long expanse, its moss- and lichen-covered surface, its low clumps of bog rosemary, and the fringe of spruce forest surrounding it. He said, "If I didn't know I was south of Washington, I would say I was back on the muskeg."

Without any intention on his part, he had recognized the relationship and given a generic name to a number of sphagnum bogs in the central Appalachians. We have been calling them muskegs ever since, and rightly so. Muskeg is an Algonquin Indian word meaning "trembling earth" (so the dictionary states) , and certainly these areas fit that definition. Furthermore, they look like northern muskeg country. The two areas have a remarkable number of identical plants and animals, and, to all practical intents and purposes, these Appalachian bogs could be bits detached from James Bay or Minnesota north of the Red Lakes.

We camped and trapped in Cranberry Glades for several days. We absorbed as much wilderness wisdom as we could, and Preble was generous. We listened as he carefully questioned Frank Houtchens, an old timber scout who happened by, drawing out all possible information about local wildlife, and weighing it for accuracy. We had a good time.

And the mouse that started it all? It was a yellownose vole (*Microtus chrotorrhinus*) , which had not previously been known south of New York's Catskills. One of its closest relatives, the yellow-cheeked vole, is an abundant mammal in the arctic prairie from which Preble had just come. Our local party went to the traplines each time in fear and trembling lest we shouldn't catch any more, but we did — five of them.

The southern muskegs occur in unglaciated portions of the Appalachians from Pennsylvania south into Virginia. Most of them are in the Alleghenies, the sedimentary rocks of this range seeming best suited to bog formation. In local terminology, these are glades. I know that this word has another meaning elsewhere, but I bow to local usage; glades they shall be, since most residents would never recognize the word "muskeg."

Glade areas usually include both swampy woods and open marsh. Some are in natural depressions in the Allegheny Table-land, a plateau that extends from Somerset County, Pennsylvania, south across Maryland's Garrett County, and into northeastern West Virginia. Two of the largest muskegs,

Canaan Valley in West Virginia, and Burkes Gardens in Virginia, occupy anticline valleys, formations dear to the heart of the geologist. Some of them, Cranberry Glades as an example, occur in closely encircled mountain valleys, the topography suggesting the onetime presence of a lake, although there is no geological evidence in support of this.

As natural refrigerators for the preservation of northern plants and animals, these muskegs rank with or surpass higher Appalachian mountaintops. Water tables are just below the surface, and soaked sphagnum moss is a good insulator; water under such vegetation is always cool. Large boggy areas hold enough moisture to affect air temperatures: Canaan Valley, at 3200-foot elevation, sometimes has frost in every summer month.

Plants and animals in surprising numbers reach the southern limits of their distribution (at least in eastern North America) in these southern muskegs. If Swainson's and hermit thrushes, Nashville and mourning warblers, northern waterthrushes and purple finches breed farther south than Cranberry Glades, we don't know about it. Dwarf dogwood, buckbean (*Menyanthes*), and bog rosemary (*Andromeda*) are here just about on their southern periphery. Varying hares are fairly common, and make their southernmost stand; if they ever occurred in the southern Blue Ridge, they have long since disappeared.

American larch reaches Cranesville Swamp in Maryland and West Virginia, but no farther south. Rose-flowered dwarf raspberry (*Rubus pubescens*) is abundant in parts of Canaan Valley. Fir trees are of the northern species (*Abies balsamea*); farther south this species is replaced by Fraser's fir (*A. fraseri*).

Because it has been much visited and much written about, Cranberry Glades stands as the prototype of these southern muskegs. It has a good cross section of bog flora and fauna, and it is fairly accessible. Furthermore, it has been set aside by the United States Forest Service as a natural area; it is likely to be preserved in undisturbed condition. No description will be adequate, but I shall set down some of my own impressions.

Cranberry Glades is in the southwestern part of Pocahontas County. It is about two miles by Forest Service road from West Virginia Route 39 between Mill Point and Richwood. The glades and surrounding area are within the Monongahela National Forest. A wet area of about 600 acres lies between Charles Creek to the south and Cranberry River to the north, these two meandering streams joining near the foot of the glades. Elevation at the valley floor is about 3300 feet, and higher mountains — Cranberry to south and east, Kennison on the west, and Black to the north — almost enclose the glades, a narrow exit being the water gap between Kennison and Black Mountains.

About 100 acres of wetland is open bog — the glades proper. There are five of these openings: the largest, Big Glade, about 56 acres in extent; three others, Round Glade, Long Glade, and Flag Glade, considerably smaller. The smallest, Little Glade, is rapidly reforesting, and can scarcely be defined at present. Between the open glades are extensive alder swamps, and around their margins are dense tangles of low spruce, Canada yew, and quaking aspen. This swampy land makes up the other 500 acres of the valley.

The Forest Service road from West Virginia Route 39 ends in a parking area along Charles Creek. A truck trail leads to the right, and the entrance to Flag Glade is about one hundred yards distant. Because many persons visiting the glades want to see them without getting wet and muddy, the Forest Service has constructed a boardwalk over a portion of Flag Glade. Fortunately for the timid and fastidious, this leads through one of the best portions of the area, botanically speaking. A visitor may remain dry-shod and still see many of the glades' characteristic plants. Those who would explore further must resign themselves to wet and muddy feet. Once the plunge is taken, it's easy, except that moss and lichens, into which one sinks, drag at the feet like heavy snow. Occasionally there are bare areas; these are to be avoided, since exposed muck is very deep and sticky. Generally, however, the mossy cover is firm, and hikers may move over it without danger of breaking through.

If the visitor leaves the boardwalk and trail through Flag Glade and bears to his left, he will reach an alder fringe that separates Flag from Round Glade. A good landmark is a grove of tall black ash trees; keep to the right of them. Round Glade, about twenty acres of open bog, has spectacular hummocks of moss, these creating a wave effect, the crests sometimes being three feet higher than the troughs.

The boardwalk and principal trail through Flag Glade leads to another alder fringe, this one enclosing Big Glade, largest and best of the bogs. There are streams through the alders; these have muddy banks, but must be crossed. The hiker soon learns to ride convenient alders down, using them as a bridge on which he may cross with wet but not too muddy feet. A visit to Big Glade is worth this discomfort anyhow. Matted vegetation, which largely covers the fifty-six acres of this bog, is composed of moss of two types — peat moss (*Sphagnum*) and pigeon-wheat moss (*Polytrichum*). Both these mosses have the habit of producing new growth on top of the old, so that continuous strands, part living, part dead, preserve the growth record of many years. Since they live in, and help create, highly acid media, decay is slowed or practically inhibited; the plants mat with dead portions constantly pushed downward as new growth appears at the top. After a while the result is peat. Back in the days when these mountains were being uplifted in the Appalachian Revolution, peat beds, under proper pressure, changed to coal.

Here and there green moss beds are interrupted by mats of grayish lichen, largely reindeer moss (*Cladonia rangiferina*). The use of "moss" in this name is unfortunate; lichens belong to a more primitive botanical class. Lichen beds support few other plants, but mosses nourish a rich flora which trails over its mats or grows upright from them. Nominate plants for the entire region are the cranberries, two species of *Vaccinium,* growing as nearly prostrate vines, bearing pink flowers in June, and abundant crops of fruit in October. Wild turkey hunters are often successful in the glades region, and they may, if they wish, harvest native cranberries whose tart sauce will accompany the main dish.

Dewberries (*Rubus*) cover the large areas of the moss mats. There are many low grasses, rushes, and sedges. Here and there are shrubby tangles — chokeberries (*Aronia*), wild raisin (*Viburnum*), and the much more interesting bog rosemary (*Andromeda polifolia*). But these are not the plants that attract visitors. Many wild tales about orchids in Cranberry Glades have become current, and during much of the year travelers to the glades who expect to see these plants in tropical profusion are doomed to disappointment. Orchids are present, of course, most of them tiny plants with inconspicuous blossoms. There are a few pink and yellow lady's-slippers in spring, and good hunting may yield yellow-fringed orchids in August. There are, however, two handsome orchids which are sufficiently abundant to create a floral display. Both are familiar to bog-trotters everywhere, both occur in far greater profusion in Great Lakes states bogs, but both are very fine in Cranberry Glades for all that. First to bloom is pink-flowered snake's mouth orchid (*Pogonia ophioglossoides*) which is at its best in late June. Don't be prejudiced by the name; this is a lovely wildflower, of interesting form and structure. Second of the pair is grass-pink (*Calopogon pulchellus*), a taller, brighter, and more conspicuous orchid, which overlaps the blooming period of the snake's mouth but is at its best a few days later. Flowers are borne in a loose spike, each one an inch or more across. Colors vary from pink through deep rose to magenta, although occasional blossoms are pure white. Fortunately for the more dilletantish visitor, both these orchids are common on the left side of the convenient boardwalk. In fact, this portion of Flag Glade is one of the best in the entire area. A trip there in early July should find them in impressive numbers. Grass-pinks are at their handsomest, and in greatest numbers, toward the center of Big Glade. I once counted seventy-two spikes within a square yard; this was the area of greatest density, but there were other good ones around it. This plant likes sunny, open spaces; snake's mouth prefers shrubby borders or the shelter of higher vegetation.

At this point I must have a word with the plant collectors. Many of my best friends are amateur gardeners; unfortunately, some of these have fingers that itch for a trowel whenever they see an attractive plant. The word is — don't disturb these, pass them by. First of all, the glades have double protection; they are within a national forest, and they are a part of a designated natural area in that forest. Permission must be granted before a plant may legally be removed. And secondly, the chances are a hundred to one against your having any luck if you try transplanting these to the home garden. A sphagnum bog is a highly specialized habitat; moisture and acidity must be just right. Bog orchids are acclimated to these conditions, and they are not likely to thrive elsewhere.

And now another word to Cranberry Glades visitors who are not botanists. These bogs have suffered from the wrong kind of publicity — they have been oversold. Feature stories in newspapers have told of orchid wealth, of insect-eating plants, and of other wonders; the visitor is led to expect marvels and monstrosities at every turn. Furthermore, he has been warned that these are places of great danger — of bottomless muck waiting to suck him down, of endless tangles in which he may get lost, even of snakes and other wild things that lurk to do him bodily harm. He arrives primed for new sights, strange experiences, and high adventure, all spiced with an element of danger. He finds a swamp where most plants are inconspicuous, none of them with strange or startling forms, and all looking vaguely familiar. He sees no vast assemblage of game; he is not conscious of having broken through barriers or of crossing new frontiers. He steps tentatively off the boardwalk, gets his feet wet, and goes home. He has been to the glades, and they can have it.

All this is unfortunate, because there is an element of truth in the stories he has heard. We have seen that there are orchids here — fine ones too, if the visitor arrives at the right time. There are a few insect-catching plants, strange and interesting enough when one looks at them closely and understands what he sees. I have seen no venomous snakes around Cranberry Glades, but there are most assuredly mucky spots in which it would be uncomfortable to get stuck.

Let's take that a little farther. One of my uncles, A. B. Brooks, was, among other things, a surveyor. He and his brothers once measured off an acre of bog land in Big Glade, placed plumb bobs on tripods at each corner, and stationed observers to watch the plumb bobs. Then one man went to the approximate center of the acre and began jumping up and down. Presently all four plumb bobs were swaying in cadence. This is a muskeg — trembling earth — all right.

I once cut a sixteen-foot sapling, took it out into Flag Glade, and, single-handed, pushed it straight down into the muck until its top disappeared. At one edge of Big Glade is an invading white pine, ten or eleven inches in diameter. Its roots escape drowning out by radiating through the mosses just beneath the surface but not actually in the water. It is a fine tree for a plant physiologist, since root ramification can be studied with very little digging. I take a class of forestry students there each year. We all stand on one side of the tree, locate a root with our feet, and begin jumping up and down in unison. Presently the white pine tree is swaying like a ship's mast in a heavy sea.

There are two ways of getting lost. In the first, the victim is completely disoriented, has no idea of direction, and knows no way out of his difficulty. This is so unlikely in Cranberry as to be ridiculous; the veriest greenhorn can work toward a mountain, at the foot of which he will find a trail. Trails always lead someplace.

The other kind of getting lost, on the other hand, is a frequent experience of visitors to the glades. It consists in not knowing how to get back to some fixed object — camp, car, or a particular trail. You are inside the expanse of Big Glade; its rim is three miles around, all fringed with alders, and all looking exactly alike. You have left your car at the parking lot outside Flag Glade, and you want to go back to it without too much walking or undue delay. Where are you going to make your exit through the alder fringe to get back to Flag Glade? This is your problem, and it may be troublesome, particularly if a severe mountain thunderstorm is threatening. No trouble at all, if you have taken a simple precaution. When you break through the fringe of this or any other of the larger glades, hang a jacket or tie a handkerchief in some conspicuous spot. This will be your orientation point, and you can return as you went in. It is simple, and it is effective.

The visitor to any of these southern muskegs (all of them have similar plants and animals) will find greater enjoyment if he knows what to look for and understands something of what he sees. He will find things with less delay and will see more if he has a guide who knows the area. If his experience of such situations is wide, he will marvel that so many out-of-range things are present, but he will also puzzle over those that are missing.

In Chapter 5 I told of some of the characteristic flowers that grow on the slopes of Mount Washington. Nearly every common wildflower there (up to but not beyond treeline) grows at Cranberry Glades, but how different are their situations! There they are on forested slopes; here in open or partially shaded bogs. Close as the correspondence is, there are some curious differences. Why, for example, is twinflower (*Linnaea*), which grows elsewhere in West Virginia, missing at Cranberry Glades?

In the same chapter it was noted that birds on Mount Washington's slopes, up to but not including the last balsam forest, would have been at home in the higher southern Appalachians. Nearly all of them nest at the glades; why, then, are myrtle warblers an exception? Why, in a wealth of bog plants, are leather leaf (*Chamaedaphne*) and sheep laurel (*Kalmia angustifolia*), both common in sphagnum bogs in neighboring states, absent at Cranberry? Why do pitcher-plants (*Sarracenia*) occur in muskegs as far as southern Pennsylvania, but not over into Maryland and West Virginia? These, and like questions, trouble the ecologist and the plant geographer; other appreciative visitors will find enough to see in any of these bog situations.

The boardwalk at Flag Glade passes over and through some of the area's more interesting plants. Round-leaved sundew grows here, one of those bog dwellers that must supply its protein needs by catching and digesting insects. Its spatulate leaves are covered with spiny hairs; at the tip of each of these is a tiny bead of syrupy exudate, attractive to small insects. When one such wanders in to dine, it is caught by the syrup, and as it struggles more and more of the spines become involved. Then a curious thing happens. Slowly, but inexorably, these spines begin to curve inward toward the center of the leaf, carrying the luckless captive with them. They press the victim firmly against the leaf's surface; a protein-digesting enzyme is secreted, and the plant is fed from the body of the insect. After the meal, the spines return to normal position in wait for another victim.

There are other insectivorous plants in Cranberry Glades. Horned bladderwort (*Utricularia*) lives along some of the streams and in damper areas. Its leaves hold small bladder-like traps, each one capable of catching, keeping, and (presumably) eating small insects or other animals that show too much curiosity concerning the bladders. Pitcher-plants in some southern Pennsylvania muskegs have been noted; there is a thriving colony of these efficient insect traps in Big Glade, but it is there through man's contrivance. Shortly after World War II, a few plants from Pennsylvania were moved to Cranberry Glades; these have increased and seem completely at home.

A handsome bog plant, Van Brunt's valerian (*Polemonium van-bruntiae*) is at or near its southern limits in Cranberry Glades. It, too, is abundant beside the boardwalk. In the same locality, Mrs. Graham Netting found an orchid rarity, Small's twayblade (*Listera smallii*), not known elsewhere in Cranberry but common in a rich (and unnamed) muskeg on Droop Mountain, about twenty miles away.

There are other plant specialties in these southern muskegs. The one on Droop Mountain, just mentioned, has thousands of plants of netted chain-fern (*Woodwardia areolata*), a species associated with coastal plains, seemingly out of place on a 3000-foot mountain. Canaan Valley has large areas overgrown with creeping snowberry (*Gaultheria*), one of the handsomest and most delicate of heaths. In a semiswampy area in Garrett County, Maryland, there is a remnant colony of fringed gentian (*Gentiana crinita*), known to few and cherished by them in the secret.

Those who visit Appalachian bogs learn to do so with expectation that each trip will bring some new experience. If I may use a paradox, they learn to expect the unexpected, and they are seldom disappointed. For example, thousands of persons, many with outdoor interests, have visited Cranesville Swamp, and there is good reason to think its bird life is quite well known. A few years ago, however, Forest Buchanan and Albert F. Ganier took a group into a much smaller glade nearby, one that had been neglected in light of the larger area, and found the first West Virginia nests of white-throated sparrows. Their record holds; not only are these West Virginia's sole nests, but they are also the southernmost ones recorded in the United States.

Late in May, some of us were in Cranberry Glades and we

decided to walk to the head of Big Glade to see buckbean in bloom. On a moss hummock in the middle of the open area stood a large shorebird with a decurved bill. Fortunately for a record, we had two things — a .22-caliber rifle, and necessary scientific collecting permits. The steadiest hand was given the gun and he collected the bird. It proved to be a whimbrel (I still prefer the name Hudsonian curlew), the only specimen ever taken in West Virginia. I marvel at this. Here was a bird presumably on its way to the tundras. Its course for hundreds of miles must have been over forest land, but when it spotted what looked like tundra it came down to feed and rest.

Sometimes there are unexpected, or unexplained, events of a different nature. On one camping trip to Cranberry, some of us started up Black Mountain with the purpose of spending the night at a fire tower on its summit. My father stayed in camp, since he had some traplines out, and wanted to look after them. We had lunch that day on a rocky spur that overlooks the glades, some thousand feet higher and two or three miles away. During our meal we spotted my father walking across Big Glade, and with our glasses we could see the slicker that he had hung up to mark his point of exit. By sheer chance, one of us was looking in the right direction to see a man come out of the alders, take the slicker, and disappear. And that's the end of the story; in a week's stay there we did not see another human being, before or after this incident.

On one rainy night we were in a tent set not far from the Frank Houtchens cabin. Since the night was warm and the rain gentle, we had rolled up the tent walls for better ventilation. Suddenly one of those sleeping in an outside position said, "Lie still, boys. I think a snake just crawled across me." It was pitch-dark, and we were afraid to move. One after another of us felt its weight as it moved leisurely along. When it came to Bill Rumsey, then state entomologist of West Virginia, it crawled across his face. That, too, is almost the end of the story, but not quite. We never saw the snake, but next day we noticed that Rumsey seemed preoccupied. He spent a long time with figures that we didn't understand, but finally he enlightened us. "Boys," he said, "I timed that snake as it crawled across my forehead last night, and if my figures are right, it was exactly twenty-eight feet and three inches long."

As had been noted, the preservation of Cranberry Glades seems assured. Others of the muskegs have been or will be protected. In Pennsylvania the very active Western Pennsylvania Conservancy is using funds (and time and influence that money couldn't buy) to safeguard beauty spots and areas of special scientific interest in the Pittsburgh region. Some of the better small bogs are now in sympathetic hands.

Cranesville Swamp, divided between Maryland and West Virginia, is receiving much attention from the Nature Conservancy. Members from the two states and the District of Columbia are unusually active; some land has been purchased, other tracts are under option, and a fund-raising campaign is having encouraging results. Happily, the pride of many local citizens has been aroused; they too are cooperating.

Canaan Valley, near Davis, West Virginia, has extensive boggy areas, and its potential as a biological treasure-house is tremendous. The valley floor has elevations around 3200 feet, and its extent is about 25,000 acres. The Blackwater Fork of the Cheat River meanders through it, and cranberry bogs are frequent. Water resources have been increasing as beavers have moved in; there are now many dams in the valley. Some of the land is under cultivation, and more is being grazed, but there is still a lot of wild land, some of it reforesting in balsam fir.

I may as well put in a word here about the local pronunciation. The name is spelled like the Biblical land of Canaan, but by local usage it is called *Ka-nane'*, with the accent on the second syllable and the second *a* given its long sound.

Canaan Valley had a tragic history, and its comeback has been a slow one. A hundred years ago valley and surrounding ridges were covered by red spruce forest of a density that is hard to imagine today. Under such a forest the sun never reached to ground level, humus accumulated through the ages, and fire was not a threat. The lumberman came, ultimately, and if total and permanent destruction of the entire area had been an aim it could scarcely have been more fully realized. An official of the company boasted that in 100,000 acres they had not left one stick of timber that would make a two-by-four. Log yields were fantastic; some acres on the valley floor scaled 80,000 to 100,000 board feet of lumber.

With all cover removed, organic material at ground level began to dry out; soon it was high-grade fuel, and the inevitable fires got started. There followed such a ground fire as this state has never seen before or since. For months this humus layer smoldered, and neither rains nor snows could stop the fire's slow advance. The village of Davis was saved by a series of deep trenches around it, these kept filled with water carried from the Blackwater River. When the destruction was complete, all vegetable material that wasn't soaked had burned, and with it all insects, worms, salamanders, mice, and other burrowing forms of life. Bare rocks remained, and thin mineral soil, this often several feet lower than ground level in the original forest. Canaan and its environs had become a desert. I have often wondered if the Pittsburgh company responsible for this has been proud of its job, and if it has enjoyed the resultant wealth. Slowly at first, then more rapidly, the processes of ecological succession began to come into play. Fireweed (*Epilobium*) appeared as though by magic, much as it did in London after the bombings and fires of World War II. For a few years it was the dominant plant, and during that period the bees thrived. Fireweed honey is among the best.

Fire cherry, too, is well named; birds must have carried in the seeds, for it began to grow around Canaan in an amazingly short time. Bracken fern is another pioneer; so are goldenrods and asters. Where there was any remaining soil, there began to be vegetative cover. Cover of a sort — true; but a far call from dense spruce forest. Then nature received an assist; the Civilian Conservation Corps went into operation, and one of its projects was the reforestation of Canaan Mountain. In places there was no soil at all to work with, so trucks ran from the valley night and day, bringing dark muck soil to the mountaintop. One bushel, sometimes two had to be used for each tree, but the roots of spruce seedlings were packed in. They lived and they grew. Twenty-five years later there is a beautiful young spruce forest overlooking Canaan Valley.

There are small but rich and interesting mountain bogs on the campus of the University of Virginia's Mountain Lake Biological Station. These are in good hands; they are the objects of study and research. Much larger bog areas are in the anticline valley of Burkes Gardens in Tazewell County, Virginia. Local residents are proud of these bogs and want to keep them.

If you decide to visit one of these southern muskegs, bring an open mind and an understanding of what you are about to see. There are marvels to be found all right, but don't expect that they will be spectacular or bizarre. These bogs and the life within them are a gift of the Ice Age; they were stocked and planted when glaciers pushed southward. As ice retreated and warmth came again to the land, plants and animals better suited to a bland climate invaded and took over. But the bogs were natural refrigerators; they resisted, and they kept their remnants. The Pleistocene was only yesterday over much of our land. In Cranberry Glades it is still with us.

10. The Shale Barrens

LEGEND HAS IT that a botanical group in New York City was once wealthy enough to send its staff members on vacation to White Sulphur Springs, West Virginia. There was a stipulation in this arrangement, however: some of the time was to be spent in a postman's holiday — plants were to be searched for and preserved, since this area had a little-known, but promising, flora.

The story continues that vacationing botanists, doing their duty to institution and profession, started up the nearest convenient mountain by the best available trail. As the first one took this path, he presently discovered a plant new to science. In great excitement he came down, took it back to New York, described it, and thus perpetuated his name in the annals of botany. The next visitor climbed higher on the trail, again found a new species, and repeated the performance. It took the plant hunters years to get to the top of Kate's Mountain; nearly every trip yielded a new plant, and thus was the sponsoring institution repaid.

As with most legends of this sort, there is a hard core of truth here. Eminent botanists did collect on Kate's Mountain, and their labors led to the discovery and naming of many new plant species. This mountain just above the resort hotel was named as type locality for the newly discovered plants, and for many years it was the only known station for some of them.

Collectors from other botanical gardens, herbariums, and universities were drawn to the area, under the impression that this was the only spot in the world to find Kate's Mountain clover, white-haired clematis, and other unique treasures. Then some more imaginative soul began to search other slopes with similar geology and topography; other colonies and stations were found, and it became clear that these botanical specialties might be local but were certainly not rare. These discoveries came, often enough, just in time to save the plants in their type localities: enthusiastic collectors were fast eradicating them on Kate's Mountain.

The discovery of one new plant species may not be an earth-shaking event, but when a single area yields more and more such finds, science begins to take notice. The area involved must have a combination of geology, soil, topography, and climate favorable to the production and retention of endemic species. The botanists were first in leading us to a knowledge of and appreciation for steep shaly ridges which occur east of the Allegheny Backbone in Pennsylvania, Maryland, West Virginia, and Virginia. These are the shale barrens — anything but barren if you ask the plant students, since so many endemic species have been found on these steep wasteland slopes.

Just west of the Appalachian Valley is a region of long, nearly parallel ridges, all separated by valleys through which streams flow. To the north, most of these streams are tributaries of the

Potomac; farther south they flow into the James, or are captured by the westward-flowing New River. This is the previously mentioned Ridge and Valley Province. It lies between the Great Valley and the higher Alleghenies; its streams form a trellised drainage pattern; nearly all its exposed rocks are sedimentary in origin, and many of them are shales. These rocks date from a geological period when life (at least in forms complex enough to leave fossil remains) was emerging. They span a period of millions of years, from Cambrian to Devonian. By the end of this last period, many of the major groups of plants and animals as we know them today had appeared; life in water was unbelievably rich and complex, and living things were conquering new media on land and in the air.

The Devonian Period was a long and intricate one. Rocks tell the story of alternate flooding and drought. Weather fluctuations must have been extreme, and storms violent. Water eroded and transported vast quantities of finely divided soil particles, deposited them in thin layers, and left the shale beds which outcrop over large parts of the mid-Atlantic states. Preserved within these thin rock sheets are the fossil remains of uncounted water creatures; on the surfaces of Devonian shales are plants that have not been found anywhere else in the world.

As we shall see, the shale barrens have many aspects and attributes of desert areas. A variety of circumstances helps to bring this about, some meteorological and others due to the arrangement of rock strata. It seems paradoxical to speak of deserts in the well-watered East, but extremely dry situations do exist. Appalachia is enriched by semideserts and the plants and animals that can find a home within them.

Much of the precipitation that reaches the eastern United States is a product of evaporation and cloud condensation over the Gulf of Mexico. Winds that blow steadily from the southwest carry these clouds inland; some are dense enough to bring rain to lowland areas, others are carried northeast until they strike Appalachian ridges. Here they are turned abruptly upward into cooler air strata. In this cooler air, clouds are squeezed like a sponge; they deposit moisture at a much higher rate. By the time they have passed above the higher Appalachians they have deposited most of their water content; little remains for eastward-facing slopes.

This pattern of precipitation may be understood if we look at the records of three weather stations in West Virginia. The first, at Huntington, is on the Ohio River, at an elevation of about 600 feet. Clouds that have traveled from the Gulf have not up to this point crossed any high ridges; they still retain a large share of their moisture. Huntington receives about 30 inches of precipitation annually. About 150 miles northeastward is the village of Pickens, in Randolph County. The weather station here is on the western slope of the first high Allegheny ridge. Cooling and condensation are proceeding rapidly; Pickens gets 69 inches of rainfall during an average year. About 75 miles east from Pickens is Upper Tract, Pendleton County. This village is on the eastern slope of the last high Allegheny crest. Clouds that pass over it have had most of their moisture squeezed out. There is little left for Upper Tract; its annual total is about 27 inches. Meteorologists use an interesting term in describing such areas as Upper Tract. They refer to them as being in a rain shadow. This is relevant to our discussion; Appalachian shale barrens are within rain shadows, and the living things found there reflect this condition.

Extremes of precipitation may have more biological significance than do averages. During the driest year of record, Pickens received 39 inches. In that same year, Upper Tract had less than 9 inches, a total that compares with many a full-scale desert. Even this is not the whole weather picture; much of the rain which falls on the shale barrens comes as a result of Atlantic hurricanes that have sufficient force to cross the Blue Ridge. One of these may give Upper Tract one quarter or one fifth of all the moisture it will receive during an entire year.

For influencing plant growth, rainfall efficiency is much more significant than rainfall total. The important question, after all, is how much of the moisture remains where it is available to plant roots. It would be difficult to create a situation better suited to quick runoff and low rainfall efficiency than is found in the shale barrens. Slopes are steep, and thin rock layers act much like shingles on a roof. Many of the strata are sharply folded; erosion tends to wear down outside edges so that water will not easily work back between shale layers. This is a country of much sunshine and high summer temperatures, so evaporation is rapid. In sum, the shale barrens retain and the plants that grow upon them can use only small quantities of the limited precipitation which reaches them.

Plants living on shale respond in interesting ways. Some, like the cacti and certain sedums, have developed fleshy stems or leaves for storage of water. Others — wild pinks are good examples — have deep, fleshy roots, advantageous in that they can store water that is available and search for it in the depths. Some ferns and their close relatives the resurrection mosses (*Selaginella*) fold up their fronds for greater protection in hot, dry weather. Many plants have tiny, awl-like leaves which may become spines as the season advances. There are plants that shed their foliage in hot weather, living for weeks in a state that might be called estivation.

I once had occasion to study adaptations that plants have made for existence under desert conditions. Russian plant physiologists, I found, had done more work on this than had any other students I could learn about. They had studied the dry lands from the steppes to the Gobi Desert, and they had listed the means by which plants conserve water. I found, somewhat to my gratification, that every major adaptation was exemplified by plants growing on the Appalachian shale barrens. Semi-arid conditions here are not a mirage.

It is noteworthy that shale barrens, with their dry-lands plants and animals, begin less than 100 miles west of Philadelphia, Baltimore, Washington, and other Atlantic Coastal Plain cities. They are within easy reach, but visitors who pass through are likely to dismiss them as starved-looking scrubby areas, without scenic or biological promise. There are times, as we shall see, when shale slopes are covered with bright wildflowers. In autumn the many species of oaks on these low ridges take on spectacular foliage coloration. But it remains true: the endemic and unusual species are often obscure, noteworthy only to those who search for them and understand what they find.

Plant life on mid-Appalachian shales might well be divided into three groups. One, the most exciting botanically, consists of true endemics, plants that have not been found anywhere else in the world. Some of the more noteworthy of these are described later in this chapter, and receive attention in subsequent chapters.

A second, much smaller group of plants is noteworthy because its members are distinctly western. Some are not found again east of the Ozarks; others have their nearest relatives in the Rockies. Such plants give eloquent testimony as to moisture conditions on the barrens. They are at home in much drier situations than can usually be found in the East.

A third and larger group of plants are those with much wider distribution in eastern North America, their best and most characteristic development often being reached on shale. In this category are many species which for one reason or another are conspicuous. We shall take a closer look at some of these. Because it is so commonly associated with deserts, we may well start with cactus. These plants are not shale barrens endemics (one race may be distinct); they occur on sandy beaches and wastelands, but it is always something of a surprise to find them flourishing on hillsides just west of the Atlantic seaboard.

Shale barrens cacti are of the prickly pear type (*Opuntia*).

They grow on rocky outcrops throughout the Shenandoah Valley, and in late May and early June masses of their showy yellow flowers may be seen from the Valley Turnpike (U.S. Route 11). Farther west the plants are locally common, often on exposed slopes near roads. In the valley of Patterson Creek, in Mineral County, West Virginia, prickly pears occupy a tract of several hundred acres. This would be a respectable cactus stand in Texas. The thick water-conserving pads look relatively harmless but are well armed with spines for all that. This will be painfully evident to anyone who handles them carelessly. One of my students brought a pad into class as a curiosity. When I asked him if he had put it through fire to remove the spines he said, "Never mind, they are all in my fingers."

Geologists and botanists are agreed that outcrops of Devonian shales may be traced by the presence on them of creeping phlox (*Phlox subulata*) in some of its varieties. This is a common spring flower in cultivation; in my home territory it has been so much planted in cemeteries that a local name for it is "graveyard phlox." Most cultivated plants have magenta flowers; some are pink or red, and there are purple, lavender, and white varieties. A few shades are garish and are disliked by some people. Wild phloxes blooming on shale outcrops are usually in softer hues. Pastel shades predominate, with lavender, pale pink, and pale blue the most frequent. Some are so light in color that at a little distance they appear white. Certain Allegheny slopes are so thickly overgrown as to appear snow-covered when creeping phlox is in bloom.

Natural companions of phlox on shale slopes are the bird's-foot violets (*Viola pedata*), the nearest thing we have to wild pansies. These plants have finely cut leaves and flowers that are large for violets. They occur in two principal varieties, but there are endless departures from the main types. In one, often called the bicolored violet, the two upper petals are deep purple, their texture velvety as in pansies. The other three petals are in shades of blue. The second common variant has all five petals blue, but there is wide range in the color values even in these. Some are pale, some intense.

On Peters Mountain, near the Virginia–West Virginia line, there is a color variety that is not yet in commerce but will be someday. Flowers are unusually large, even for a bird's-foot violet. The two upper petals are royal purple, velvety as usual, and the three lower ones are nearly pure white, their only markings being small purple dots at their throats. White petals have the same texture as do the purple ones. I have not seen many wildflowers that are more beautiful.

Another handsome plant characteristic of the shales is wild pink (*Silene pensylvanica*), the name "pink" describing both flower color and the notching on the petals. Blossoms are borne in low rosettes, and open with the violets and creeping phloxes. A collector who tries digging up wild pinks will learn about root size and penetration. Apparently these plants have to go deep for their moisture, and must conserve what they find.

Attractive wildflowers on shale are by no means restricted to the spring season. In midsummer butterfly milkweed (*Asclepias tuberosa*) is common, its glowing orange blossoms living up to its name as magnets for butterflies. One of the region's most eye-catching endemics, shale barrens evening primrose (*Oenothera argillicola*), has a blooming season that extends from June to October. Its abundant buttercup-yellow blossoms are nearly two inches across, far larger than other evening primroses. Shale stonecrop (*Sedum telephioides*) bears white or pale pink flowers in August and September. By this time its succulent leaves are reddish and look like flower rosettes at a little distance.

Woody plants that grow on shale reflect unfavorable conditions of soil and moisture; most are dwarfed, some (locusts for example) extra spiny, and some have branches that lie on the ground. Dwarfing is well displayed by hackberries (*Celtis*), large trees on favorable soils but only low, twisted shrubs on shale slopes. Whether these shale barrens plants are a separate species or simply a well-marked form has not been determined. In any event, hackberry butterflies (*Asterocampa celtis*), obligates of this tree, are common characteristic insects of the barrens.

Where forests can form, trees are essentially a mixture of oaks and pines, most of them scrubby and low-growing. Bear-oak (*Quercus ilicifolia*) is often abundant, its tangles about as impenetrable as a Great Smokies rhododendron slick. When bear-oak is mixed with scrub pine, the resultant cover is excellent for wild turkeys and good for deer. Some of the best hunting in central Appalachia is to be found in shaly areas.

Among the select group of plants whose associations are western, none is more interesting than yellow buckwheat (*Eriogonum alleni*), a species that has been found only in six Virginia and two West Virginia counties, but whose close relatives are abundant and widespread in the Rockies. Another is tall grama (*Bouteloua curtipendula*), a grass important on western ranges as a contributor to the nutritious forage which once supported mid-America's buffalo herds.

Some shale barrens endemics are inconspicuous plants; these would include a wild onion, a forked chickweed, and a golden ragwort. Some are species closely resembling other, more common plants. In this category a goldenrod and a wild morning-glory are notable; also, Buckley's phlox, a remarkably handsome plant in flower but one of the famous Appalachian "lost" species that we shall look at in Chapter 16.

That leaves two of the Kate's Mountain group whose discovery helped create an interest in the shale barrens. One is Kate's Mountain clover (*Trifolium virginicum*), obviously a member of the white clover group but very different from its relatives in important particulars. It was discovered along the Kate's Mountain Trail by John K. Small in 1892. Its leaves are narrowly oblong, the length often three or four times the width. The greenish-white blossoms are borne in large heads that often rest on the shale. The plant grows in the driest, most exposed places, and is easily eradicated when collectors become too enthusiastic. In its type locality it is now something of a rarity, but fortunately there are many less visited shale slopes in Virginia and West Virginia, and a few in Allegany County, Maryland, and in Bedford County, Pennsylvania, where the plant flourishes.

Second of the plants whose type locality is Kate's Mountain is one of the leatherflower clematises, the white-haired clematis (*Clematis albicoma*). First collected in 1877 by Gustav Guttenberg, it was renamed by Edgar T. Wherry, the foremost student of shale barrens plants. Its floral parts are dull purple, thick and leathery, and covered with silky white hairs which persist on the seed-heads. In addition to its type locality, it grows in a few other Virginia and West Virginia counties. Any botanist who finds a new station of this still-rare plant considers the day eventful.

The many plant endemics on the barrens are not paralleled by numbers of unique animal species. Wider spaces, it seems, are required to produce endemic animals. This is not to say that shale areas are without an interesting and abundant animal life.

Showy flowers and open sunny spaces encourage large and varied butterfly populations. Tiger beetles of many species are conspicuous. Collectors of those aristocrats among beetles, the longhorns (*Cerambycidae*), will have good hunting. Many common plants on the barrens serve as hosts to these insects; there are cerambycid species on milkweeds, goldenrods, locust, pine, and other plants. A particularly handsome one is the gold and blue elder borer; another common species, a black one, is among the largest of American longhorns.

Salamanders generally find the barrens too dry for their needs; their place is taken by lizards, most of them of the genus *Eumeces*. Broad-headed skinks (*E. laticeps*) may be found

under pine and oak, running swiftly along the ground or up
the trunks of trees. Occasional adult males reach lengths of a
foot or more; their swollen head and jaws are coppery red, and
they excite attention whenever they are found. Coal skinks (*E.
anthracinus*) are locally common on shale slopes. These stout-
bodied lizards have blackish-brown bodies and dull blue tails.
They sun themselves in the hottest weather and on the most
exposed outcrops. When disturbed, they dart into crevices in
the shale, their movements extraordinarily fast. I have tried
striking behind a disappearing lizard with a geology hammer,
to throw him out if possible. I have never been quick enough to
find traces of a single specimen in this manner.

Another reptile much at home in shaly areas, particularly in
the scrubby oak-pine forests, is the wood turtle (*Clemmys
insculpta*), locally called "redleg" because of the orange-red
coloration on neck and legs. Although it may go to streambanks to deposit the eggs, this turtle is largely terrestrial, almost
as much so as the smaller, more familiar box turtle.

Breeding birds are those one would expect in low brushy situations or in mixed forest. Pine and prairie warblers are common, as are chats. White-eyed vireos nest in low tangles, and
blue-gray gnatcatchers frequent the oaks. Where hawthorne
thickets, mixed with red cedar, dot the slopes, often there are
mockingbirds. Shrikes find spiny vegetation suited to their
feeding habits and are locally common. Carolina wrens are
everywhere at all seasons, and during spring and summer
elevated valleys in between shale ridges are as good spots to
look and listen for Bewick's wrens as any in the region.

This is rewarding country for the geologist. Mountain folding has displaced and disarranged many ancient strata; these
are beautifully exposed in the water gaps that are characteristic
of the Ridge and Valley Province. Where the New River cuts
through a high Allegheny ridge at Narrows, Virginia, thousands
of feet and ages of geology are to be seen and studied by those

who can read the story of the rocks. This area is a magnet for paleontologists as well, since fossils in many strata tell the tale of invertebrate evolution. Especially fine crinoids and trilobites are turned up from time to time.

There are other scenic gaps — many of them nearer the Atlantic seaboard. In West Virginia, Greenland Gap, Petersburg Gap, Cosner Gap, Judy Gap, and the Smokehole are all scenic areas, locally famous but deserving of wider attention than they have received. Some of the most exciting botanical finds have been made in these and similar areas. Ferns, some of them of restricted distribution, cling to rock crevices and talus slopes, the many varieties of exposed stone contributing to the flora's diversity.

It is interesting to speculate about the variety of names for these gashes where mountains have been riven and eroded. In the mid-Atlantic part of Appalachia they are gaps — water gaps if a stream passes through, wind gaps if there is no present flow. Such areas in New England are notches, often deeper and more rugged because of harder rocks. Franconia, Crawford, Pinkham, and Dixville all are famous notches in the White Mountains, and Smugglers Notch, one of the East's wildest and most rugged, is a featured attraction in Vermont's Green Mountains. In western mountains, these formations are passes, the name having, possibly, more alpine connotations. South Pass, Berthoud Pass, Loveland Pass, and Donner Pass are names to be reckoned with in the history and the commerce of the West. I know of few local uses of the name "pass" in the southern Appalachians; most are gaps, or, if they are deep enough, gorges. By whatever name, however, they are wonderful places for biologists and geologists. Some of them may have provided entryways for slow-moving species such as the wood turtle. Certainly they have facilitated man's commerce; he has built his highways, his railroads, and his canals through them.

The Shale Barrens, warm and sunny for the most part, have

areas and formations that are in vivid contrast to dry, almost semidesert, conditions. None is more sharply contrasting than Ice Mountain, in Hampshire County, West Virginia. This anomaly is at a modest elevation, less than a thousand feet, along the North River, a Potomac tributary. A peculiar folding of the rocks catches winter rains, holds them until they freeze, and then retains ice, some of it near the surface, until midsummer, or, in exceptional seasons, until late August.

Visitors to Ice Mountain have good opportunities to experience the changes that a few feet make. Their approach is by dirt road, over shaly ridges, and through oak-pine scrub. In summer the temperature will often be above 90 degrees. Suddenly the approach pitches down steeply to the stream, still with no warning as to what lies directly across. There is a bridge of sorts, although the water is shallow and fordable. Then suddenly there is an unexpected coolness and freshness to the air. From crevices on the rocky east bank, cold currents pour out. Air temperatures drop from 90 to about 55 degrees. It is unbelievable, but it happens. The unwary, who would rest and refresh themselves in this coolness, should be duly warned. Such abrupt temperature changes take their toll of the body; many a visitor to Ice Mountain has had a heavy cold to remember it by.

In the days of homemade ice cream, it was quite the thing to bring an old-fashioned crank freezer and some salt to Ice Mountain, then with pick or mattock to uncover ice among the rocks and use it in freezing the picnic's dessert. I have seen two hundred families using this natural refrigerator and its product on a summer day. There was no shortage of ice, nor was it difficult to remove. The refrigerator was well stocked.

Those with an understanding of plants and their distributions will find much to marvel at in the flora of this cold niche. All around are species of warm lowlands, but here is an enclave of the North, another one of those striking remnants left from glacial times. Twinflower and dwarf dogwood are abundant; so is oak-fern (*Dryopteris disjuncta*), a species that would be completely at home in cool forests of Newfoundland or the Gaspé. There are other boreals, some of them hundreds of miles or thousands of altitudinal feet out of their normal ranges.

Not quite so sharply contrasting, but still striking enough, are the differences in plant life on the lower, shale slopes of some of these ridges and in the flora at the ridge's summit. Northfork Mountain, in Pendleton County, West Virginia, is a good place to see these transitions. Lower slopes of this range have fine examples of shale flora. In places are found some of the most austral plants known to occur in West Virginia. In the Smokehole, for example, some cliffs are covered by the little gray polypody (*Polypodium polypodioides*), a fern that is abundant in the New World tropics, and farther south habitually grows on the trunks of trees. Another southern species is an orchid, crested coralroot (*Hexalectris spicata*), here at or near the northern limit of its range and not known to occur elsewhere in the state.

Shale outcrops persist almost to the top of the ridge, and shale-dwelling plants go with them. Here and there are exposed steeps covered with resurrection moss (*Selaginella rupestris*). Table Mountain pine (*Pinus pungens*) is a common species in the overstory. Near the summit of the ridge things change abruptly, and an amazing variety of more boreal plants occur. On a trip to Northfork Mountain, my father and I found the first West Virginia station for white birch (*Betula papyrifera*), and the small three-toothed cinquefoil, which has so frequently been mentioned. Near the same time, and on the same slope, a party of foresters found a vigorous stand of red, or Norway, pine (*Pinus resinosa*), here several hundred miles farther south than it is known to occur elsewhere. An even more remarkable discovery was made nearby by P. A. Rydberg. At an elevation above 4000 feet he found a colony of beach-heath (*Hudsonia tomentosa*), a species typical of northern seacoasts.

An elevated ridge connects the stations for red pine and white birch to the next southward high point. The ridge, above 3000 feet, is covered with a next-to-impenetrable stand of bear-oak. A climb of a few feet from this typical shale-slopes plant leads into a very large and thriving colony of dwarf Canada dogwood. Few areas have so many ecological complexities.

As evidence of the mountain's ornithological possibilities, we once watched seven golden eagles in the air over Northfork. One flew from a ledge less than a hundred feet from us, and we were hopeful that we had at last discovered an authentic southern Appalachians nest of this great bird. But, as always before and since, we were disappointed. Three or four decades ago there was a good population of these birds in eastern West Virginia and southwestern Virginia, but one sees them infrequently today. They have fallen victims, I suppose, to sheep-raisers, who seem determined that not one golden eagle shall remain alive.

On first thought it seems a pity to apply the name "barrens" to so diversified and rich an area as is this shale section just west of the Great Valley. And yet the name need not be regretted. New Jersey has its pine barrens, and these hold some of the finest botanical treasure along the Atlantic Coast. There are heath barrens on many southern peaks — gardens of beauty, attractive to visitors. Barren and forbidding some shale slopes certainly are, but they may hold more unique plants than does any other area of equal size in the long sweep of the Appalachians.

This is ancient country. Its rocks began to form when vertebrate life on the planet was first appearing. Its strata span millions of years — first as they were formed beneath the sea, then as they were wrested up by the forces that folded mountains. They have been above water for a very long time. When glacial ice moved southward, they just missed being overwhelmed.

These valleys and ridges have stood through the ages — islands above the surrounding seas and places of refuge for fugitives from advancing ice. Creatures of dry land and freshwater here found their sanctuary. Time and space have been theirs — the shale barrens have formed a stage for the drama that we call evolution.

11. The Waters under the Earth

"HE CLAVE the rocks in the wilderness, and gave them drink as out of the great depths. He brought streams also out of the rock, and caused waters to run down like rivers." It was written about the Siniatic wilderness, but it applies equally well to

Appalachia. Where great beds of limestone occur, particularly from Pennsylvania to Tennessee, the rocks have been riven; there are caverns and hidden streams, narrow passageways and colonaded halls, all a tribute to the erosive force of water. Here and there the streams will not remain pent up; they flow out as springs, some small, some running many thousands of gallons each day.

Ask a group of people, young or old, what they remember about Tom Sawyer. My guess is that most will recall the adventure of Tom and Becky in the cave. Some years back, crooners all over the land mourned the death of Floyd Collins, while millions of listeners wept, for various reasons, in accompaniment. There is something about a cave that touches our emotions and our hidden fears.

But where darkness becomes light, where underground waters gush forth, there man has built his spas, created his playgrounds, erected his shrines to healing and health. Caverns and springs, then, are important to man; in the Appalachians they become facets in a way of living.

The older Appalachians, with metamorphic and igneous rocks, are not suited to cave formation; underground reservoirs of great size do not form, so there are no sources for large springs. But west of the Blue Ridge, in newer Appalachia, water has searched out tiny breaks and crevices in the limestone, enlarged these where weaknesses were discovered, and through vast ages since the Cambrian has worn tunnels miles in extent and sometimes hundreds of feet in depth. Streams that flow through these may be only remnants of once mighty torrents, but they still break from the earth for the refreshment of living things. Thus the caverns and the springs are cognate: related manifestations of natural forces.

That both contribute to ways of living is abundantly proved in Appalachia. Only a few of the larger and more spectacular caverns have been developed commercially. Even so, not many

regions in the world will match the Appalachian Valley and
nearby areas in cave exploitation. Virginia's Shenandoah region
is outstanding, but there are developed caverns of note in Pennsylvania, Maryland, West Virginia, and Tennessee — other states
touched by the Great Valley.

This leaves the "wild" caves, thousands of them, for professional speleologists and for amateur cave explorers who do not
pretend to any scientific purpose or interest. Speleologists, those
who scientifically study cave formation, structure, and life, are
a hardy and adventuresome breed, and their numbers are wax-
ing. So also is amateur interest; where New England students
on holidays go hiking, Middle Atlantic college men and women
go "spelunking." I have seen caves in which almost every em-
bryonic stalactite had been broken off — graphic evidence of
misguided enthusiasms and too many geologists' hammers.

Large limestone springs in the Appalachians became centers
of social life and commerce long before caves were exploited.
Luxury seekers who know White Sulphur Springs and Virginia
Hot Springs may forget that there are, and have been, many
other such spas, some of them still in operation, many more once
flourishing but now almost forgotten. Some springs were named
to describe colors of mineral deposits which their waters left —
White Sulphur, Red Sulphur, Blue Sulphur. Some described
the physical condition of outflowing currents — Warm Springs,
Hot Springs, Salt Sulphur Springs, Old Sweet Springs, Sweet
Chalybeate Springs. Some — Pence Springs is an example —
commemorated the owner's family; some, as Berkeley Springs,
indicated a location; a few — Healing Springs is one — implied
pleasing results in a name that must have appealed to sufferers
from vapors, rheums, phthisis, and other miseries that beset
mankind.

In carriage days before the Civil War, southern planters in
the Carolinas, even as far away as Louisiana, loaded their
families, their best clothes, and numerous slaves into coaches

and were off for the Virginia springs. Here they met others of their own rank and station, some even from north of the Mason and Dixon Line. Flirtations led to marriages; when the war came, northern men were owner-managers of southern plantations and southern belles were housewives to Philadelphia bankers or Wall Street brokers.

For the time being, at least, we shall leave the waters above the earth and turn to those below by visiting one of the undeveloped caves, an easy one at first, accessible, relatively simple in structure, and well explored. McClung's Cave will do; it is near Maxwellton, Greenbrier County, West Virginia, and if after that beginning further cave exploring seems desirable, the facilities are at hand; there are some 105 other explored limestone caves in the county, and perhaps 20 more that have been reported but not explored.

The people who live fifty yards or so from the entrance are used to cave explorers; they are hospitable, and will allow you to park your car in the driveway. They will expect you to stop at the house and ask permission to visit their property, a common courtesy too often neglected. They will view with some misgivings any geologist's hammers that may be in evidence; thoughtless visitors have broken or marred many interesting rock formations inside the cave. These, of course, will be replaced in some similar form in another million years or so; the owners are becoming rather impatient of waiting.

Once the amenities have been observed, entrance to the cave is quick and easy. McClung's is at the bottom of a limestone sink, a fairly steep-walled saucer-like depression. It was doubtless once filled with water (there are hundreds of similar potholes in the region that still are), but the water in this one either broke through into an existing cavern or else helped create the one that drains it. The opening is about ten feet wide and four feet high; a slight stoop will clear it. Save for the sudden comparative darkness (to which your eyes will quickly accommodate) , the first impression is of coolness on a summer day, or warmth in winter. There is a gentle air current flowing out of the cave, and it maintains about the same temperature, 54° Fahrenheit, throughout the year. Contrast with air temperature and moisture content outside is further heightened by the fact that cave air has about 100 percent humidity.

Until your eyes are adjusted, artificial light is of little service, but as you become accustomed to the twilight you find yourself in a large chamber, the roof thirty feet above your head and the walls sloping away so as to leave a wide expanse. You are at the top of a slope leading down to a small stream. Beyond is a sharp turn in the passage; you can see one hundred feet or so, but not beyond that.

As you start down toward the stream you make another discovery, painful if you are unlucky, but more likely to provide mirth for your companions — until they have the same experience. Water flows in through the opening; it brings deposits of finely divided yellowish clay which coat all the rocks and fill in the openings between them. A steep-pitched roof, well covered with a good grade of soap, would have about the same physical attributes. Chances are, you will do some sliding, painlessly, unless you hit a rock. In any party some will have this experience; let those who haven't remember about a haughty spirit.

Once you are securely anchored in a good spot, however, it is well to turn your light in all directions; many cave features are in evidence. From the roof, in innumerable places, drops of water are falling. Some have begun this drop recently; there is wetness on the roof above and curious little pits in the clay where drops strike. Older depositions, in contrast, have begun to change the shape of roof and floor. This water contains dissolved calcium carbonate; as the water accumulates for its drop it leaves a minute deposit; when the globule of water strikes the floor another deposit is made there. Cave decoration has begun.

Icicle-like deposits depending from the ceiling are stalactites; those which build up from the floor are stalagmites, usually blunt cones rather than pointed formations. The mineral involved is travertine, and in the large entrance hall to McClung's Cave there are stalactites and stalagmites in almost every stage of development. Unhappily, many of those within reach have been broken off, testimony to the souvenir mania of thoughtless visitors. When stalactite and stalagmite meet, a column is formed. McClung's Cave has few of these, but in Organ Cave, a commercial venture a few miles away, there are many. When these are struck lightly they give off resonant musical tones; hence the name of the cave.

Although the cave we are visiting has few columns, it does have other interesting and characteristic travertine formations. Where water slowly seeps over a boulder or other obstruction, it creates a formation suggesting an arrested waterfall. The resultant rock is fluted, often with wavelike irregularities. Such formations are called flowstone; in commercial caves strong artificial light often brings out striking colors; our flashlights or head lamps are too weak to show these here.

To the visitor's right as he enters McClung's Cave is a clay platform, and a part of this is occupied by one of the cave's handsomest features, a series of water-filled stone terraces, each wall sinuous and knife-blade thin but strong enough to support a body's weight. This sort of travertine formation is called rimstone; some of the terraced pools created by the delicate rock tracery are a foot or more in depth.

Most of the cave life in this, as in other Appalachian caves, is concentrated in the twilight zone where light from outside still penetrates. On steep walls, and clinging to the ceiling, are cave crickets, medium-sized insects with long legs and excessively long antennae, these constantly waving as they receive stimuli. The nature of these stimuli and their receptors remains a matter of speculation, so far as we are concerned. Cave crickets are not limited to caves; there are species that feed at night on forest floors, but there they are scattered and infrequently seen; in undisturbed caves one may find them by the thousands.

Other insects present are smaller and less conspicuous. Tiny midges dance in the beam of a flashlight. There are larger flies, sometimes in numbers to make themselves a nuisance, since they seem to like alighting on a human face. They do not bite; they simply annoy. Under rocks and in dark crevices there often are small beetles, usually some species of the scarab group. Related to insects are the granddaddy longlegs, frequently abundant on cavern roofs. Their many-lensed eyes gleam as they reflect light directed on them.

Most zoologists who visit caves will be interested in salamanders, and McClung's Cave has (or had) its complement of these ancient amphibians. Three species are known — two restricted to the twilight zone and one found in water throughout the cave. Most sought after is the large, handsomely marked cave salamander (*Eurycea lucifuga*). This is a famous inhabitant of Appalachian limestone caves, occurring from eastern West Virginia to Georgia and Alabama. It is not restricted to the Appalachians, however; cave salamanders occur in suitable habitats across Kentucky, and are common in parts of the Ozarks uplift to the west. Strangely enough for a creature of the twilight, this salamander is brightly colored, the general body hue being orange, liberally spotted with black. The similarly colored and marked tail is as long or longer than the body. Eyes are (for a salamander) large and prominent, as befits an animal that must find its food in low light. Another adaptation is for travel over damp rocks, the toes are long and slightly disced. Cave salamanders like dark crevices just inside the cavern's opening, and may sometimes be seen traveling along the roof, their bodies upside down. Juveniles are more yellow than orange, and may be found where springs break out of the limestone.

It should be emphasized here that cave salamanders are not blind. Except in Pennsylvania, no blind vertebrates of any kind have yet been found in Appalachian caves. This is strange in view of the age of these caverns; there are blind fish in Mammoth Cave in Kentucky and blind salamanders in Ozark caves. There also are blind salamanders in underground waters, these troglodytes occasionally brought to the surface by strong-flowing artesian wells. Texas and Georgia have produced such animals; there seems no reason to suppose similar ones might not be found in subterranean Appalachian waters.

The second salamander species found in the twilight zone of McClung's Cave is the black or dark brown, white-spotted Wehrle's salamander (*Plethodon wehrlei*). This is an Allegheny Mountains species, found from southwestern New York to Virginia. It is common in the red spruce forest of the higher Alleghenies; it occurs in cool gulches and ravines, and is found just inside many limestone cave openings. Cave populations of Wehrle's salamanders present interesting possibilities. All the factors for isolation are here; presumably the animals have been in cave openings for a long time; populations are relatively small, and complete separation from other populations might be expected more often than not. In at least one case this set of circumstances has led to a new race. In Dixie Caverns, in southwestern Virginia, Jim Fowler found salamanders obviously close to Wehrle's but differing in several particulars. He described the new animal as the Roanoke salamander (*Plethodon wehrlei dixi*). In Arbuckle's Cave, in West Virginia, N. Bayard Green found thick-bodied, atypical Wehrle's; these may represent an undescribed race. Unfortunately, this cave is no longer open to the public; the owners felt that visitors were abusing the privileges given them, so they clogged the entrance with debris. There have been other instances of the same nature.

The third salamander known to have been collected in

McClung's Cave is the spring salamander (*Gyrinophilus por-phyriticus*). Often called the purple salamander because of the reddish body shades, this is a creature of the water, and is likely to be found anywhere in the stream that runs through the cavern. This species, when it dwells in caves, is frequently pale in color, so much so that in the weak light of an electric torch it may appear practically colorless. In a number of Appalachian caves good observers have reported white salamanders; all thus far collected have proved to be poorly pigmented spring salamanders.

In streams within limestone caves there often are crayfish and a few fish. These, with animals already mentioned, just about make up the cold-blooded fauna of Appalachian caves. There are a few additions on occasion; wood frogs are more or less regular where there are standing pools, and long-tailed salamanders, close relatives of the cave species, occur at some openings.

That leaves the warm-blooded vertebrates, bats being by far the most numerous of these. There is such a wealth of misinformation, coupled with so good a supply of superstitious fear, concerning these animals that one scarcely knows what to write about them. First of all, there are bats, of several species and at times in fairly large numbers, in many Appalachian caves. Some appear to be permanent residents, resting in the darkness during summer days, remaining to hibernate throughout the winter. Others appear to be migrants that congregate at caves for the long winter's sleep. How extensive this migration may be we do not know; certainly there are species of bats in some caves in winter that have never been found there in summer.

At rest, bats normally hang head down from cave ceilings, although I have seen them crowded into small crevices, perhaps for conservation of heat. Roosting groups all may be of one species, or may be of mixed kinds. They are much more numerous near cave entrances, but they also may be back from the twilight zone.

Although eastern caves have no bat flights comparable to those of New Mexico's Carlsbad Caverns, populations are large enough in places to have caused a considerable accumulation of guano. These deposits constitute one of the more unpleasant features of caves; the guano is finely divided, and when it is disturbed clouds of very strong ammonia-laden dust fill the air. It may be advisable to dampen a handkerchief and use it as a respirator. From some caves bat guano has been removed for use as fertilizer.

An old belief was that bats disturbed in a cave would fly at candles, open torches, or acetylene lights, putting them out and leaving the unfortunate explorer in darkness. This, of course, is fantasy; bats are too surely oriented by their built-in radar systems to strike solid objects. Occasionally one shaken down from its perch when not fully awake will strike a human being; I have never heard of anyone being bitten in such an encounter. Bats do have a mouthful of sharp teeth; they will bite if they are seized, but they are not often the aggressors.

The only other regular mammalian cave inhabitant is the Allegheny woodrat (*Neotoma magister*). This native rodent builds its nests in caves, and is often abundant but seldom seen. It has a long hairy tail, huge eyes, and is yellowish brown. Unlike many other species listed above, it is not at all confined to limestone caves; shallow caverns and cracks and crevices in sandstone are just as acceptable. Where any of the native magnolias are available, woodrats feed on their seed pods, often dragging large quantities into caves. They are completely inoffensive, do not invade buildings or harm crops, and ask only to be let alone in their retreats.

Bats and rats as regular cave inhabitants may be lacking in appeal; they are not mammals that inspire affection. On a casual basis, nevertheless, caverns can do a little better. Raccoons, foxes, and groundhogs sometimes shelter there. No doubt more formidable species did in earlier times. A well-preserved bear skeleton was turned up by archeologists in one West Virginia cave. It is easy to imagine that panthers once used such natural openings for denning.

Limestone caves in Pennsylvania, Maryland, and Virginia have extensive deposits that date from Pleistocene times; certain of these have yielded treasure in the form of animal skeletons. Some bones come from species present in the area today, others from animals that were obviously here during the Ice Age and have since disappeared or moved. For some unaccountable reason, West Virginia caves have yielded few fossils; in one a peccary skeleton was found, but that is the best discovery to date.

That earlier man made free use of caverns and shelters is shown by charcoal deposits in many situations. Near my home is a large sandstone overhang that was called Indian Camp by early white settlers. There must have been good reason behind the name. The charcoal layer was thick, the shelving rock above

---

Winter. Biologically speaking, winter in our latitudes is a resting period. For the animals, the drives of pairing and of familial duties are over, migration has ceased, and the matter of sheer survival occupies their whole attention. But not all nature is sleeping: rabbits, squirrels, and many furbearers are about, and under the snow meadow voles are as busy as ever they were during the summer. In the bark of trees and logs insect larvae and pupae await the stimulus of spring to resume their development, unless a passing woodpecker, chickadee, or nuthatch finds them first. Most plants are in a state of suspended animation too, outwardly lifeless. But although the tempo has slowed, the "dead" of winter is pure illusion. Life is everywhere. Much is happening of interest and great beauty, not the least of which is the snowy brilliance of the winter panorama itself. Note the evidence of activity in the tracery of rabbit tracks.

A farm scene such as this will evoke memories of plowing roads, carrying in wood for fires, and the job of feeding and watering cattle. But spring will come and the maples are waiting to be tapped.

If most animals and plants are resting during the winter season, humans in increasing numbers certainly are not. Winter sports have become big business in Appalachia, with ski runs in operation as far south as West Virginia, and occasionally into Tennessee. The ski lodge (opposite, above) overlooks Stowe, Vermont, a center for all sorts of outdoor activity at all seasons. Except at the coldest times, water still flows (opposite, below), and brook trout eggs deposited the previous autumn are aerated for spring hatching.

Snowflakes and crystals seem infinite in their variety of forms. If perfect, snowflakes are hexagonal, but usually one or more of the six points have been broken. South to Georgia and Alabama, the Appalachian country sees manifestations of snow and ice.

Pines like these, as forests or as
individual trees, mean life itself
to wintering wildlife. Much
snow is held up, so seeds and
grit are available under the
spread of conifers; needle-bear-
ing branches offer safe cover during long nights. This is a typical
New England winter scene.

Evidence of good construction is
in this last summer's songbird
nest. But it has served its purpose, and the maple twig may
shelter a similar one next spring.

For mammals as basic to the wildlife food chain as hares and rabbits, one of the best defenses against natural enemies is camouflage. The brown summer pelage of the varying hare, or snowshoe "rabbit" (left, in white winter coat), would be a liability in winter. This is the only mammal resident as far south as the Virginias to change regularly from summer color to winter white.

The cottontail (above) couldn't change clothing, so fell victim to a winter-hunting red fox. Unlike the hares, true rabbits are born blind, naked, and with undivided feet and toes.

During recent winters at about two-year intervals, big, colorful evening grosbeaks have been wintering in the Appalachians as far south as Georgia. They are gregarious, lively, and sometimes quarrelsome, but welcome for all that. The sturdy conical bill is a superb instrument for opening tough seeds — and for defense, as many birdbanders can testify.

During recent winters at about two-year intervals, big, colorful evening grosbeaks have been wintering in the Appalachians as far south as Georgia. They are gregarious, lively, and sometimes quarrelsome, but welcome for all that. The sturdy conical bill is a superb instrument for opening tough seeds — and for defense, as many birdbanders can testify.

darkened by smoke. This was the scene of one of those senseless massacres that marked border warfare. A group of thirteen Indians, apparently on some peaceful mission, slept one night at Indian Camp. As they awakened at dawn, a group of white hunters, concealed on top of a nearby rock, shot them all down. Border reputations were built on such butchery.

In my own boyhood the owner of Indian Camp told me that he helped haul away eighteen wagonloads of wood ashes from beneath the rock, and that the family collected a gallon of arrow points, scrapers, and other stone implements as they worked. I saw some beautiful points from the collection; of course they are long since scattered. No one thought of any possible value in these finds; no records were kept, and archeological exploration (at least near the surface) would be meaningless at this late date.

We have spent a long time at the entrance and in the twilight zone of McClung's Cave. There is more to be seen, but we must carry our own light now. Most of the cave's life is behind us; from here on there are only mineral deposits and manifestations. Beyond the first large chamber, but around a bend in the stream, there is a second spacious room. Beyond this a narrow passage extends for about 1900 feet, the cave's stream occupying much of the space but leaving steep (and slick) claybanks. A breakdown of rock almost closes the passage at this point, but determined spelunkers may crawl 240 feet along a very dusty passageway into another opening. This trip is for cave *aficionados*; others will have turned back long ago.

Fortunately for the visitor, McClung's Cave has its best features in that easily reached first room. These are representative of formations in other limestone caves; in other caverns some formations are better developed and there usually is much more beauty. But McClung's will do for a beginning. As previously noted, anyone who develops a taste for further cave work will find abundant opportunities nearby.

I am not content that Appalachian caves, so far as is known, have no blind salamanders. This requires further investigation, and will get it. A few caves in Pennsylvania harbor blind catfish; it seems reasonable to expect that both blind fish and blind salamanders should occur elsewhere in Appalachia. There are some leads; local people near Slaty Fork, West Virginia, tell of a cavern (a tough one to find and get into, by the way) which has blind fish. Maybe so — the speleologists who have been there haven't found any.

Once Ruth and I thought we had struck pay dirt. A visiting geologist from Ohio, together with some local people, walked through the 3000-foot passage of the Sinks of Gandy. They reported white salamanders in Gandy Creek, and we took the first opportunity to see for ourselves. We went, we found lightly pigmented salamanders, and we thought we had them at long last. It was not to be: when we got them to the surface they were pale spring salamanders, apparently with perfectly good eyes. But some day . . .

Suppose that you want to go spelunking. What should your procedure be? Once again, I venture some suggestions. First, visit one or more of the developed caves. All are beautiful, all have features in common, and all are run by people who know their business. You will be safe and comfortable, you will see representative cave features, and you will be instructed by guides who tell their stories well. Many are geology students on summer jobs; all have learned from competent scientists. Their patter may be long on fantasy (these underground features assume queer shapes and are given picturesque names), but it will have little false information.

Once you have found out what a civilized cave has to offer, try a wild one if that appeals to you. But take certain steps before you do. First of all, wear the oldest clothes you have. You will be muddy when you come out. Have shoes with clinging soles, to cope with slick rocks or steep mudbanks.

Above all, never go alone; you could need help badly, and you will certainly need some extra light. If you can secure an experienced local guide, or if you can join one of the regular trips scheduled by speleologists, do so by all means. It is like hiring a guide for alpine work; these people know their way around, and they will get you out if you get into trouble.

Just in case you are really serious about caves, the state geological surveys (in the Appalachian region, at least) have elaborate publications that give detailed information. Each explored cave will be described, its approximate dimensions noted, special features will be stressed, and warnings given if there are unusual danger spots. Sketch maps with compass bearings will be available for larger caves. You will know whether you are dealing with a straight or a branched passage; whether or not the cave has more than one known level (some have three or more) ; and whether there are alternative exits. Once you begin to approach a cave with this information, you may call yourself a spelunker.

Now that the atomic age is upon us, a great deal of attention is being given to bigger caverns. This is particularly true of those near Washington, and fortunately some of the country's best are in that area. But the speleologists and their kind have gone far afield. They are always on the scent of new caves.

Some years ago James J. Murray bought a tract of land along the Maury River, a few miles from Lexington, Virginia. On this property the ornithologist built a summer home and spent much time looking for birds and flowers on his holdings. One day by sheer chance he stumbled on a cave opening, and when he made his way inside he found an extensive cavern. Excited over his discovery, he made inquiry of local people as to any records or any knowledge of his cave. None had ever heard of it; it was evidently unknown and unexplored.

Filled with pride of discovery and possession, he told some of his friends about it. A few weeks later one of them, an officer at the Virginia Military Institute, brought him a publication of one of the service's Corps of Engineers. In it was an account, complete with map and dimensions, of his "unknown" cave. Apparently the government thinks such information may come in handy some day.

I spend a part of each summer teaching in a camp school, attendance at which is a requirement for graduates in professional forestry. My school's camp is ten miles from White Sulphur Springs. Few regions in America are richer in limestone caves, and in the mineral springs that sometimes break from them. Much of our work is field ecology — we like students to see every niche and every facet that may be explored in the time at hand. Every summer we visit one or more of the nearby caves, and to many students this is a revelation. Here is a new world, a threshold to be crossed, and they want more of it. Once they have started, many take their own time for more cave exploring. Hard hats and acetylene lamps are much in demand, and everyone wants them on weekends. During some years our son was with me in camp; he followed the students as they explored one cave after another, and he became a fairly accomplished spelunker. He will admit, when pressed, that he hasn't seen anything in his beloved West quite like a limestone cave. Exploring in Appalachia does have its points.

On the mountain slope just above camp there are many springs of cool, sweet water, a gift from hidden caverns that collect and release winter snows and summer rains. Flow from these springs is channeled into a reservoir; from that it is pumped for use in the great resort hotel at White Sulphur. There are sulphur springs on the hotel's grounds. The resort, of course, was built around them. Their waters are for bathing and medication, and only the hardy will drink them. But Anthony Springs are untainted; guests and townspeople use these waters, and there are none better.

I like to think of the way in which caverns and streams have here combined to build a community and a way of gracious living: those who stay and play in luxury at the hotel, those who make their living in the community, those who sojourn there as students, campers, or fishermen — all in some measure are debtors to the waters under the earth.

12. A Land of Broad-leaved Trees

THE STUDENTS, each year a different group, who come to our camp for professional forestry training, are from diversified backgrounds. Some have spent their lives in Appalachia, others are from far away. I take pleasure in watching them as they discover the Appalachian forest, and through their eyes I too see it in a new light. Through experience the conviction grows that this is one of the vegetational wonders of the world.

During the ten weeks of their instruction, students leave camp for daily trips, visit selected forest areas within easy reach, and return to their own beds that night. In the course of a summer's work — this is the crux of the matter — they will have studied in every major forest type in eastern North America save only the tropical hardwoods of peninsular Florida. This is the priceless gift of the mountains and their variations in elevation.

Long before the Appalachians were folded and uplifted, there were forests over this land. They must have been wonderfully vigorous, since they supplied the raw material from which coal, natural gas, and perhaps petroleum were derived. But their trees were not such as we know today; seed plants were just appearing on the earth, and this dominant plant cover was made up of trees somewhat like giant clubmosses and other fernlike growths. We know them today as fossils, *Lepidodendron* and other tree-proportioned species which have been preserved in the coal measures.

Plants that bear seeds have many advantages over those that

reproduce from spores, so the seed-bearers gradually increased in size and numbers and after a time came to dominate the plant kingdom. Slender-leaved species such as pines, spruces, firs, cedars, and larches were early on the ground, and they have persisted so that we know them as living members of the community. Gradually, however, plants of more complex structure and reproductive parts appeared; some of these grew to tree size, and so the stage was set for today's broadleaf forests. In the Appalachia of today this is the dominant and most abundant plant growth.

People who have spent their lives in eastern North America are sometimes surprised to learn that they are dwelling in a forest formation which is comparatively rare on this earth. Most of our broad-leaved trees shed their foliage in autumn and are reclothed in new dress in spring. This rhythmic succession is not followed by most tropical trees; it is a product of the changing seasons in midlatitude regions. There are deciduous broad-leaved forests in Europe, in central China, and in a few other areas that lie 30 to 60 degrees of latitude from the Equator, but the best and most extensive of these forests is in North America, on the slopes of and to either side of the Appalachians.

This will bear further emphasis. My native state of West Virginia, when the white man first saw it, was forested throughout, a fifteen-million-acre stand of trees. By the best calculations we can make, only about 11 percent of this area was in needle-foliaged species — pines, spruce, hemlock, cedar, and the like. All the rest, 89 percent of the entire state, was covered by deciduous hardwoods.

If I travel northward, I gradually find broad-leaved trees less prominent, until tiny stands of willow, aspen, and dwarf birch are mere islands in a sea of conifers. When I go southward, I enter pines almost as soon as I leave Appalachian highlands; the great southeastern pine belt begins in New Jersey and extends along Atlantic and Gulf until the forest disappears on the southern Texas coast. There are stands of oak, sweet gum, and other hardwoods, but these are merely interruptions to the dominant pine cover. If I go westward, I leave prairie groves of oaks and hickories, I cross the grasslands, and when I again enter forested country, all important tree species are conifers. Oaks, maples, and other broad-leaved species are scrubby, too small to concern any lumberman.

Another ancient mountain mass, the Ozark uplift in the central United States, has deciduous hardwoods, but it has abundant pine as well. Its broad-leaved trees cannot compare either in extent or variety with those in the Appalachians.

Lest this become too concentrated an exercise in forestry, I would like to mention some by-products of the deciduous forest, any or all of which may interest a wider public. One of the glories of eastern autumn is the annual fall foliage display; this can occur only where there are deciduous trees. In spring our hillsides are covered with masses of wildflowers — violets, anemones, hepaticas, phloxes, lilies, trilliums, and a myriad others. These plants are brought to blossom by warm sunlight which strikes the earth. If there were a closed forest crown above, there would be no such wildflower display. Coniferous forests have few spring blooms beneath their shade.

When settlers along the Atlantic seaboard had conquered land, wild animals, and Indians, they began to seek some of the graces of living. One result of this quest was the burgeoning of cabinetmakers, designers of fine furniture made from enduring wood. Among American cabinet woods, three have been in a class by themselves — sugar maple, black cherry, and black walnut. All of them reach their best development on Appalachian slopes and in rich, well-watered mountain coves. These, and other similar matters, will be returned to; they are here inserted to emphasize that a forest is more than merely trees. But we still have some forestry lessons to learn if we are to know and appreciate Appalachian landscapes.

Among students of the deciduous forest, none perhaps has had so wide an experience as has Professor Lucy Braun. Certainly no other person has so influenced thinking as to how this forest originated, developed, and spread. I am aware that there are those who will differ with her in detail; nevertheless, I shall follow some of her ideas in the next paragraphs.

According to Professor Braun, there was a vast and varied deciduous forest over much of eastern North America in the time before Pleistocene glaciation, a period the geologists have called Tertiary. When the Ice Age came, this forest was of course greatly modified and vastly reduced in size. The glaciers, after all, reached New Jersey on the Atlantic seaboard and extended almost to the Ohio River in mid-America. One sizable portion of this flourishing Tertiary forest was, however, far enough away from glacial margins to escape major alterations brought about by climatic changes and resultant ice. This remnant woodland covered the Cumberland Plateau and the southwestern portions of the Allegheny Plateau — parts of eastern Tennessee, eastern Kentucky, and the southwestern sections of the Virginias. During a million years or so of glacial advance and retreat, this forest, according to Professor Braun, remained relatively stable and unmodified. As ice withdrew northward, the Cumberland area served as a distribution center from which reforestation took place.

Reforestation, when it came, proceeded in three major directions, each advance showing its own peculiar features. Northeastward there was ice, retreating slowly but still potent in its climatic influences. Trees that followed closely upon glacial retreat had to be hardy species, able to withstand arctic winters, driving winds, and late frosts. In general, the birches, maples, and beech were best able to meet these requirements. Rugged trees, these have found homes high on mountain slopes and far northward. They flourish on good soils on New England hills, in Adirondack valleys, on ridges of the Canadian Shield, and around the Great Lakes. One of their finest stands is on the southern shore of Lake Superior, cold country by any standards. From the lumberman's standpoint these are the pioneers, the last important timber hardwoods to the north.

Foresters refer to this timber type as "northern hardwoods," a good term when used in proper perspective. Its justification becomes manifest following one of those severe late-May or early-June frosts that plague Appalachian highlands, even pretty well southward. After one of these, oaks, hickories, poplar, walnut, and sycamore all show foliage injury. If the freeze was severe, they may stand defoliated for several weeks. But throughout all this, birches, maples, and beech are unaffected, their foliage unburned and their growth unchecked. They are true northerners, and deserve the appellation.

A second pathway for reforestation lay eastward and southeastward. Along this route the problem was different. During colder and damper periods, spruce-fir forest stretched farther south, and farther downslope, along the Appalachians. When warm, dry times came these northern conifers disappeared, except in a few favored spots. Their replacements, after a time at least, were oaks and American chestnut, strong and hardy trees, tolerant of almost all conditions but low temperatures. They did well on the original plateau, they thrived in the coves, they climbed the slopes to 4000 feet or more, and they found passages through the mountains to occupy eastern sides and the piedmont hills beyond. Their nuts fed bears, squirrels, turkeys, grouse, and other game species, making this an Indian Happy Hunting-ground.

Still a third reforestation movement took place to the west. On this front the critical problem was water supply, which tends to decrease with each degree of west longitude gained. At first, throughout the valleys of the Ohio and its principal tributaries, there was sufficient moisture for the growth of an unbroken forest, oaks and hickories dominating but elms, sycamore, and a few other species being present. In western Ohio, however, certain areas were occupied by tall grasses. Where moisture gathered, there were island-like groves of oaks and hickories, the "oak-openings" just west of Toledo being good examples of this mixed vegetative covering.

Westward, prairie groves grew more scattered, until only the watercourses were bordered by trees. Struggling to occupy each available acre (this is not anthropomorphic — it is a struggle, as will be clear to anyone who sees this area), mossy-cup oak, elms, and ash-leaved maple have pushed a tongue along the Red River Valley through Minnesota and North Dakota into Manitoba. This is the northwestern extension of the oak-hickory forest, a type foresters call "central hardwoods."

Professor Braun would be the last to claim that her system explains all the problems of hardwood-forest distribution. There always are local factors to upset a pattern, and every experienced field student can cite dozens of instances of nonconformity. The fact remains, nevertheless, that present distribution is along the lines she suggests, and no other proposal yet made seems so logical to forest botanists who have lived and worked in the eastern deciduous forests.

If an ancient forest on the Cumberland and Allegheny Plateaus was capable of expanding to cover nearly half a continent, what was it like? For just a moment, look once more at the three forest types already discussed, birch-beech-maple, oak-chestnut, and oak-hickory. In each the species or groups named are dominant; other trees occur, but they are not prominent or very numerous. Competition, it would seem, is largely intra- rather than inter-specific.

So far as one may judge, conditions in the old Tertiary forest must have been very different. As we find it today there is no one species, nor any small groups of species, holding dominance over the others. Twenty or twenty-five tree species are common, another twenty or twenty-five species less common but present.

Where soils are good and moisture is abundant many of these trees make rapid growth and reach near-maximum sizes. No other area in North America may be so favorable to deciduous forest development.

This is a highly complex forest, and it has received special classification. Ecologists use the term "mixed mesophytic forest," but that will not likely find much general acceptance. Some writers have simply called it the "Appalachian forest," and that is far too exclusive. Foresters and lumbermen speak of it as "cove hardwoods," and, properly understood, that name may be the best one yet proposed. Appalachian coves produce as good examples of this rich woodland as can be found anywhere.

One very special characteristic of this cove-hardwoods forest must be mentioned. Dominant trees in the three other forest types named (birch, beech, maple, oak, and hickory) are not notable for showy flowers. Chestnut, when it still covered the hills, was spectacular in blossom, but few people younger than my own generation have seen a large American chestnut tree in full creamy-yellow display. In contrast to these plants of less striking flowers, the cove hardwoods include twenty-five or thirty trees that bear handsome blossoms. More remarkable even, their flowering periods are distributed throughout the growing season. Serviceberry (*Amelanchier*) may open its snowy-white blossoms in March on warm slopes; witch-hazel's (*Hamamelis*) yellow flowers may still show color when December's freezes arrive.

It seems necessary to list this floral wealth in order to emphasize its variety. Some species mentioned receive more detailed discussion later on. A summarizing of them will do for the present. Excluding shrubs, and naming only those plants which reach tree proportions, a southern Appalachian cove might hold redbud, serviceberry, magnolias of several species, black cherry, pin cherry, wild plum, hawthornes of many species, tulip poplar, two or three species of buckeye, flowering dogwood, and other dogwoods with good flowers, locust (both white- and pink-flowered), crabapple, mountain ash, black haw, yellowwood, fringe-tree, silverbell, lindens of two species, sourwood, Hercules-club, and witch-hazel. On the border between trees and shrubs (these reach heights of thirty feet occasionally) are rhododendron and mountain laurel. This profusion is tropical, there is no other way to describe it. Although no one should expect all of these to be growing side by side, I expect that Cades Cove in Tennessee, throughout the season, could show most of them.

Fruits both handsome and useful are about as much a feature of cove hardwoods as are fine blossoms. Serviceberries offer their purple-red fruits just about the time hungry young birds are learning to find their own food. Following (not in the order given below) are red mulberries, wild plums, wild cherries, sassafras, hawthornes, pawpaws, black haws, Hercules-club, mountain ash, persimmon, several species of holly, and a great variety of nuts. It is not surprising that fall migrants among the birds swarm to a feast so freely offered.

Except at very high elevations, it is safe to say that broad-leaved trees will be dominant in parts of Appalachia which offer them good soils and fair moisture conditions. Parts of the Shick-shocks and of New England may be exceptions, but southward the hardwoods will take over unless soils are too cold, too wet, too dry, too sandy, too acid, or too rocky. Under any of these conditions, conifers may grow where hardwoods cannot.

Borderline conditions for hardwoods are to be found on many drier eastern Appalachian slopes. Oaks are persistent, and they will grow (in scrubby form, perhaps) where other hardwoods cannot compete. They are often joined by one or more species of pine, and foresters know this as the oak-pine type. It is found on the Atlantic Coastal Plain, it occurs in the piedmont and sometimes on the Blue Ridge, but it reaches its best development in the Ridge and Valley Province, an area sometimes dominated by shale barrens. Belts of oak-pine forest occur on poor, dry ridges west of the Allegheny Backbone. George Washington describes such a forest along the Ohio River in his journal for 1770, and conditions there today are much as he found them nearly two hundred years ago.

Although our primary concern in this chapter is with the more characteristic broad-leaved trees, we cannot completely neglect coniferous forests. Spruce and fir have been mentioned many times, on high points southward, lower on the slopes northward. Firs generally are small and useful mainly for pulpwood. Red spruce is, however, a valuable timber tree, reaching great size and producing tremendous lumber yields. Northern pines are abundant in New England and in parts of Canadian Appalachia. White pine, an important source of lumber, extends south in mountain valleys to the hill country of South Carolina and Georgia. Unlike the hardwoods, it often occurs in pure stands. In the southern Appalachians, short-leaved pine becomes valuable to lumbermen. Canada hemlock grows to large size, and often in pure stands, under many situations in the mountains. Northward it may cover the slopes, but farther south it has its best development along streams. Carolina hemlock, a species of the southern mountains, is handsomer but smaller. Red cedar prefers sites that are alkaline. Its well-known use is as a lining for moth-repellant chests and clothes closets. At one time it was much used for long-lasting fence rails. Larch, a conifer that sheds its needles in winter, occurs south to West Virginia and Maryland. These are the principal Appalachian conifers, all interesting, sometimes valuable, but overshadowed in abundance and importance by the broad-leaved trees.

Once more I must beg your indulgence if the foregoing reads like a lesson in elementary forestry. It is just that, and it has a purpose. I see no way to explain certain facets of Appalachia except through forests and their influences. Forests covered most of the land, from eastern Canada to southern coastal areas. Trees and their products built the soil, and determined the nature and abundance of wildlife. In a large measure they were responsible for lesser vegetation — shrubs, vines, and herbs — which found homes beneath their spread.

From the forests, settlers took their first building materials and their first food and clothing. For a century and a half Appalachian woodlands barred the way to the West, compressing eastern white settlements into a narrow band along the Atlantic Coast. When roads, canals, and — later — railroads were built westward, these largely followed streams that had cut water gaps through the ridges, or sought out wind gaps for easier passage over when there was no pathway through. In short, forests created a way of life, and molded a people who adapted to that way.

My hope is that as you drive your car up a mountain, in New England, New York, West Virginia, or Tennessee, you will note the way in which forests and the life they support change at different levels. There is a further step if you want to be highly practical about the matter. As you drive along you might note how many of the trees around you would furnish a sixteen-foot sawlog of good diameter. Perhaps that will give you an inkling as to why you pay such prices for oak or maple flooring, pine paneling, or good solid-cherry furniture.

Having done my duty to my profession, I shall turn to some of those forest-caused or forest-oriented sights and activities that have become rich parts of our heritage. Maple sugar seems a good starting point; eastern Indians had learned to make it, and it may have been the first luxury that white settlers took from the forest. Sugar maple and its close relative, black sugar maple, grow from Quebec to Georgia, abundantly northward, in mountain coves southward. Throughout its range it produces sap that flows freely in late winter and early spring and has dissolved within it a considerable quantity of distinctively flavored sugar. When condensed to a certain point by boiling, this sap yields rich, heavy syrup. If it is heated a degree or two higher, the product solidifies on cooling to form maple sugar.

That is the situation in its simplest form, but it misses telling the whole story by a long way. Maple syrup may be heavy, or it may be light. It may be dark, or it may have a clear, light golden color. It may have smooth texture or it may contain sandlike sediment. All of these things are determined by the time when the tree is tapped and the manner in which the sap is boiled down.

Maple sugar may be dark and coarse-textured, or, if it is properly timed and stirred as it is cooling, it may be a soft, creamy-brown delight that must rank among the finer things life affords. Furthermore, there are all sorts of refinements — maple cream, maple butter, granulated maple sugar, and many others — and each is delectable. Possibly you have guessed by now: I like maple sugar.

Sugar-maple trees spread in beauty over the hills of Vermont, and, through some clever advertising, that state has fixed an idea in the public mind. Vermont syrup and sugar are the standards by which these products are judged; prices are determined there, and for many a consumer all really authentic maple products must stem from the Green Mountain State.

If I trace my ancestry far enough back, I can find a number of Vermont forebears. I hope, therefore, that I shall not be disclaimed when I set down this heresy: good maple syrup is good maple syrup, whether it is made in Vermont, New York, Pennsylvania, Ohio, or in Virginia. No matter what its origin, if it meets certain standards established through the Pure Food and Drug laws, it may be graded as Number 1, or "Fancy."

There is a big maple syrup industry in the Allegheny Mountain county of Somerset, in Pennsylvania. Syrup as clear, sweet, heavy, and pure as may be found anywhere is produced in Highland County, Virginia. In my own state, we have had a situation that is almost laughable, but not quite so. Several counties on the Allegheny Tableland produce quantities of syrup. One country merchant at Mount Storm, West Virginia, undertook to market it. He received it, stored it in steel drums, and then discovered that the consuming public did not want West Virginia maple syrup. Finally, in desperation he shipped 17,000 gallons to St. Johnsbury, Vermont, where it was promptly graded and marketed as "Vermont No. 1."

Nut kernels (black walnuts the most important, but hickory nuts and butternuts also of commercial value) are Appalachian forest products that are finding increasing public favor. One hill county in Tennessee has a black walnut cooperative; Roane County, West Virginia, has a black walnut festival; there are walnut-cracking plants and marketing centers in many places. At Knoxville, Tennessee, one of those ingenious Scots who seem born with a wrench in their hands has developed a plant for making nut-cracking machines, and he now supplies these devices to a good portion of the world.

In earlier times, of course, country boys and girls earned their pocket money by gathering American chestnuts and selling them for a few cents a pound to the local merchant. I had thought these days were over, but a correspondent from Hendersonville, North Carolina, tells me that he bought a good many pounds of native chestnuts in local stores during the fall and winter of 1961. I am beginning to hope that the American chestnut is never quite going to disappear from the Appalachians.

Makers of fine furniture have buyers at strategic points throughout the eastern mountains. Hard maple, black walnut, and black cherry are the three premium cabinet woods, and if they locate a tree of curly maple or curly walnut they will remove even the roots, and will pay very fancy prices. Competitive bidding for walnut comes from firearms manufacturers, who value this wood as a source of gunstocks.

Makers of baseball bats conduct an active search for white ash, the wood of which imparts that extra spring so valued by the long-ball hitter. Cucumber magnolia is highly regarded as a raw material in the making of panel-truck bodies. Woodcarvers like to work in American holly, basswood, tulip poplar, and sourwood.

The Appalachian country ham, cured in a salt and brown-sugar brine and slowly and lovingly smoked over burning hickory chips, is still produced and still valued by those who know. For purposes best known to their users, high-grade white oak casks are made, charred on the inside and used for storage purposes. This is a considerable wood-using industry in Appalachia, and the ultimate product is valued by many. A Tennessee enterprise of repute varies the formula — it uses sugar maple in addition to white oak.

One never knows when and where a particular need for a particular kind of wood will arise. During the dark days of World War II, when German U-boats were sinking Allied shipping and Allied seamen at an appalling rate, the magnetic mine appeared as a new refinement in destruction. There was a fatal attraction between this instrument and the steel hull of a ship. Suddenly it was realized that we must have wooden-hulled minesweepers to seek out and destroy these menaces. White oak was the wood most desired for hull timbers, and the best white oak was growing in Appalachian coves. The institution in which I teach had few forestry students during these years; most students and a good many staff members were in the services. Those who remained civilians took as one of their tasks the scouting out and making available of large white oaks for use by the Navy.

We have one story that we like to tell. Back in a sheltered valley in Doddridge County, West Virginia, there was a fine stand of mature white oak. We arranged the cutting and handling of these trees, a technical lumbering job since the Navy wanted very large and very long timbers. Not many trucks could haul such logs, and not many sawmills had carriages to handle these outsized sticks.

One morning a magnificent old white oak was felled, and from its trunk a 42-foot log was cut. It was skidded to a landing, loaded on a special truck, and that afternoon moved to Parkersburg to the only mill in the region with facilities to shape and saw it. The sawing was done, and an outsized truck was used to move the squared timber, all 42 feet of it, to Ashtabula, Ohio.

Here the stick was placed in an accelerated-action dry kiln, given a quick seasoning, and used in the construction of a United States Navy minesweeper. Eight days from the time it was a growing tree on a Doddridge County hill it was afloat on Lake Erie.

Autumnal foliage color is accepted, enjoyed, even exploited. In this eastern broad-leaved forest country we take it for granted, not realizing that much of the world will never see such displays. I remember accompanying two visiting European botanists on a trip through October woodlands. As we reached a high point and saw the soft shading of color produced by thirty or forty plant species, each with its own tinting, we paused to look about us. After a time of silence one visitor said, "We have heard about it; we have seen pictures of it; we never did believe it."

Fall coloring in the northern Appalachian forests differs from that found in southern Appalachia. I have no intention of comparing the two. Both are wonderfully satisfying, and by seeing both you can greatly extend the season of bright foliage. No doubt the natural settings help. It seems to me that I have never seen the maples and birches as blazing elsewhere as they appear in and around New England's and New York's famous notches. Wilmington Notch in New York, Smugglers in Vermont, and any of the eight or so best known in New Hampshire are often at their peak of color during the first ten days of October. Along the Blue Ridge Parkway and in the oak-pine areas of eastern slopes, color may still be vivid a month later. Between those dates the Catskills and Poconos, then the Allegheny ridges in Pennsylvania, Maryland, and West Virginia will have their days of glory. Southward the sweet gums will still flaunt scarlet, purple, and gold — the three colors sometimes on the same tree — in mid-November. It is a gift of the Appalachians that we may enjoy so long a season.

In other chapters I have had, and shall have, occasion to speak of spring flowering. Here I shall confine myself to one tree, the silverbell (*Halesia carolina*). It is a favorite of mine, and for years I have wondered that it is not better known and in wider horticultural use. It grows best on rich, moist woodland slopes, from West Virginia and Virginia south. Northward it is usually a small and slender tree, but in the Great Smokies there are giants 70 or 80 feet tall. In late April or early May, before leaves are fully out, each twig bears many pairs of white bell-shaped flowers, their exteriors often tinted a delicate pink. Flowers are of good size, an inch or more in length. They are borne in such profusion as must be seen to be believed.

In West Virginia's New River Gorge country there is a fine show of these plants, probably brought there by the waters of New River, which rises in the mountains of Ashe County, North Carolina. Along the Blue Ridge Parkway in Virginia and North Carolina there are good displays, but, as with so many other plants, this one seems to reach its climax in the Great Smokies. There are belts of trees along the western slopes so dense that when they are in blossom the whole mountainside appears white. I do not know of another Appalachian tree that presents an equal display.

Many things have happened to the Appalachian forests since white men first came to them. Some — wild fire, destructive lumbering, fumes from manufacturing plants, and in recent years the curse of strip mining — are destructive, but the picture has its bright sides. Nature is adept at healing scars, and if left undisturbed for a hundred years or so many of our woodlands will appear as virginal as they ever were. There is a growing determination that these good areas shall remain protected, some of them undisturbed. Provincial and state parks and forests, national forests and national parks, these have under their care millions of acres in Appalachia. More and more privately owned land is coming under good, sound conservation forestry. The public wants it that way, and there will be trees for tomorrow.

13. Mountain Heaths

I SUPPOSE some homesick Scot planted them there, the Scotch heather and cross-leaved heather growing in a lonesome spot high in the West Virginia Alleghenies. These mountains may have reminded him of his native heights and moorlands. With so many heaths growing naturally, he may have felt it a shame that two others — his favorites from the Old World — were not among them.

This is speculation, and we may never know the full story. What we do know is that in 1942 Harry A. Allard found both these plants, Scotch heather (*Calluna vulgaris*) and cross-leaved heather (*Erica tetralix*), growing on Cabin Mountain, on the Tucker-Grant County line in West Virginia, a spot now some miles from the nearest human occupancy. The plants are at home, so far as one can judge from their vigorous growth. There are indications that they have spread somewhat in recent years, and they are an established part of the plant community.

For many years there has been speculation as to whether Scotch heather is of natural occurrence anywhere in the New World. Spurred on by old reports, Merritt Lyndon Fernald went with great anticipation to investigate the flora of Newfoundland. He found a wealth of heaths in the western portion of that island, northern outpost of the Appalachians, but no heather, even in places where it had formerly been reported.

When the West Virginia discovery was made, hopes were again stirred that these might indicate a genuine natural occurrence of these storied plants. Roy Clarkson, who has investigated the reports of heathers in North America, points out that the West Virginia plants are growing in what seems a spur of an old logging railroad, that the soil there had been disturbed, and that no plants have been found away from this graded area. We have no choice but to fall back on the guess about the lonesome Scot.

If this may seem to some people a lot of fuss over an unimportant matter, let me offer a few words for the defense. Heaths are true mountaineers throughout much of the world, at home in upland country, prized features of highland floras. They are nearly cosmopolitan; there are representatives in the ancient plant life of Australia, and Table Mountain at the Cape of Good Hope has one of the richest heath floras in the world. Some members of this group — Scotch heather is notable — have come to hold treasured places in the lives and affections of people who dwell among them.

It is not surprising, therefore, that heaths are so characteristic a part of the Appalachian flora. They abound from Newfoundland to Alabama, and they include some of the showiest native plants. They stand, some at least, in special relationship to Appalachia, since many are endemics. Along with the Appalachian spleenworts among ferns, the lungless salamanders, and to some extent the wood warblers, these living things reach a peak of development in the mountains of eastern North America. Gray's *Manual of Botany* recognizes twenty-two genera of the heaths in the northeastern area it covers; of these, all but one are found in the Appalachians, many of them being restricted to these mountains. It is scarcely possible to visit any area — mountain summit or slope, forest or rocky headland, swamp or dry cliff face — without finding heaths.

Previous chapters have already made mention of heaths under many circumstances. It could not be otherwise; heaths are so prominent in the flora as to demand attention. Arctic-alpine gardens above and beyond treeline hold them in abundance; so do the muskegs far southward. From cove to bald they decorate the landscape in southern Appalachia, and where Appalachian foothills break down to the coastal plain they are still flourishing.

Since the family holds so many highly decorative plants, attractive in the wild and valued in cultivation, it seems desirable to point out here some of the places and times of their greatest abundance. People come by the thousands and from distant points to see the "pink beds" of North Carolina, the rhododendron "gardens" on Craggy and Roan Mountains, and the flame azaleas along the Blue Ridge Parkway. There are many other fine heath displays, most of them not so well known. I am certain that as they are discovered they will be cherished.

"Rhododendron" is derived from the Greek, and means "rose tree." As it is usually defined, it includes both evergreen forms, which we regularly refer to by the generic name, and also related plants (many of them deciduous), which we know as azaleas. The average gardener will not be concerned with these bo-

tanical niceties; he uses evergreen rhododendrons for one purpose and azaleas, native and exotic, for very different ones.
Furthermore, if his interest in plants is deep, he is willing to
travel to see new plants of both branches of this genus. Let us
look at some members of each group.

Catawba rhododendron (*Rhododendron catawbiense*) is a
southern Appalachian endemic found from West Virginia and
Virginia to Georgia and Alabama, always in the mountains but
in a surprising variety of locations. It has been mentioned so
frequently in these pages that any further discussion might seem
superfluous, but that isn't quite the case. First of all, it and its
relatives have been responsible for a characteristic piece of
southern mountain terminology. Beds of rhododendrons growing on exposed slopes and rocky crests, so densely as to be almost
impenetrable, are called "slicks" in local parlance. When they
grow as an understory to heavy woodlands, a trial to the hunter
or hiker, they may be called (and for good reason) "hells." Only
those who have tried walking through such a growth can fully
appreciate this term.

Travelers along the Skyline Drive and the Blue Ridge Parkway will be greeted by Catawba rhododendron in bloom in late
May. If they continue south they will find the plant becoming
more a feature of the landscape, open then only at the 2000–
3000-foot level. It will be a month before the high summit
"gardens" are at their best, so the season is a long and gracious
one.

Although the purple-flowered Catawba rhododendron reaches
its natural distributional limits in the Virginias, it is hardy
much farther north, successful in plantings in Ottawa. Because
of this hardiness, and because it is remarkably free-flowering, it
has been used as one end-member to hybridize with many frost-
tender rhododendrons from other portions of the world, particularly some handsome exotics from the Himalayas. These hybrids have resulted in most of our named horticultural rhodo-

dendrons, plants with colors ranging from white to deep red. Chances are good that the plants you have growing in your garden are influenced by the native Catawba strain included in their breeding.

Blooming a month or more after the Catawba species, rosebay rhododendron (*R. maximum*) opens blossoms that are white, pale pink, or even rose, one petal of each flower marked with chartreuse-green spots, in late June or July. This plant, West Virginia's state flower, is somewhat hardier than its close relative; it grows naturally in southern New York and is able to adapt to coastal plains southward. For all that, it is a true mountaineer, reaching its best development on rich wooded slopes and in dark ravines. It is an open question whether rosebay rhododendron should be treated as a tree or as a shrub. Throughout much of its range it is shrubby, but in the Southern Highlands its stems become treelike, sometimes 30 feet or more in height and many inches in diameter. Tree or shrub, nonetheless, this evergreen is a handsome plant, affording food and cover for deer, turkeys and grouse in winter weather. Its blossoming is not so profuse as that of the Catawba species, nor is it so well suited to hybridization. Notwithstanding, it is a fine plant, an ornament to many a planting in America and abroad.

There are many places in the Appalachians where rosebay rhododendron displays its flowers. A favorite of mine, an interesting drive at any season but particularly fine in late June when rosebay is open, is a mountain loop road built by the Forest Service about seven miles east of Elkins, West Virginia, and branching off U.S. 33. It first climbs near the summit of 4000-foot Bickels Knob, then continues along a high Cheat Mountain ridge until it rejoins U.S. 33 in about fifteen miles. Beginning in the cove forest along Shavers Fork of the Cheat River, it passes into northern hardwoods and reaches red spruce on the summits. Much of the way is wooded, although the road passes through a cleared section, the Greenbrier limestone bench so characteristic as an outcrop along the Cheat Mountain range.

Rosebay rhododendron grows at all elevations along this road, from about 2000 feet at the river to 4000 feet on Bickels' summit. It is particularly fine in some ravines just at the start of the climb. It is also abundant in a rocky tangle (known as "Bear Heaven") at the top of the ridge, although flowering will be nearly a month later at this elevation. There are many fine things to see along this Forest Service road; rhododendron is a highlight.

Lapland rosebay we have already seen in the alpine gardens of Mount Washington. On southern heights there is handsome pink-flowered Carolina rhododendron (*R. carolinianum*), and perhaps one or more closely related species. Botanists do not agree as to classification of some of these forms. No matter — all of them are worth seeing, worth planting too, if you have the acid soils they demand.

Our native deciduous rhododendrons are known commonly as azaleas, and they include a greater range in species, distribution, and color than do the evergreen members of this genus. Nearest to the evergreen species, botanically speaking, are two handsome plants, rhodora (*R. canadense*) of the north country and Vasey's azalea (*R. vaseyi*) of the southern mountains. But for Lapland rosebay, rhodora is the most boreal of all our native rhododendrons. It is at home on summits from Newfoundland to eastern Pennsylvania, and it is equally at home in bogs or on barren lands. Its lilac-rose flowers open before the leaves have developed, and they look particularly attractive against a background of New England granite near the summit of some northeastern Appalachian peak.

There are colorful beds of rhodora in the Notre Dame Mountains of eastern Quebec and there are fine displays in northwestern Connecticut. My favorite country for this plant is the Connecticut Lakes area of extreme northern New Hampshire. This northern extension of the Granite State, tucked in between Quebec and Maine, is well known to the outdoor brotherhood. It is Big Woods country, heavily clothed in forests that are mostly coniferous, but with enough northern hardwoods to break the monotony. The lakes are in deep valleys between ridges, and they are bordered by pines, spruces, fir, and hemlock, with abundant white birches for accent. Wildflowers run riot in this well-watered land, particularly on forest margins or where open bogs interrupt the denser cover.

Olin Sewall Pettingill, Jr., recommends this area as the best place in New Hampshire to look for certain birds of northern affiliations — pine grosbeaks, spruce grouse, three-toed woodpeckers, gray jays, and boreal chickadees are some. Handsome yellow, white, and black evening grosbeaks remain during some summers, although I have found them in greater numbers in the nearby Quebec Notre Dames. I remember particularly one June evening along the Second Connecticut Lake when there was a heavy hatch of mayflies. The resident warblers went wild, darting in to make wing catches of these insects with little regard for the humans watching them. There were blackpolls and baybreasts by the dozen, along with Cape Mays, myrtles, magnolias, and others. All were in full breeding plumage, a boon for which bird students could be duly grateful. Across the highway from the warbler banquet hall was a swamp and bog area, its entire expanse overgrown by rhodora just coming into full blossom. This was a fine heath bed for North or South. Our pleasures were enhanced when just before dusk loons out on the lake began to call.

Vasey's azalea belongs to the southern mountains as does rhodora to the northern ranges. Its flowers are clear pink, and the long exerted stamens give a butterfly effect to the blossoms. Like so many plants, it is hardy north of its natural range, able to live where it cannot reproduce itself. As with rhodora, Vasey's azalea grows and thrives on open mountain crests, but (also like its near relative) it will adapt itself to a variety of circumstances.

Most native azaleas are judged by and compared with the flame species (*Rhododendron calendulaceum*). This is not altogether fair; a plant can be beautiful without being superlative. Flame azaleas, nevertheless, remain the standard by which other flowering shrubs, hardy in midlatitude regions, are judged. Flame azaleas begin to appear as natural parts of the plant community in the Allegheny Plateau country of southwestern Pennsylvania and southeastern Ohio. Down the mountains they extend to Georgia and Alabama. According to elevation and latitude, they bloom from mid-May to late June, although a closely related form of the Cumberland Plateau in eastern Kentucky (usually regarded as being of another species, *R. cumberlandense*) opens its flowers in July.

Actually, azaleas are a plastic group, subject to free natural hybridization. It is impossible to be sure how many separate species there were, or are. They have crossed naturally until the genetic makeup of any individual plant is a puzzle. Plants classified as flame azaleas may be of any conceivable shade in the spectrum between palest yellow and deep brick-red, may be pure white, or white with one yellow or one pink petal, pink with one yellow petal, deep red with one lighter petal, or just about any combination you might imagine. Whatever their coloring, they are strikingly beautiful plants.

Fortunately for the motoring public, flame azaleas are abundant along many miles of the Blue Ridge Parkway. Their season corresponds to, or overlaps, those of Catawba rhododendron, mountain laurel, and, in spots, flowering dogwood and black locust. All the southern ranges have azalea displays, some particularly rich ones being in the Nantahalas, the Cowees, and the Snowbirds. Art Stupka recommends Gregory Bald as the Smokies' best spot for this show, with more accessible Andrews Bald not too far behind. Every park or forest ranger knows this plant, has his own favorite place for seeing it, and will share his information with you if he believes in your good intentions. Natives in the mountains also know the plant, but they will call it honeysuckle.

Among native pink azaleas, the pinxter-flower (*R. nudiflorum*) is well known and widely distributed. It is inclined to have whitish or pale pink blossoms at lower elevations, but in the highlands it is often much deeper in color. This may be due to genetic crossing with another species, rose azalea (*R. roseum,* although that name is in question), a rose-pink clove-scented heath of mountains from Maine to Virginia and Tennessee. This plant is a contributing member of the famous Carolina "pink beds" community, a specialty of Pisgah National Forest slopes in the Asheville region.

For those who find a trip to North Carolina in early June an impossibility, there are also pink beds not too distant from Washington and Baltimore. Through eastern West Virginia, the main ridge of the Alleghenies often widens into a broad plateau. One such elevation is near the junction of Grant, Pendleton, Tucker, and Randolph Counties, a region whose parts are known as Roaring Plains, Flatrock Plains, Red Creek Plains, the whole often spoken of as Huckleberry Plains, in tribute to the abundant blueberries that grow there.

There are Forest Service roads (this is within the Monongahela National Forest) leading to the mountain from east and west, points of departure being Petersburg and Lanesville. Once on the summit of the mountain, at elevations near 4000 feet, a rock-based road follows the crest for eighteen miles, one of the most scenically and biologically rewarding drives in the mid-Appalachians.

This once was spruce country, and these northern trees are making valiant efforts to re-establish themselves. Much of the land is still open, with low growths of blueberries, Allegheny menziesia, mountain laurel, rosebay rhododendron, mountain ash, serviceberry, and pin cherry as prominent parts of the flora.

In swampy places all along the way are cranberry bogs, rich places for northern plants of many kinds. Toward the northeastern terminus, there are acres of three-toothed cinquefoil. And in this area are hundreds — thousands — of bushes of rose azalea. In most years they would be at their height of bloom on June 15.

There are two white-flowered azaleas in the eastern United States, both fragrant and both blooming in early summer. Both include some individuals whose corollas are pink rather than white, although these are uncommon. One of the two, clammy azalea (*Rhododendron viscosum*), grows from Maine to South Carolina, and is more common in lowland situations. The other, smooth azalea (*R. arborescens*), is found along mountain streams or at the borders of swamps from Pennsylvania to Georgia. U.S. Highway 250 crosses Shavers Fork of the Cheat River in Randolph County, West Virginia, at an elevation of 3556 feet. Along the riverbanks, up- or downstream, there are hundreds of smooth azaleas, and in late June they perfume their surroundings.

American laurels of the genus *Kalmia* constitute another group of highly ornamental heaths. Because it is widely used horticulturally, mountain laurel (*K. latifolia*) is perhaps the best known of these. It grows locally in New England and in the Catskills and becomes abundant in upland areas southward. Although not restricted to mountains, it certainly reaches greatest size and abundance there. This is another puzzling arborescent species. In rich Appalachian woodlands these plants may grow to be 30 or 35 feet tall and may have trunk diameters of a foot or more. It is difficult not to regard these as trees, although most plants will remain of shrubby growth.

Mountain laurel blooms from May to July, its opening time determined by altitude. A profusion of blossoms is borne, white or pale pink at lower elevations, much deeper rosy pink at high ones, each bloom with ten folds into which a red-tipped stamen is inserted. From the center of each flower rises a pistil, longer than any of the stamens. This presents a problem in fertilization and seed development: How is the pollen from inferior stamens to reach the elevated stigma? The difficulty is readily taken care of, since nature has worked out a system. As was noted, each stamen is held within a fold of the corolla, bent into an arch and awaiting ripening of its pollen. It also awaits a releasing stimulus, this usually provided by bees, which come to the blossom for nectar. When nectar forms, pollen is ripe and the stamens are ready for release. A bee, probing the center of the flower, touches first one, then another stamen. As each is stirred, it flies upward like a rod relieved of stress, throws the pollen into the air, and some of this pollen inevitably sticks to the hairs on the bee's body. When the bee goes calling on the flower next door, its pollen-coated body brushes the blossom's stigma, and the transfer is completed. Thus do the plants and their parts perform the life function.

Mountain laurel is the state flower of Pennsylvania, growing in tremendous natural beds on Allegheny slopes. Around Ligonier or Altoona it is often open, or well in bud, by Memorial Day. The graves of thousands of Union soldiers have been marked by mountain laurel sprays in the years since the Civil War.

From the Poconos northeastward, swamplands, old pastures, and barrens are often overgrown with sheep laurel (*K. angustifolia*), a smaller member of the laurel group. This species, with narrow leaves as the name indicates, has deep pink flowers, their parts built on a plan similar to those of mountain laurel. In mid-June a dense stand of sheep laurel is highly decorative. According to botanical literature, this species is supposed to extend southward along the mountains to Georgia. I have never seen it south of Pennsylvania, although it doubtless occurs in favored places.

The third of the eastern kalmias, pale laurel (*K. polifolia*), is a true northerner, transcontinental in the subarctic and extending along the mountains into New England, New York, and extreme northern Pennsylvania. The common name is unfortunate — some flowers are pale pink, but in the White Mountains many are deep pink to crimson. In boggy spots, this small laurel is at home above treeline on northeastern peaks. Fell-fields in the Shickshocks sometimes have dense stands, and in blossom these make a fine display of color over peaty and rocky slopes.

Pipe smokers in this country, some of them at least, owe a debt of gratitude which they may not realize to heaths of the genus *Kalmia,* chiefly to mountain laurel. During World War II, when Italian and German armies had cut off supplies of briar pipe blocks from North Africa, the industry turned to burls on mountain laurel roots as a source for American-made pipes. North Carolina was the center for this activity, and mountain people who discovered laurel burls (they call the plant "ivy" down there, by the way) could sell them at good prices.

Another ornamental heath, native to southern mountains, is fetter-bush (*Pieris floribunda*). I wish that this handsome evergreen shrub had a more appealing common name. Dense growths of it are hard to travel through, and I suppose that gave rise to the name. It deserves a better one. Leaves on this plant resemble those on mountain laurel, although they are lighter green, with a polish as though they had been waxed. In habit of growth also there is a resemblance to mountain laurel, but the flowers are distinctive. The white, bell-shaped blossoms are borne at branch tips in dense racemes, closely crowded, and highly attractive. Bud clusters for the following year are formed in summer and are prominent throughout the winter. In May they open, suggesting a bushy lily-of-the-valley. A Japanese relative of this American plant is much used horticulturally; both are fine for brightening a winter landscape.

Common names of plants vary from community to community; their use without scientific names could lead to all sorts of misunderstandings. As a case in point, take plants of another evergreen heath genus, the *Leucothoe*. These shrubs, several species of them, are also called fetter-bush. The leucothoes too bear clusters of lily-of-the-valley-like flowers, although these clusters hang from the stems and are partially concealed by foliage. Leucothoes grow on well-watered mountain slopes from the Virginias south. They are abundant in the Great Smokies, their gracefully arched branches being especially attractive in winter. Evergreens they are classed, but this needs some qualification. Leaves are retained throughout the year, but in winter they often turn a rich dark red, much prized for accent notes in floral arrangements.

The only American heath that is without question throughout its range a genuine tree is sourwood (*Oxydendrum arboreum*). Appalachian areas of Pennsylvania and Ohio are at the northern limits of this tree; it becomes increasingly abundant southward. In the Cumberland and Allegheny Plateaus, sourwood forms a major element in the flora. It bears racemes of white, bell-shaped flowers, similar to those of the last two heath genera mentioned. In sourwood, however, flower masses are gracefully curved, suggesting the lines followed by Japanese pagodas. After flowers have dropped, the seed capsules persist, still grouped in these arching designs.

Sourwood blooms in July, when it has little competition from other native woody plants. Those who travel south along U.S. 25 from Berea, Kentucky, and on through Norris, Tennessee, may think that not much besides sourwood grows on some of the hills over which they are driving. If they retrace the route a couple of months later, they may still hold to this belief. Beginning in September, sourwood foliage turns brilliant scarlet, one of the brightest elements in autumnal foliage display.

Sourwood in blossom is visited by bees, those in man-tended stands, and those swarms that have gone wild, living and storing their sweets in some hollow tree. Many who care about such things consider sourwood honey among the finest honeys. There is a tradition that has grown up around bee trees, a custom that has the force of law. The finder of such a wild swarm must notify the owner of the tree; then the owner has no choice. The tree must be cut, and the honey divided equally between finder and owner. Woe to the landowner who refuses to honor this tradition! His tree will be cut anyway, he will have no part of the honey, and the fire that is built to smoke out the bees just might escape to run through his woodland.

Right here I want to say a word about mountain honey. Most of us have grown up on the bland sweet that bees gather from clover and alfalfa. I have no spite for this product, but it is lacking in character. Honey made from wild plants is likely to have distinctive color and flavor, particularly since bees when they start on one honey source continue working on that plant until its nectar is no longer available.

Sourwood honey is yellow, and just a little of the oxalic acid which the host plant contains comes through to give the sweet a certain piquancy. Basswood honey, a favorite of many, is very light yellow, its flavor mild. Tulip poplar is the source for a heavy, reddish honey, delectable if the bees haven't also taken honeydew from aphids, which sometimes infest this plant. Buckwheat honey is dark and musky, the flavor too strong for many, especially if frost has touched the blossoms before bees have removed their nectar. One of the fairest and most flavorsome honeys is made from fireweed, a pretty magenta-flowered plant that seems to appear spontaneously after fire has swept over the land. And one final word — in the Appalachians it is still possible to get honey in its natural comb, not the vapid stuff that we pour out of bottles.

But we were talking about heaths, and we return to one that holds a distinctive place in human affections. There is something special about trailing arbutus, mayflower, fleur de mai to the Quebec *habitant, Epigaea repens* to the botanist, a delight under whatever name it bears. I suspect that the regard in which this small wildflower is held springs from a combination of factors. It shows its white or pink blossoms early in spring, a promise of the longed-for warmer weather to come. It has to be searched for, and, when found, it is often in pleasant surroundings. The flowers have an odor that seems paradoxical — it is delicate, and yet pervasive. For New Englanders and their descendants it holds a suggestion of the vessel that brought colonists to these shores. There can be no doubt about it, trailing arbutus belongs.

Ruth and I were married during the depths of the Great Depression. She was in college in New England; I was teaching in West Virginia. It seemed wise that she finish her graduate course, and I had to continue teaching. We agreed that at the Easter season we would meet in Philadelphia. Easter came fairly late that year, and I decided to take her a corsage that would be unmatched among the sons and daughters of Brotherly Love. I knew a warm hillside on which trailing arbutus grew, and I watched these plants as they opened their flowers. To my deep satisfaction they were ready for Easter, so I gathered some, carefully packed them in moss, enclosed them in tin, and carried them to Philadelphia. They arrived all right, and were appreciated. But we made a discovery. On every downtown Philadelphia corner there were street vendors offering bunches of trailing arbutus from the Carolina mountains. My gift suggested the swain who sends his best girl in Charleston, South Carolina, a camellia.

This listing of heath favorites could go on and on. One of spring's taste delights is provided by the new tender leaves of wintergreen, or teaberry (*Gaultheria procumbens*), a sturdy little evergreen whose aromatic red fruits are eaten by humans, if the grouse, turkeys, bears, and other wildlife have spared any. Botanists now place the delicate white-fruited creeping snowberry in this same genus, although I liked the suggestive name *Chiogenes* — "beginning in the snow."

The bearberries (*Arctostaphylos*) are true mountaineers and cannot go unmentioned. Two species, common bearberry and red bearberry have bright scarlet fruits. A third species, alpine bearberry, reaches New England's treeless summits, and bears purplish-black fruits. These plants have western relatives that help make up the stubborn vegetation called chaparral on Pacific slopes.

Blueberries and their close relatives, huckleberries, are widely distributed, highly useful to wildlife, and commercially important. Their season of fruiting fairly well spans the summer, and when autumn comes their foliage becomes ornamental. In Chapter 16 I have more to say about one of these shrubs, the famous box huckleberry.

Most of these mountain heaths grow in acid soils, and they help to create a habitat favorable to many ferns, orchids, lilies, and other woodland ornamentals. It would be difficult to imagine Appalachia without its heaths. Fortunately, one needn't try; the plants are there, many of them decorative and all interesting. Somehow they fit the mountains, and they dwell in harmony in the community of living things.

14. Ferns

SOME YEARS AGO Abram S. Margolin and I wrote a bulletin about ferns and their allies, and, hoping that it would sound learned and important, we titled it *The Pteridophytes of West Virginia*. I have lived to regret that title. Occasionally, I speak to groups of various kinds, and when I am representing my university in any official capacity, the school's information office duly sends out a publicity blurb, recording my authorship of the volume. For years I have suffered as I have heard luncheon club presidents, high school principals, and garden club chairmen struggle with the word "pteridophytes." They nearly always lose, and I have learned my lesson. This chapter is about ferns.

Any discussion of Appalachian ferns must cover a rather wide field. This is a highly variable area with which we are dealing, and the soils and outcropping rocks are of many different origins. Generally speaking, it is well watered, a place in which ferns have proliferated. A fair portion of the region's fern population is at home in the Arctic, being found on lands that encircle the Pole. Another segment comes up, evidently, from the New World tropics. There are species so widely spreading as to reach New Zealand. Most interesting of all, perhaps, is a large group of Appalachian endemics.

Fern people have their own organization — the American Fern Society — and its members are just as enthusiastic and dedicated as are those of any other interest group. I learned with some surprise that a number of copies of their publication,

American Fern Journal, go to Soviet Russia. It is not for these devotees, however, that I am writing. They don't need it. It must be abundantly clear by now that a purpose of this volume is to encourage closer looks at the Appalachians and the features found there. I hope you will look at the ferns; they deserve attention.

Ferns are comfortable plants to live with, restful to the eye and a solace to the mind. They suggest coolness on a hot day, and water in a dry land. A good growth of ferns tells a story of rich soil, of interesting accompanying plants, and of a healthy ecology. In this situation, we seem to sense, things are going well with the community.

Suppose that you are lucky enough to find the nest of a ruby-throated hummingbird. This tiny structure, its top exactly the size of a silver quarter, will most likely be lined with the brown fuzzy material from the stems of cinnamon ferns, a substance that is soft enough to cradle the two white eggs. You may recall from your school days a physics laboratory experiment in which the instructor sprinkled yellowish-white powder over the top of a glass of water, then inserted his finger to the bottom of the glass, and withdrew it without its getting wet. The powder he used came from a fern relative: it was the spores of a *Lycopodium* — clubmoss — a product of nature which has the property of greatly increasing the surface tension of water.

Perhaps you purchase a spray of flowers from an eastern florist and find that it is arranged with a backing of ferns. These may have been gathered in the redwoods forests of California, or under Oregon's Douglas firs. When your daughter is married, it may be before an altar banked with ferns. There are many of these associations; ferns and their relatives do not live in a vacuum.

There is a fine enthusiasm for fern gardening, and justly so. Ferns, many species at least, are easily transplanted and established. There are species that will be at home in almost any conceivable site — around the garden pool, under the heath border, in exposed sunny spots, in crevices of a dry stone wall, or in the rock garden. Devotees have an active exchange system by which members may secure plants from other portions of the country. And, if you leave the rarities strictly alone, and stay away from those species that are highly exacting in their requirements, you will be able to collect wild material without doing violence to whole populations.

One of the finest of native fern gardens in the Pennsylvania mountains was planned, planted, and carefully tended by Dick Harlow, sometime coach of football at Harvard University. James Logue, a dentist in Williamsport, Pennsylvania, was an enthusiast of fern variations — forms with forked or crested pinnae, outsize individuals, and other natural freaks. His garden attracted visitors from far places. Years ago, two others and I went in late winter to Owen Sound, Ontario, in quest of birds from the northland. We stayed in the home of two delightful Scottish women; their name was Buchan and their family included John Buchan, onetime Governor-General of Canada. With great pride they showed us their fern garden, a prized portion of which was a colony of hart's-tongue, abundant in their native Scotland and found locally in Grey County, Ontario, a place sought out by fern hunters throughout North America. Some twenty years later we again visited Buchan Manor, and one of the sisters again showed us the hart's-tongue plants that had persisted through the years in her garden border.

As is true of most of us, I suppose, I cannot think of interesting plants without associating them with interesting places and people. So is it with the ferns; I shall be writing about areas where significant finds have been made, and about some of the people who have extended our knowledge by making these discoveries. If some of this material is personal, I know of no way to avoid mentioning it.

I grew up in a fairly remote section of West Virginia. My

father, whose outdoors interests were unlimited, became especially aware of ferns when he undertook a local collection to be exhibited at a county fair. I tramped the woods with him on many of his searches, so I too became interested. On one of our trips we found a beautiful colony of what appeared to be a hybrid spleenwort, the hybrid growing between fine plants of pinnatifid and mountain spleenworts. Knowledge of these Appalachian rock ferns and their possible hybrids was just developing, and interest in them was very great. As a result of this find we began to have visitors, botanists eminent in their field and amateurs who did their work with professional excellence. Some of them have become lifelong friends; all were pleasant acquaintances. Certainly they would not have come to our hill country had it not been for the accident of the fern discovery. Early visitors included the dean of American fern students, Edgar T. Wherry. With him was Francis W. Pennell, exploring for members of the figwort family, which he so ably described in a monograph. On later occasions the colony was visited by Harry W. Trudell, Harold Rugg, and many others. It meant something to us to have such people around.

Later I shall have several occasions to speak of Edgar Wherry. I cannot pass up this opportunity of paying tribute now to his tireless explorations, extraordinary knowledge of rare plants, and uncanny ability to find them. A case in point: he was traveling through West Virginia along country roads when the car in which he was a passenger had a flat tire; while repairs were being made, he climbed a bluff along the highway — and discovered the first-known West Virginia colony of rusty woodsia, a fern abundant far northward. If any American botanist has greater serendipity than Edgar Wherry, I don't know about him.

The Mountain Lake Biological Station of the University of Virginia has long been a center for the study of Appalachian plants and animals. It is in Giles County, in a wooded area on the summit of Saltpond Mountain. The elevation is about 4000 feet, and nearby is Mountain Lake, one of the few natural bodies of water in the Southern Appalachians. The station's founder, Ivey F. Lewis, has, I am convinced, never met a worthy person or encountered a biological problem in which he did not take an interest. Furthermore, he has had the ability to communicate his interests. His influence has made the Mountain Lake station a wonderfully stimulating place for work. At the station there have been field courses devoted to study of the pteridophytes, and some of the best fern students in the country have taught them. When able instructors and groups of active students go to work in an area discoveries are likely to be made.

Saltpond Mountain stands about 2000 feet above the valley of the New River. Much of the mountaintop was covered with a fine stand of oak-chestnut forest, the chestnut persisting in sprout form and the oaks now dominating. Nearby, however, are fine forests of northern hardwoods and remnant stands of hemlock and spruce. Boggy areas have cranberries and other northern heaths. There are many exposed cliffs, both of sandstone and limestone. The lake and its borders is unique in this elevated region. The nearby valley has oak-hickory and oak-pine forests, with an element of southern hardwoods brought in by the New River. There are shale slopes, limestone caverns and sinks, and slow-moving streams. Sixty miles away is the Blue Ridge with its metamorphic and igneous rocks.

Present, therefore, is just about any niche for ferns (and other plants and animals) that one might imagine in a mountain country. As a happy result of these circumstances the local fern flora is rich and varied. New finds are constantly being made, and it seems that there are no limits to things that may turn up.

One of the first major discoveries, Alabama lipfern (*Cheilanthes alabamensis*), was made by John M. Fogg, Jr. and his classes. This southwestern fern grows on cliffs along the New River;

here it is at, or near, its known northeastern limit. Near this locality, in wooded limestone plateau country, Robert Patrick Carroll found Engelmann's adder's-tongue fern (*Ophioglossum engelmanni*), another species more common to south and west.

These are plants of the lowlands. On the heights there have been finds of equal significance. Warren H. Wagner, Jr., has had extraordinary success in finding grape-ferns (*Botrychium*), wood-ferns (*Dryopteris*), and clubmosses (*Lycopodium*), many of them of northern affiliations, and some at the known southern limits of their ranges. Save for subtropical things in Florida, he is convinced that almost any eastern fern might be found in the Mountain Lake region.

Since we have a particular concern with living things that have originated, or had their best development, in Appalachia, we must consider a confusing but fascinating aggregation of rock-inhabiting ferns which Wherry has called the "Appalachian spleenworts." At the risk of seeming pedantic, I want to explain that "wort" in a plant's English name means "plant." Some herbalist, or practicer of physic, seeing a real or fancied resemblance to the human spleen in certain ferns (or their parts), called them "spleenworts," and no doubt viewed them as sovereign remedies for ailments of this organ. We retain the name, but so far as I know these ferns have no standing in modern pharmacology.

Some rock spleenworts are plants of wide distribution. Green spleenwort (*Asplenium viride*) comes down from Newfoundland and is a treasured find in the Green Mountains and the Adirondacks. It also clings in limestone crevices in Alaska, Greenland, and Eurasia. American wall-rue (*A. cryptolepis*), another plant of calcareous rocks, is close kin to the widely distributed wall-rue of Europe. Maidenhair spleenwort (*A. trichomanes*), a delicate and beautiful fern, ranges farther south, and is not restricted to limestone, although it may be more abundant on that substrate. It, too, is common in Eurasia.

Ebony spleenwort (*A. platyneuron*) is a highly variable plant, some of whose forms have been reported in the West Indies, South America, and Africa.

Walking fern, a rock dweller that often reproduces itself vegetatively, taking root and forming a new plant where the tip of a frond touches soil, has been by tradition placed in the genus *Camptosorus*, but fern students regard it as a spleenwort for all that.

According to Wagner, who has brought genetics and cytology to his study of American ferns, there are three basic spleenworts in southern Appalachia — mountain spleenwort (*A. montanum*), ebony spleenwort, and walking fern. These have what seems an almost infinite capacity for forming varieties and for hybridizing. Many of the hybrids are fertile, or partially so. They in turn are capable of hybridizing, and there is no telling what may develop. Many of these crosses have extra complements of chromosomes, another factor in the appearance of new and unusual individual plants. As a result of this genetic mix-up, new Appalachian spleenworts are frequently discovered, and if they are sufficiently distinctive, and particularly if they demonstrate the ability to reproduce themselves, they have to be given names. Pity the fern student who has to keep up with all these developments!

Assuming that one has an interest in ferns, the quest for rock spleenworts in the Appalachians, their varieties and their hybrid forms, is a thrilling pastime. It involves climbing and exploring cliffs, tracing out wooded ledges, visiting areas well away from beaten paths. If one does not live for ferns alone, there are other interesting plants to be found. And there is always the possibility of finding something new: evolution has not reached a standstill in this group at least.

Mountain spleenwort, very lacy and fragile-looking, but hardy for all that, grows in cracks of sandstone ledges from the Berkshires of Massachusetts south to Georgia. It spills over a bit into northern Michigan, but for the most part it is a dweller in Appalachia. In shady and moist sites, the fronds may reach five or six inches in length; in full sun these will be reduced to an inch or less, and it is surprising to find such tiny fronds with heavy crops of spores.

Ebony spleenwort grows in all sorts of places, sun or shade, limestone or acid soils, rock crevices, wooded slopes well away from any rocks, just about anywhere it can find a foothold. If you build a stone wall, it won't be long until spores of this fern lodge there, and if crevices are sufficient these will germinate, and you will have a new decorative plant.

Walking fern is a beauty — a long, slender frond that is often auricled at the base and attenuated at the tip. It is evergreen and has, I am sorry to say, suffered from overenthusiastic fern collectors in areas where it is scarce or restricted. It is most abundant, perhaps, on limestone, but it grows well on sandstone and in other situations. Small plants have been found growing on old bark of mature trees.

These three (so Wagner believes) are the genetic stock from which any number of variants have arisen. Some, like the highly regarded pinnatifid spleenwort, are well established and of fairly wide distribution. Another, Bradley's spleenwort (*A. bradleyi*) is something of a rarity, much more frequently sought for than found. Some plants may be genuine novae, recent crosses which have become established in only one locality.

If living fronds or pressed specimens are not available, pictures, not words, must be used to delineate these ferns. Even with specimen in hand, it may be difficult to determine the parentage of a hybrid. Many of the named forms are remarkably close to each other in appearance; Wagner calls the differences "subtle," and I think he has found the *mot juste*.

I suppose it is apparent to any reader of these pages that when we talk about the geographic ranges of living things, particularly of some of the Appalachian endemics, we are actually defining the ranges of collectors, not the organisms themselves. This is a big country, and the number of field students is limited. Those who do work here tend to concentrate in areas where transportation of a sort other than wild-land hiking is available. All this is natural; if your time is limited you don't want to spend half the day hiking through the burned-out area of a mountain. You go where there are roads, you see what you came to see, and you are satisfied.

All this, however, adds up to some pretty distorted ideas concerning the distribution of living things. Let's examine the Harpers Ferry, West Virginia, area as a case in point. Harpers Ferry is strategically located. The Potomac River, having just been joined by the Shenandoah, cuts a water gap through the main Blue Ridge. This gap facilitates two-way movement of living things between the Appalachian Valley and the piedmont, thus obviating the necessity for climbing over a mountain range. Animals and plants alike have made use of this freeway. Its strategic possibilities were recognized by John Brown on a certain occasion, and they were no secret to Robert E. Lee: he sent "Stonewall" Jackson there to capture 11,000 Union soldiers. Furthermore, Harpers Ferry is close to Washington and Baltimore, easily reached by train or highway, and once reached by canal boat for those who were not rushed. As scientists in seaboard cities began to widen the scope of their investigations, it was only natural that Harpers Ferry should receive a lot of attention.

A Harpers Ferry doctor, T. C. Stotler, developed an interest in ferns and began to explore the many sandstone and limestone ledges the region holds. He became something of a pioneer in the field of Appalachian spleenworts. One of his discoveries, presumed to be a hybrid between pinnatifid and ebony spleenworts, was named *Asplenium stotleri* by Wherry. This discovery, and others like it, started something. Plant students, especially those interested in ferns, swarmed to the area.

I remember a meeting of the American Fern Society which was held there. Wherry led the field trips, and among those attending were Mr. and Mrs. Charles A. Weatherby, Campbell Waters, and other important figures in pteridophyte botany. Temperatures during that late summer weekend were in the hundred-degree range; mountain slopes were steep, and cliffs were shadeless. Nevertheless, Wherry showed us the plants we all wanted to see, and I, for one, was delighted to be there. The results of all this publicity were, I suppose, inevitable. Many local rarities were highly restricted. Each visiting botanist took just one small plant or frond for his collection; each fern gardener was careful about taking too much and yet took a sample. Presently some of the more celebrated plants were gone from their known stations; rarities had become absentees.

As this region lost some of its attraction for plant hunters, there were fewer visiting collectors. Other areas began to be explored, and Stotler's and other Appalachian spleenworts were found. I think it is safe to say that every serious fern hunter who has really worked a suitable area has found one or more of these hybrids. Meanwhile, Harpers Ferry was recovering. Joseph Gambino, naturalist of the Harpers Ferry National Monument, has rediscovered most of the species and forms once so eagerly sought after there. Plants that are no longer regarded as unique are not nearly so exciting.

It is obvious, I think, that Appalachian fern rarities (other supposedly rare and restricted species also) are not so scarce or local as they seem to be in the present state of our knowledge. In other connections I have had occasion to mention that vast areas of the Appalachians have had very little biological exploration. There will be new finds and many range extensions. Not all the possible crosses and recrosses of Appalachian spleenworts have yet been seen. I haven't lost my enthusiasm; I hope to see some more of them myself.

As with other living things, ferns include certain species

which have that indefinable thing that we call glamour. Each
student of the ferns will have his own list of plants that for
some reason or other stir his emotions, but on one they are
likely to agree. This is the climbing fern (*Lygodium palma-
tum*), the only native species with a vining habit of growth. It
isn't so much that vining is an unexpected trait in a fern —
this one is a gem in every way, and throughout much of its
range it is elusive enough so that finding a colony is an event.
From north of Mount Mansfield, Vermont, to northeastern
Georgia the climbing fern has been found, often growing as a
single isolated colony, far from any other known station for the
plant. Fronds are sometimes a yard or more in length, twining
around any vegetation that may be nearby. They bear palmate
blades, the sterile ones light green and up to two inches across,
the spore-bearing blades much reduced in size. Perhaps because they usually grow in fertile spots, the plants have a
healthy, vigorous appearance, which is certainly a part of their
charm.

Fern literature is likely to assign this species to moist thickets,
swampy streambanks, or other damp and shaded places. In the
Appalachians at least, these restrictions do not hold. I know
of two flourishing colonies in open mountain pastureland, and
I have seen other colonies in dry woods. One thing does seem
to be necessary: the soil in which the plant is growing must be
strongly acid.

Cumberland Falls State Park in Kentucky is a famous station
for this plant. In this portion of the Cumberland Plateau,
climbing fern comes about as near to being common as I have
ever seen it. As already indicated, it has been reported from
northern Vermont and also from southern New Hamsphire. It
grows along certain waterways in the New Jersey Pine Barrens.
It has been found near Mountain Lake, Virginia. In West Virginia we know eight or ten stations, all well separated from each
other. Since it seems to do well when once established, and since

it tolerates a wide variety of growing conditions, the fact that the species remains so local is amazing.

It would be worthwhile, I think, if fern students were to record the plants over which climbing fern is vining. In two of the most recent stations I have seen, hay-scented fern was furnishing the support. In another, recently found by Kenneth Carvell, climbing fern is growing over bracken. Still another station, in swampy woods, has climbing fern using cinnamon fern as a support. Perhaps the association with other ferns has some meaning; no one seems to have explored this possibility.

Another fern group holding special attractions are the hardy northerners, ferns that occur in the true Arctic and spread southward through the mountains. Nicholas Polunin, in a study of arctic pteridophytes, lists thirteen circumpolar ferns (as well as a number of fern allies) which also occur in the Appalachians. A few of these — the fragile fern (*Cystopteris fragilis*) an example — are common and widely distributed in eastern North America. Rusty woodsia (*Woodsia ilvensis*) reaches North Carolina. Slender cliff-brake (*Cryptogramma stelleri*) was discovered in West Virginia by Wherry and Trudell. To find some of the major prizes, however, it is necessary to visit northeastern Appalachian peaks.

Mountain cystopteris (*Cystopteris montana*) is highly regarded by British fern lovers, who search for it in Perthshire and other Scottish Highlands counties. It is fairly common in Gaspé's Shickshocks, and has been found in the hills adjoining Quebec's Notre Dames. Green spleenwort and fragrant fern (*Dryopteris fragrans*) reward the searcher on cliffs high in the New England mountains and in the Adirondacks. Holly-fern (*Polystichum lonchitis*) is a special prize; it seems to grow in company with other attractive plants.

A surprising number of these northern ferns follow the Canadian Shield around through the Bruce Peninsula of Ontario, both shores of Lake Superior, and into Minnesota's iron-range country. Many published ranges list the Thunder Bay district of Ontario, rugged country on Superior's north shore. There is a reason for this, of course. Thunder Bay has attracted botanists from Minnesota, and has had special attention from very active biology groups in Fort William and Port Arthur. Lists of plants from this area read much like those made in the Shickshocks.

If arctic plants find their way south along the Appalachians, so do some tropical groups reach northward. Among the ferns no group probably would be more representative of the tropics than the filmy ferns (*Trichomanes*). These thin-bladed plants creep over rocks and fallen vegetation in tropical or subtropical rain forests. One species, *T. boschianum* (call it simply filmy fern), occurs in widely scattered Appalachian stations. It reaches Webster County, West Virginia, and Hocking County, Ohio, and there are vigorous colonies in Kentucky's Cumberland Falls State Park.

Another species of tropical associations is the little gray polypody, already mentioned in Chapter 10 as growing on rocks in an area close to Appalachian shale barrens. Often called resurrection fern, this dusty-looking plant folds its fronds to resist drought, then opens when rains return. It ranges widely through warm portions of North, Middle, and South America, and it reaches Wirt and Pendleton Counties in West Virginia. Northward it usually grows on exposed rocks, but southward it is at home on trunks and in crotches of trees. Just in front of the Wren Building, on the William and Mary College campus at Williamsburg, Virginia, are old trees well overgrown with resurrection ferns.

No fern in America has, I suppose, received more attention than has the straplike evergreen hart's-tongue (*Phyllitis scolopendrium*). In England this has been called one of the four commonest ferns, and it abounds throughout much of western Europe. In North America it is fairly widespread but is usually rare and local. No one has offered a good reason as to why this should be. The American form of hart's-tongue, regarded as varietally different from the European form, was once recorded from New Brunswick, where it is now probably extinct. It was discovered in the Syracuse, New York, area, and seems to be persisting there, under difficulties. And, marvelous to relate, husky plants were found in limestone pits and sinks in Marion County, Tennessee, in hill country near Chattanooga. This single known occurrence allows us to include the species as a member of the Appalachian flora.

Near the base of the Bruce Peninsula between Georgian Bay and Lake Huron proper, hart's-tongue is locally abundant; although even there one has to know where to look. The plant has also been found in Michigan. And, curiously enough, hart's-tongue (some form of it at least) is known from tropical Mexico, near the Guatemala border. Sporelings of the American form have been distributed to fern gardeners. If any have succeeded, I do not know of this. Those that I tried in West Virginia persisted for a year, then disappeared.

Among the fern allies, clubmosses are conspicuous and abundant in many Appalachian situations. There are alpine forms and there are species that seem to prefer the pine barrens. Some grow in rocky places, others in swamps. They are evergreen, they are decorative, they have been much used in Christmas decorations, and near cities they have become scarce. Towns often contract with some local florist or plant collector to furnish their street decorations at holiday times. These, or their agents, go into the woods, rip up whole colonies of running-pine and other species, braid the strands into ropes, and hang them over streets so that we may all be merry and enter more fully into the spirit of Christmas.

Like many of the ferns, some clubmosses are widely distributed. *Gray's Manual of Botany*, after recording Carolina clubmoss from the Atlantic coastal plain of North America, goes on to list it as occurring in the West Indies, Central America, eastern South America, tropical and southern Africa, Mauritius, Ceylon, Australia, and New Zealand. I have been in our mountains with botanists who know the Alps well; they feel right at home, so far as clubmosses are concerned.

Horsetails (*Equisetum*) are other ancient fern-related plants. They may be as close a link to forests that grew in the Carboniferous Period as anything we have today. A number of species and forms grow in the Appalachians, some abundant, others restricted. The fertile spikes of a common species are seen in early spring along streams, in railway ballast, and in waste places generally. After a time, these brown spikes are followed with very different-looking green, branched, sterile shoots. Despite their ancient lineage, horsetails come close to bridging the gap between spore-bearing and seed-bearing plants. Some of them have structures remarkably suggestive of flowers.

Spikemosses (*Selaginella*), like clubmosses, are fern allies. The common names, with "moss" in them, are unfortunate, since they are far removed from true mosses. There are many tropical species, and there are some in the Arctic too. One that resembles a small clubmoss (*S. selaginoides*) reaches the far tip of the Appalachians in Newfoundland, then reappears in the Bruce Peninsula and westward. A spikemoss which is often called resurrection moss (like the similarly named fern, it folds up in dry weather) grows on exposed rocky slopes in the Ridge and Valley Province of the Appalachians.

Quillworts (*Isoetes*) grow in water and are very unfernlike but related, nevertheless. Although most of them are found in lowland situations a few get into mountain rivers and ponds. There are occasional colonies of water fern (*Marsilea*), a four-leaf-clover-looking aquatic plant that reproduces by spores not seeds. And that is about the list of the fern tribe.

I have visited no spot in the Appalachians where there are not ferns or fern relatives. There are clubmosses above treeline; there are ferns under every forest cover, and on every geological variety of rock formation. Fern allies grow in streams, and cover the driest slopes. Some of them are Appalachia's own children, at home in these mountains and nowhere else. I have had a lot of pleasure in searching for and finding some of them. There are still unexplored places, and discoveries waiting to be made.

15. Orchids That Aren't in the Tropics

AUGUST HAS COME, and summer is in pause. All during the warm season heat units have been building up, the accumulation now at its peak. Days are still long, and late summer's morning fogs have not yet reduced the hours of sunlight. The tropics have come to midlatitude regions and will linger for a short time, even in a mountain meadow.

High in the Alleghenies, the meadow now has its fullest display of summer flowers. Were it not for the white pines which surround it, it might be a bit of tall-grass prairie. Blue-stem grasses, both tall and short, are dominant species, just as they are (or were) over millions of acres in America's Grain Belt.

In among the grass stems are spikes of purple-flowered blazing-star (*Liatris*), growing here as though this were Minnesota's Red River Valley. There are other prairie species also — mountain mints, sunflowers, asters, and goldenrods.

Turk's-cap lilies are scattered over the meadow — more abundant in moist places — and in the partial shade of wooded borders. Some of the more primitive greenish-flowered lilies are here too, featherbells (*Stenanthium*) on the margins, bunchflowers (*Melanthium*) in open grassland. Along the stream that meanders through the opening, vivid spikes of cardinal lobelia are attracting hummingbirds, winged sprites drawn irresistibly to red flowers. Blue monkey-flowers (*Mimulus*) are there also, and on drier banks above them are clumps of pink- and yellow-flowered meadowbeauty (*Rhexia*).

Visiting the meadow flowers are dark-winged regal fritillary butterflies (*Speyeria idalia*), aristocrats among the Lepidoptera. Along the trails and woods roads back in the forest, there is a chance to see an even greater prize among butterflies, the Diana fritillary (*S. diana*). In this mountain species coloration of the sexes is radically different. Males have wings that are dark brown toward their centers, their outward borders rich orange-brown. Females are essentially black, with whitish spots on the forewings and larger pale blue markings on the hind wings. Occasionally an individual will venture out into the open, although Dianas prefer areas of lower light.

And there are orchids in and around the meadow. Earlier in the season there were many of the ragged fringed species (*Habenaria lacera*), but their greenish-white spikes have faded. Back in the woods there are round-leaved orchids (*H. orbiculata*), the whitish spikes rising from a basal pair of large flattened leaves. Slender ladies'-tresses (*Spiranthes gracilis*) thrive in sunny areas, their white flowers in spirals which may ascend either to left or right, an unusual thing in plants. Best of all, the meadow holds two of Appalachia's finest summer orchids, the purple fringeless (*H. peramoena*), and the yellow fringed (*H. ciliaris*).

This is not a community of living things dreamed up by the author. I have seen a number of these woods-bordered meadows, some of them with every species that I have listed, and many more as well. They contrast strikingly with the dominating forest, and they serve excellently to introduce native orchids. Here most of the flowers are easy to see, and some of them are very beautiful. Those words "very beautiful" are an exact translation of the specific name *peramoena* borne by the purple fringeless orchid.

If your mental image of orchids insists on limiting them to tropical jungles, liana-entwined, insect-infested, probably with lurking deadly reptiles draped over branches, or if you judge all orchids by exotics in hothouses and by gorgeous things so freely flown in from our fiftieth state, you are doomed to considerable disappointment in the Appalachian species. A few of our northern kinds are lovely, but many are inconspicuous, likely to elicit the derisive remark "Don't tell me that ugly little greenish thing is an orchid!"

Appalachia has no orchids that vine over, or support themselves, on trees or bushes — although the region doesn't miss this very far. Just east of North Carolina's Sandhills, at Lake Waccamaw, there is a colony of *Epidendrum conopseum,* a true epiphytic orchid which goes partway toward meeting the tropical aspects on which some persons insist. This is the closest approach to the image. All Appalachian orchids are ground dwellers, most of them independent green plants, a few of them without chlorophyll and therefore dependent upon other organic matter for their nourishment.

As orchid populations go, ours in Appalachia is not a great one. Orchids have their best development in tropical regions; they flourish in both hemispheres and they number perhaps fifteen thousand species, making them among the largest of plant families. Away from equatorial lands their numbers drop off sharply, and midlatitude areas see no such orchid wealth as is found toward and in the tropics. And yet orchids do persist northward. A single rich Great Lakes state's bog may hold fifteen or twenty species. My home community in West Virginia has twenty-two known species, and I imagine that we have missed one or two. Six of our northeastern orchids cross the Arctic Circle to find homes on the tundra. And, interestingly enough, some of the more boreal species are among the loveliest we have.

So far as I am aware, no orchid species is restricted to the Appalachians. Small's twayblade (*Listera smallii*) is a mountain plant in North America, growing from West Virginia to South Carolina and Georgia, and it also grows in Asia. Southern Appalachia has a number of endemic lilies, botanically speaking, not too far removed from the orchids. Perhaps orchids' lack of restricted species is due to the minute seeds they bear. Orchid seeds are so tiny as to be easily transported to distant spots. A characteristic of the family is that many species are found in isolated colonies.

For some casual students of the outdoors, native orchids begin and end with the lady's-slippers (*Cypripedium,* or Venus' shoes). True enough, these are the largest of showy eastern orchids, just common enough in many sections to be well known but usually sufficiently local to be prized. They are also the orchids that most suffer from the attentions of overenthusiastic wildflower gardeners.

Since it is found in Newfoundland and the Gaspé, and since its range extends to Georgia and Alabama, the pink moccasin-flower (*C. acaule*) is probably the best known of eastern lady's-slippers. Its large flower is borne above a basal pair of rounded leaves. Southward these flowers are usually some shade of pink, pale in the dense shade of spruce or fir, deep rose on pine-clad piedmont hills. The plant is remarkably tolerant as to its growing situations: it is found at all elevations, under varying conditions of soil and moisture, on dry sandbank or in a shaded sphagnum bog. As we have seen, occasional plants northward bear blossoms that are pure white or only faintly brushed with pink. In one area near the base of Mount Katahdin, I found a colony in which nearly half the blossoms were white. Here there were plants of both color phases standing side by side. I leave the effect to your imagination.

When I go looking for pink moccasin-flowers, I have the best luck in two types of niches. One is where some forest tree has been uprooted, the hollow thus created filled with drifting leaves. After the leaves have accumulated and their decay has provided a thick humus layer, these pink orchids often become established. Such a colony may have a dozen or more thriving plants. The other favored site is in the decaying wood of a fallen tree. Once decay is far advanced, lady's-slipper seeds germinate and take root. I have seen such a fallen log almost exactly outlined by these plants.

Next to pink moccasin-flower, yellow lady's-slipper (*C. calceolus*) is most widely distributed, and, in the Appalachians, best known. As a species this orchid is found throughout America and Eurasia — in the Himalayas ascending to 12,000 feet, according to Donovan Correll. A number of American varieties have been named, some authors listing a "large" and a "small" yellow lady's-slipper. There is certainly wide variation in the size of blossoms, but since plenty of intermediates occur, this is not a satisfactory means of separation. An interesting variety is found in Newfoundland on the north shore of the Gulf of St. Lawrence, and sparingly elsewhere in boreal situations. It closely resembles the European yellow lady's-slipper, another link in the circumpolar flora of this north country.

In much of Appalachia the common form of yellow lady's-slipper is a plant of rich, well-watered coves, usually under stands of deciduous trees. In my "sang"-hunting days, I used the orchid as an indicator plant: where I found a colony of the orchids, I began to look for ginseng. If such sites are preferred, they are by no means restrictive. One of the most extensive yellow lady's-slipper colonies I have ever seen was on an oak-pine slope of the Alleghenies near White Sulphur Springs. Nearby were some of the shale barrens endemics, but in small hollows on the hillside there were hundreds of the orchids, their blossoms a deep vivid yellow.

The little ram's-head lady's-slipper (*C. arietinum*) is an orchid which few, even among enthusiasts, have seen in the United States. It does occur in New England, New York, and the Great Lakes states, but colonies are sparse and local, their locations usually well-guarded secrets. Incidentally, don't blame local plant students if they are indefinite in giving locations of rare plants. Many of them have had unfortunate experiences with plant collectors; their caution is justified. You might look for ram's-head in nearby Quebec; it is much commoner there. Another complicating factor in seeing this strangely formed orchid is the shortness of its blooming season. Each blossom is at its best for just one day, and a sudden warm spell in late May or early June will wither all the flowers in a good colony. With an orchid photographer I once went to Montreal, our purpose to see and photograph this plant. On white cedar slopes south of the city we found the plants all right, but we were one day too late. Not a single blossom was perfect, and most were completely dry.

Barely entering our area, and not really a resident of Appalachia, is the small white lady's-slipper (*C. candidum*). This handsome orchid is most at home in marl and limestone situations, in open bogs or on prairies. By stretching things a bit, we might regard it as reaching our territory in Pennsylvania, but bogs on lake plains in New York, Ontario, and Michigan are better places in which to search. Yet, it does occur in Kentucky; and a West Virginia woman who was an enthusiastic orchid collector told me she had found a colony near her home, transplanted it to her garden, and promptly lost it. She may have been correct in her identification, although I think it unlikely.

This leaves the queen lady's-slipper, an orchid which many persons consider the most beautiful of North America's wildflowers. Queen, or showy, lady's-slipper (*C. reginae*) follows the Appalachians from Newfoundland to North Carolina. South of the Adirondacks it is local, known in some states from one or two colonies. West of the mountains it is common in parts of the Lakes states, and, like many orchids, it reappears in Asia.

With colored illustrations so freely available, I am not foolish enough to try to describe this orchid. To neophytes of the orchid cult: gaze longingly at the pictures, but see the plant in nature if you can. Fortunately, it is not rare in northern states, and in Canadian bogs it is often positively abundant.

One of my forester friends told me of visiting a logging camp in the Adirondacks. The cook had surpassed himself in more ways than one. The table held five kinds of pie, and it also held a washtub filled to the brim with queen lady's-slippers. Obviously these lumberjacks were not to live by pie alone.

I was once fishing on a Michigan river that flows into Lake Superior. Trout were abundant and luck was good, but presently I saw a sight that stopped my fishing. The stream flowed through a steep-walled ravine. Cliffs were covered with delicate slender cliff-brake, a favorite among northern ferns, and that made me pause. Then I saw the real spectacle: in the moist talus below the cliffs were huge colonies of queen orchids, hundreds, thousands perhaps, and nearly all of them at the peak of their blossoming. All the shades of rose-pink, magenta, and royal purple were in the pouch-shaped lips, the color perfectly set off by the waxy white of floral parts above.

Knowing how much he would appreciate the sight, and knowing also that he was a member of the Huron Mountains Club and so might be in the area, I told Bayard Christy about my find. Sixteen years were to pass before he could visit the colony, but when he did they were there, hundreds of blossoms in full perfection. He wrote an article about it for one of the horticultural journals. He did admit that the display was in Michigan — farther than that he would not go.

The fate that overtakes colonies of rare and attractive plants is well illustrated in my own state. During my lifetime I have known of four queen lady's-slipper stations in West Virginia. Two of them were found by one plant enthusiast; he promptly dug all of them for his home garden, and all died within a short time. A third colony was found by the orchid gardener who told me about also finding the small white species. She, too, took all the plants she found. I saw some of them in bloom the next year, but they disappeared shortly thereafter. That leaves one colony, possibly a hundred plants in all, cherished by a few persons in southern West Virginia. I hope its location continues as a closely guarded secret.

Perhaps a word about transplanting lady's-slippers and other orchids is in order. When it can be done properly I have a good deal of sympathy with this sort of thing; I've done some of it myself. My father and I used to visit areas that were being lumbered; we carried home basketfuls of yellow lady's-slippers, planted them in places that looked suitable, and some of those plants have lived and bloomed for twenty-five years. With the pinks we weren't so successful, although by using the decaying wood of a fallen tree we did establish several colonies. None to my knowledge lasted more than a few years. We tried a good many other orchids; a few, like the rattlesnake plantains, were easy — but most were complete failures.

If you must have orchids in your wildflower corner, buy them from a nursery that is in the business of producing them. You will get good plants, properly handled, and, more important, you will probably get a fair portion of the fungus (or fungi)

Wildlife.

From the Gaspé to the Carolinas, Appalachia offers a broad spectrum of wildlife. In winter, snow buntings from the Arctic find southern balds to their liking. Spruce-fir forests with their resident winter wrens and golden-crowned kinglets sharply contrast with deciduous woodlands, which shelter nesting worm-eating and Kentucky warblers. Limestone caverns have their special inhabitants, and the lungless salamanders of isolated mountains are prized by herpetologists.

Its spotted coat, like dappled forest sunlight, will protect this young whitetail deer until its mother returns to nurse it. If she has twins, the doe will hide them in separate places. Though a fawn can walk at birth, it rarely ventures far during the first month or so. Then it begins to follow the doe, and will remain with her during the winter.

Ovenbirds are warblers but they look and behave more like thrushes, and build domed nests on the ground. Their ringing "teacher, *teacher, TEACHER"* songs are familiar sounds in hardwood forests.

The wild mink, a prized furbearer, no longer is threatened by trapping. Most pelts now come from ranches. Minks vary widely in color, usually hunt near water, and will catch fish.

Despite hunting to the point of persecution, black bears have maintained themselves pretty well throughout Appalachia. Bears in the wild are almost always harmless to humans; those in national parks often become spoiled and dangerous. Properly respected, however, they make fine tourist attractions.

Whitetail deer have adapted to, and thrived under, man's use of the land. Lumbering and fire, with the sprouting that follows these, encourage heavy deer populations; there are probably more deer in New York and Pennsylvania than occupied these areas when Columbus landed.

Opposite: Beavers are remarkable engineers, but their dams do break. Like whitetail deer, they now occupy most of their ancient range in the Appalachians.

Above: Moose, largest of the deer family, occur in Appalachia south to New York and New England. They feed in swamps and along lake margins.

Stories of golden eagles nesting in the Appalachians are like will-o'-the-wisps — they recur, but they are always applicable to the next county. These, and their relatives the bald eagles, still fly above Hawk Mountain and other ridges. However, their numbers have been tragically reduced by hunting, by unwise use of pesticides, and by people whose trigger finger twitches at the sight of any large bird. The golden eagles pictured here are immature birds.

Opposite: This is a view from Hawk Mountain, in eastern Pennsylvania, a spot that marks the triumph of conservation dreams. So many visitors have watched with pleasure as soaring hawks, accipiters, falcons, and occasionally eagles have flown past that their influence has been felt. Many eastern states now have laws protecting hawks, due in part to the fine teaching of Maurice Broun and his associates. Even at Hawk Mountain it is difficult to predict the occurrence of a heavy flight day, but when one does happen, passing hawks are numbered in the thousands.

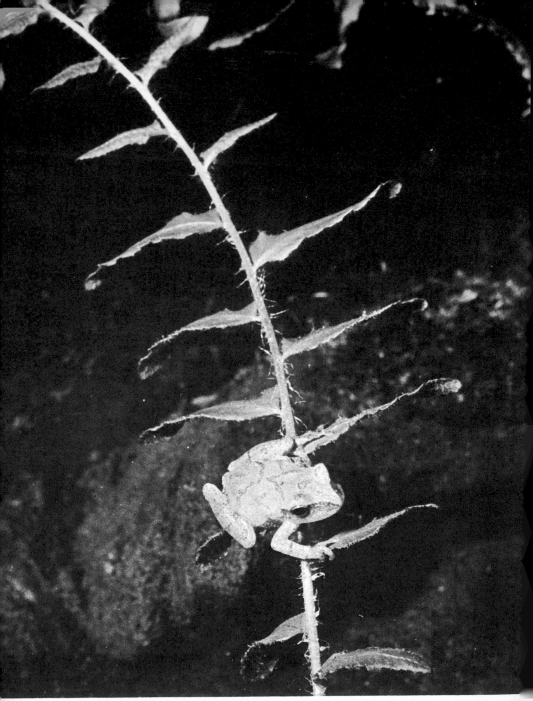

An inch-long spring peeper demonstrates the climbing ability of the tree-frogs. X-shaped marks on the backs of these spring harbingers inspired the scientific name *Hyla crucifer*. They sing in chorus throughout Appalachia.

Farm people call gray tree-frogs "rain" frogs, and with some reason. When summer air becomes humid, these frogs start calling, and if rain follows they descend from the trees to breed in any convenient water. They change color to blend into the ridged bark patterns of forest trees.

Wood frogs, always showing dark masks through their eyes, are among the earliest Appalachian amphibians to emerge in spring. Quickly they assemble in forest pools for calling, courtship, and mating. In the constant temperature and humidity of limestone caves, they often remain active all year.

None of the three salamanders here figured is lungless, but they are typical Appalachian dwellers for all that. The red-spotted newt pictured above is an adult in its aquatic breeding stage. In its land existence it was bright red, and during this eft stage it may have traveled far from water. Both efts and adults have red spots bordered with black. Newts occur practically throughout Appalachia.

Opposite, above: Strongly marked in gray and black, marbled salamanders are also widely distributed in the Appalachians. In late summer and early fall they assemble at the margins of shallow ponds, often depositing their eggs under soaked black-willow leaves.

Below: Spotted salamanders are darkish, with light spots on the dorsal surface. Like so many amphibians, they are tied to water for reproduction. Females deposit their masses of glassy-green eggs, each mass with a cottony cover, in shallow pools often just after the ice has melted.

Copperheads and rattlesnakes, almost all of these latter of the timber species, make up the venomous snakes of Appalachia. Copperheads (above) do not occur very far beyond the line of glaciation, hence are seen mostly in the South. Their bodies are marked with hourglass figures, the narrowest portions of these bands falling along the snake's spinal ridge.

Slitlike vertical pupils mark the eyes of rattlesnakes, and, if one is close enough, these may be seen, along with the heat-sensitive pits below the eyes. Most people will prefer greater distances between themselves and the snake's hollow fangs. Timber rattlers occur from southern New England to Georgia.

which orchids must have on their roots if they are to take food from the soil. This is a subtle plant interrelationship; not much is known about it in any case, and for some species nothing is known. One thing is sure, the fungus must be present. Orchid growers have it in their nurseries; if they didn't, they wouldn't have plants long.

At one corner of my house I have a rhododendron and fern bed that seems well suited to orchids. Fifteen years ago I bought a strong clump of queen lady's-slippers from a nursery in North Carolina. I asked them to include as much dirt as possible, and the clump arrived with the roots well covered. It produced two blossoms the first year, then four, then none. In an effort to save it, I began gathering live sphagnum moss and placing this green growth around the orchid clump. Nothing happened the first year, but the next I again had two blossoms, and I have had four, five, or six each year following. By now the sphagnum must be a foot deep around the stems. There are, of course, no guarantees attached to this, but it has worked for me.

The genus *Orchis*, from which the orchid family takes its name, is best represented in Europe and Asia, only two members occurring naturally in the Appalachians. One, the round-leaf (*O. rotundifolia*), is a northerner, just reaching our north-eastern states but occurring southward along the Rockies. The other, showy orchis (*O. spectabilis*), follows the mountains from Quebec to Georgia and spills over into contiguous areas as well. Both are attractive wildflowers, much appreciated by people who find them.

Roundleaf orchis is surprisingly rare in states along the Canadian border — and just as surprisingly common in provinces north of the boundary. Above a single basal leaf there is a spike of pink (sometimes almost white) flowers, their lips spotted with magenta or purple. Southward this is a plant of spruce and white cedar forests, the best growths being at bog margins or along streams. In Newfoundland and around the Gulf of St.

Lawrence, however, this orchid, like others of the family, is often found in open places, completely exposed to light. Moisture must be abundant for such colonies and soils must be alkaline or neutral.

This pretty little orchid is one of the floral prizes around Percé. It is probably just as abundant in other portions of Gaspesia; I can speak only for the Percé area. Tumbling down from 1200-foot Mont-Ste-Anne and other nearby summits are many streams, some of them dignified by the name of "river" before they reach the Gulf. During the last ten days of June, choose one at random and follow up it for a short distance. Small roundleaf grows along all of them, most abundantly where white cedar swamps border the stream.

It would be easy to dwell at length on other plant and animal finds to be made along almost any of these tumbling streams. There are holly and Braun's holly-ferns, male ferns, and, when one reaches the limestone cliffs, green spleenwort. I think I shall remember longest the finding of another orchid. Tiny round-leafs were just opening and we were searching for suitable plants to photograph. As we worked through a cedar thicket, we found rough going and we had to do some crawling. Fortunately so, for in front of my eyes as I ducked under a log was a fully open and perfectly formed Calypso orchid, surely one of the fairest.

The much more southern showy orchid is to be looked for in woodsy places favored by yellow lady's-slippers. It blooms early, usually in May, and its white and purple-pink flowers rise on a short stalk above two basal leaves. I used to find it frequently on my hikes but now I seldom see it. The plant, I think, holds a fascination for amateur gardeners, one they do not resist. Since it is easily found, I suspect that it gets transplanted. My orchid-gardening acquaintance who tried the lady's-slippers had good luck with showy orchis; she had dozens of them around her grounds, and so far as I could see all were thriving. I believe, however, that she had an exceptionally favorable spot for them.

After the lady's-slippers, the native orchid group most likely to attract public attention is the genus *Habenaria*, the so-called rein-orchids. All members of this genus bear flowers in spikes, some showy, some decidedly inconspicuous. All flowers include in their parts a spurlike structure; to some imaginative soul these spurs suggested a bridle rein, hence the name rein-orchids. One of the graces of the habenarias is that many of them bloom in open places — bogs, marshes, meadows, or prairies — where their flowers may be seen. Another notable thing is that some members of the group have developed along three color patterns — white, yellow, and orchid-pink. Finally, many of these plants are widely distributed and locally common. Any amateur of the wild orchids may expect to find some members of the genus in his territory.

In one respect, at least, it is unfortunate that so much of the good early writing about America's outdoors was done by persons from New England or New York State. Quite naturally, they judged the abundance or scarcity of a plant by what they saw near home. I grew up on botanical literature that listed cranefly and three-birds orchids as among the rarest of their kind. It was always something of a shock to find them both abundant in the woods through which I hiked.

It must have been startling to any of these northeastern writers who may have found themselves in an orchid bog in Ontario's Algonquin Provincial Park, in a wet marl meadow in southern New Jersey, or in one of the great swamps near Wilmington, North Carolina. Concerning many species their ideas of rarity would have faced considerable revision.

Because this chapter makes no pretense to being a catalogue of the orchids, I have chosen to write briefly about a few representatives in each of the three bright-colored rein-orchid groups. So, if you have no quibble at considering white as a color, we shall begin with white-flowered species. Fortunately widespread from north to south and from mountains to lowland, the white fringed orchid (*H. blephariglottis*) is in bloom somewhere in eastern North America from June until September. It grows in Newfoundland, and on the Gulf of Mexico coastal plain. It thrives in Lakes states bogs, and in the Great Smokies. And in whatever place it may be growing, its deeply cut white flowers are handsome and conspicuous.

Because so many people live within easy reach of southern New Jersey, the peninsula between the Atlantic and Delaware Bay, because this area holds so great a wealth of orchids, and because industrial and housing developments are taking some of the best of the orchid sites, I would suggest that the beginner in orchid study might consider this area in August and early September. It is of course not in Appalachia, but, as we shall see, most of the orchid specialties found near Cape May are also growing in the southern mountains. White fringed orchids are locally common in swamplands, especially in the Pine Barrens. In the famous Bennet bogs, before some of them were destroyed, another one of the white rein-orchids, the snowy (*H. nivea*), was abundant. It is still found locally, its pure-white spikes justifying the common name, snowy orchid. It is largely a coastal plains species, but, like so many of its genus, it reaches the mountains in Habersham County, Georgia.

A more northern plant, the tall leafy white orchid (*H. dilatata*), has milk-white flowers and is most at home in wooded bogs from Newfoundland to Pennsylvania in our area, widespread elsewhere across the continent. It is often called scentbottle, and for good reason: its flowers have a rich, spicy fragrance, quite unusual in northern orchids. Still another handsome white-flowered species, the prairie white fringed orchid, just misses the Appalachians, approaching our territory in Maine and New York, where it is rare, and in the Great Lakes region, where it becomes more common.

The yellow- or orange-flowered rein-orchids occupy a rather special place in the interest and admiration of wild-orchid cultists. None of the three species grows far northward, all are particularly handsome, and all have that special trait of growing in company with other attractive plants. Plant students from northern areas look on these with just a bit of envy. Commonest of the three is the yellow fringed orchid (*H. ciliaris*), barely reaching Canada in the Point Pelee area (that bit of Canada's "Dixie" is farther south than Erie, Pennsylvania, after all) but becoming common to absolutely abundant in the southern Appalachians. This is one of New England's rarities; until actually seen, it will be difficult for that region's plant students to believe that yellow-fringe is a characteristic plant along mountain roads from Virginia south.

Actually, these flowers are more orange than yellow. Their deeply cut floral parts and their long spurs give them an insect-like appearance. They open in late July, and a few spikes will still be bright in early September. They seem tolerant as to light, soil, temperature, and moisture, thriving in open bogs, dry pine woods, wet meadows, or on shale slopes. We met this plant, you may recall, in the mountain meadow whose description opened the chapter. That meadow, by the way, existed just as I described it, in Greenbrier County, West Virginia. Unfortunately for plant students, it has become an artificial lake for fishermen.

Yellow-fringes are something of a specialty around the University of Virginia's Mountain Lake Biological Station. They grow around the buildings and along every road that traverses the mountaintop. Formerly it was easy to find colonies of ten, twenty, fifty, but in recent years the plants have suffered. The station is within a "natural area" of the Jefferson National Forest, a tract set aside for special handling because of its scientific values. For good reason, it seemed, deer were given complete protection on the area; now they are increasing and they are causing a problem. They feed on tender plants, orchids and lilies seemingly the favorites. Many of the more noteworthy wildflowers are becoming scarce, and the station personnel would be glad if deer weren't so tame and ubiquitous.

Crested yellow orchid (*H. cristata*) is the second of the orange-flowered species. It too grows on the coastal plain from New Jersey southward, and also in the Southern Highlands in Alabama, Tennessee, and North Carolina. Near Flat Rock, in the last state, it climbs to elevations of 2500 feet or more. Here in a small sphagnum bog Correll collected this and thirteen other orchid species, some of them considered great rarities.

Few wildflowers are so vividly orange as are those of crested yellow orchid. This species is another one of the southern New Jersey specialties, preserved north of its usual range by equable climate and warm bogs. Its season of flowering coincides with that of two of the whites and the other two yellows; all five may be found in bloom at one time if the searcher is fortunate.

Third of the select orange-flowered species is yellow fringeless orchid (*H. integra*), still another plant of coastal plains and Southern Highlands. It is a New Jersey rarity, becoming commoner southward. It reaches elevations of 3000 feet in North Carolina, and occurs in Tennessee's Cumberland Plateau. Paler in hue than the other two in this color group, it approaches true yellow. The spikes are remarkably trim, the flowers quite different in appearance from those on fringed species. Interestingly enough, there are fringeless representatives in each of the three major colors — this one, the snowy among whites, and the purple fringeless among the purple-pinks.

This seems the place to re-emphasize a matter already touched on. Botanical literature contains much wonderment that so many species (orchids and others) spoken of as "typically coastal plain" also occur in isolated colonies on Appalachian highlands. These mountain sites are certainly more ancient, geologically speaking, than coastal areas. To me it seems obvious that many plants survived floodings, and much later survived the effects of nearby glacial ice in the unglaciated Appalachians. Because of highly varied habitats they could live only in scattered places. When coastal plains were exposed, there often were much more extensive areas — bogs, swamps, sandbanks, pine barrens — to meet the special needs of some plants. These species moved downslope, established themselves widely, and so became "typical."

If orchids should have the colors that we call "orchid," these next species meet the requirement. The purple fringed orchids are lilac-lavender, purple-pink, soft rose — almost any shading in which blue and red mix. A widespread species is the small purple fringed orchid (*H. psycodes*). Whether a larger form, more common northward and in the mountains, is a separate species or variety I shall leave to the specialists to decide. Both are things of beauty, common enough so that beginners may expect to find them. The smaller form likes partial shading afforded by roadbanks through forested country. I enjoy driving Forest Service roads in June, since I am fairly certain to see these flowers along the way. Larger plants, usually somewhat paler in color, grow at the fringes of mountain swamps — Cranberry Glades, for instance.

In sharp contrast to these shade dwellers, purple fringeless orchids, the "very beautiful" ones, are plants of the open, growing in full sunlight. Correll says of this species, "I have seen [it] so abundant in a small meadow above the falls at Linville Falls, North Carolina [Grandfather Mountain area], that the flowers gave to the whole landscape a rich red-purple color. Some of the undisturbed meadows and swamps in the vicinity of Caesar's Head, South Carolina, abound with hundreds of these plants." The high meadow in Greenbrier County held many of these orchids, and I am sorry that they were flooded. Fortunately, there are other similar mountain meadows, some of them along the Blue Ridge Parkway. They are rewarding places to visit in August.

I hate to take leave of the habenarias; there are so many whose distribution and flowering habits are noteworthy. But this story has been long, and there are three special gems that must be exhibited. Spreading pogonia, justly called rosebud orchid (*Cleistes divaricata*), is one of the more southern species, scarcely to be found north of Virginia, and at its best in the Carolinas — mountains, piedmont, or coastal plain. Flowers are pink, white, and brown, varying somewhat but always pleasing. Blooming is early, sometimes in April. The Great Smokies are proud to claim this plant as a resident.

No common name is needed for *Arethusa*. It is an individual, and there is no other orchid, save its close relative in Japan, with which to compare it. Blossoms combine yellow, white, and magenta in harmony. Many an orchid enthusiast has yet to see it; it is one of our greatest prizes. Were it not for some North Carolina stations, we could scarcely claim this as an Appalachian species, although it probably occurs in the Shickshocks. There is a colony in a bog on the slope of Cadillac Mountain, in Maine's Acadia National Park. It has been found at low elevations in Vermont. For the most part, however, one who sees this orchid in abundance must do so in Canada.

The Terrills took us to a bog northeast of Montreal which held hundreds of Arethusas. I remember that the photographer, in his eagerness to capture this plant, stood squarely on top of a great clump of queen lady's-slipper as he took some of his pictures. I recall also that two male Wilson's warblers were singing in the thickets which surrounded this Quebec orchid garden.

Last of the distinguished trio (many would say the best of all) is *Calypso*, another plant that needs no common name, although fairy-slipper has been used. There is only one *Calypso*, widely distributed but standing alone. I have mentioned finding it near Percé, and I have seen it in New Hampshire's Connecticut Lakes country. It likes the white cedar areas and grows where the sun breaks through to bring light for at least a little while during each day. It is another of the yellow, white, and red orchids to be seen but not described.

So much of an event is finding this orchid in the East that it seems slightly disrespectful to say that Calypso is sometimes quite common in western mountains. One June my wife, our son, and I were at Kaibab Lodge, back from the North Rim of the Grand Canyon. Fred and I decided to take a walk. Snow was still deep on northern sides but southern slopes were bare, the early flowers joining those of midseason as they do in these northern situations. Oregon holly-grape was in bloom and open spaces held displays of coral-root orchids such as I had never seen before. Largest of this group, striped coral-root, I had found on the Gaspé and near Munising, Michigan, but never in splendor like this. Suddenly Fred found a Calypso, his first, and after that we found numbers of them. We didn't look at much else. When we went into the dining room for dinner, we saw that our table held a bouquet of Calypsos. Local people knew them all right, and took them for granted.

I have had to skip some orchids that I like best — the tway-blades, the whorled pogonias, and species that orchid hunters really have to work for, like the adder's-mouths. But I promised that this would not be a catalogue. One final word. Orchid colonies, many of them at least, are evanescent things, flourishing one year, gone the next. Enjoy them when you find them; it may be a long time until you see them again. Once you have come to know wild orchids, you will search and you will find — something.

16. Something Lost

THERE IS sound psychology in the story of the lost sheep that caused more excitement and received more attention than the ninety-and-nine that stayed home minding their business. Let a thing — almost anything — become lost, and suddenly it takes on new and unsuspected values. We seem to resent the fact that anything might be hidden from us; we want to know, and the sooner the better.

In Arizona they make an annual social event and stunt of searching for the Lost Dutchman Mine; but don't bet that a good many of the solid citizens who join the hunt aren't hoping to find this fabulous lode. All through the Appalachians there are stories of buried treasure, usually gold buried by retreating British during the Revolution, and I have seen places where the earth was pitted with shallow openings, the work of treasure hunters. They always have a map, the directions obscure and the characters faded, and some day the right number of turns will be made, the combination will open the secret, and wealth will be revealed.

Or, on a less commercial basis, take the "lost" plants in the Appalachians. For the most part these were in southern Appalachia, since that is the area with the most endemics. The area holds, I suppose, 3000 or so flowering plants, most of which are easily found and are familiar to anyone who cares to go looking for them. But a handful were lost after some pioneer scientist-explorer discovered them, and these have excited boundless curiosity, have been the subjects of many papers, and, in the search for them, have caused the expenditure of a tremendous amount of energy. Seemingly as a demonstration that hard work should be rewarded, every so often one of these lost species is found.

There scarcely could be a better place where things can become lost than southern Appalachia, especially before the still recent coming of good roads and the national forests and parks. Settlers were so few and scattered that many places were still unexplored. Topographic features — mountains, streams, rock ledges, and such things — had not been named. By what means, and in what terms, would an explorer pinpoint the exact location of his discovery?

Everyone who travels through the complex system of ridges and valleys in the Southern Highlands will understand how difficult it is to remain directionally oriented. If the journey is through thick forest, densely undergrown with rhododendron and other rank shrubbery, most persons will have little idea of the distance traveled. The wonder is that Michaux, Bartram,

Pursh, Rafinesque, Gray, and others could be as accurate as they were. All of these factors combined to produce a situation in which specific plants (other living things too) were discovered, then mislaid for a time. Many people have enjoyed painstakingly pouring over old journals, retracing the routes of these early explorers, and then, perhaps, rediscovering some lost botanical prize. Most species of which specimens were taken and preserved have been rediscovered; some, particularly those only described in someone's journal, have not. And, as we shall see, there is still hearsay evidence to be examined, still report of things yet unknown.

Shortia (Oconee-bells), should probably stand as the archetype of Appalachian lost plants. We met this plant briefly in Chapter 5, "Alpine Summits." It is a botanical relative of diapensia, so prominent above treeline on Mount Katahdin and Mount Washington. It is also related to *Galax,* a connection its specific name *galacifolia* shows. And, as time has shown, the only other known member of its genus is in Japan.

Shortia was discovered by André Michaux; whether the year was 1787 or 1788 remains in dispute. This matter is of importance to botanists, for on it depends which of two areas should be designated as the type locality for the species. Both areas have had their claimants, and students are still trying to match journal descriptions to present-day topographies. Michaux placed his specimens in a folder of unidentified plants, these being deposited in the Jardin des Plantes in Paris. The Shortia folder bore the notation "high mountains of Carolina," with an abbreviated suggestion that it might be a pyrola or a species new to science. Asa Gray examined this material, determined that Shortia was undescribed, and in 1842 named it in honor of a colleague, Charles W. Short, of Kentucky. Presently the search was on in earnest. As we have seen, Gray and his associates, followed by many other plant students, worked long and carefully in the high mountains of Carolina. Someone

misintepreted Michaux's label, for soon, through some mis-
interpretation, it was changed to "high in the mountains of
Carolina." This led to a concentration on the higher summits
— Grandfather, Roan, Mitchell, and others.

Meanwhile, Gray had found a picture of the Japanese relative of Shortia, and from that and other evidence had placed it
in the family with galax and diapensia. This was encouraging;
but he could not know that he was many miles from, and often
some thousands of feet above, the place of Michaux's discovery.

As repeated explorations in the high mountains failed to
yield Shortia, the search spread farther afield, still in the mountains but at much lower elevations. In 1886, Charles Sprague
Sargent, student of American trees, explored for plants — always
with Shortia in mind — in southwestern North Carolina, not far
from the South Carolina border. And there Shortia was rediscovered, still in the high mountains, but not high in the mountains.

Ninety-eight (or was it ninety-nine?) years had passed since
any botanist had seen this plant growing. Once found, it proved
to be locally abundant, although the student must still know
where to look. Michaux had found the plant out of its blooming season, so its flowers were unknown, although reference to
the Japanese relative afforded a fairly good idea of them. The
rediscovery having been made, botanists were soon familiar with
the pretty little white flowers, so suggestive of diapensia. The
season of blossom is early, late March or April. Leaves are
evergreen, so it is another of the multitudinous species that
prevent southern Appalachia's being drab in winter.

The search for Shortia was by no means over. In addition to
the area of first rediscovery, a territory that included small parts
of North and South Carolina and Georgia, Shortia was presently
found more than sixty miles northwest, along streams that flow
into the Catawba River. And, to add a bit of confusion, flowers
in the newly discovered situation were slightly, but constantly,

different from those farther southeast. This gave point to the botanists' quest for Michaux's type locality. Since his plants were sterile, no one can know from them, so investigators again had to fall back on his journals. I do not know whether a determination satisfactory to everyone has been made; if not, I am sure that plant students will keep trying.

And now a pattern that has become familiar to students of plants and animals in the Appalachians once more repeats itself. A rarity once found may remain a rarity for years; then someone at a distance, possibly by pure chance, finds it in a new place and thus extends our knowledge of plant geography. It happened with Shortia, just as might have been expected. The year was 1956, the discoverer was Dorothy L. Crandall, and the place was Amherst County, Virginia — still in the hills but a long way from the earlier-known localities. That other discoveries will be made, even farther removed, I have no doubt.

One of our projects on the family's West Virginia farm was to plant specimens of as many of the Appalachian "lost" plants as we could lay our hands on. We tried Shortia of course, placing it in acid soil at the edge of a mountain laurel and rhododendron stand, where *Galax* had done well. It lived for several years, bloomed freely, sometimes when snows still came to cover the blossoms, but gradually it died out. It is, I think, very much worth trying in home plantings. Few American plants have gathered unto themselves more romance and tradition. Flowers and foliage are attractive. The plants are being produced commercially, so no one need despoil a natural growth.

Another of Appalachia's "lost" — well, almost lost — species is a particularly handsome evergreen heath, box huckleberry (*Gaylussacia brachycera*). Named for the French chemist Gay-Lussac, plants of this genus produce edible fruits; most of the "huckleberries" of commerce are really blueberries, however. The box species is the only one in our territory with evergreen foliage. The common name, of course, is in reference to its resemblance to ornamental box (*Buxus*).

The tireless Michaux first discovered box huckleberry in 1790, his type locality given as around Winchester, Virginia, although the label on his specimen indicates another location, possibly the present Berkeley Springs, West Virginia. Mathias Kin also found it, in a region which in his inimitable way he called "Krien Preyer," by which he presumably meant Greenbrier. Pursh collected specimens at Sweet Springs, Monroe County, West Virginia, in 1805; then for 116 years it was completely lost sight of by West Virginia plant students. A few scattered plants were known elsewhere, in Delaware and Pennsylvania, but, like so many of the blueberries and their relatives, these were almost self-sterile, spreading through roots but not often seeding. These plants, by the way, when growing in clumps have extensive underground root connections. Wherry has estimated that stands of box huckleberry, all essentially one plant, may be among the more ancient of living things.

In 1921, Fred W. Gray, a minister affectionately known as "Parson," was dining with friends in Monroe County, West Virginia. Gray was an enthusiastic amateur botanist and his interest was aroused when he was served a section of pie whose principal ingredient he could not name. The cook assured him that it was "juniper" pie, and that the fruits were borne on low evergreen bushes that grew nearby. She remarked casually that they had already picked about sixty gallons from the patch, and expected to get about forty more. Parson Gray was doubtless aware of certain uses of juniper berries, but he had not heard of them in a pastry connection. He asked to see the plants, was taken to them, and, after some investigation, realized that these were box huckleberries.

The local name "juniper" was useful in his next investigation. Using it in advertisements in local country weekly newspapers, he asked that anyone who knew of patches of these plants get in touch with him. He received prompt answers, and a surprising number, from five West Virginia counties. As a result of his curiosity, more than seventy-five separate stations were made known to botanists. Gray immediately got in touch with Edgar T. Wherry, and this started a lifelong friendship. Later he and Wherry collaborated on a catalogue of West Virginia ferns.

Box huckleberries are light blue, the fruits heavily coated with the whitish waxy material that we call bloom, which is abundant on grapes and plums. Fruiting is heavy, the berry-like drupes being sweet and highly acceptable as food for humans. Big colonies (all a single plant in some cases, at least) may cover half an acre or more. My father moved a portion of a plant one hundred miles or so northward; it is still alive after twenty-five years, but it has not spread. It has borne sparsely, but I do not think the seeds are fertile.

I might as well revert to being a teacher for a moment. Since huckleberry and blueberry equate for most people, it may be pointed out that huckleberries have ten relatively large seeds, whereas blueberries are many-seeded. We are more comfortable, generally speaking, eating blueberries.

It is a matter for wonderment that a brightly colored wildflower, very showy and obviously a distinct species, should for so long remain unrecognized botanically. This happened to Buckley's phlox (*Phlox buckleyi*), a particularly handsome plant that grows in West Virginia and Virginia in shale barrens territory, but not actually on shale slopes themselves. Buckley's phlox has long slender leaves, causing it to be called swordleaf phlox in some literature. The manuals call its large flowers purple, but to me they look bright rose-pink. Samuel Botsford Buckley, so the story goes, was one of those New England schoolteachers who chose to teach in the upper South. He walked (also by choice) to his schools in eastern Tennessee, spending winters in the classroom and using springs and autumns for his journeys. Along the way he collected plants, one of them the phlox that now bears his name. (I hope that someone has written about the influence of these Yankee teachers who took schools in the South. In every case of which I know the communities where they taught were centers of Union sympathizers when the Civil War came.) Buckley's specimens lay unnamed from 1838 until after 1919, when Marian S. Franklin, of Lewisburg, West Virginia, rediscovered the plant, brought it to the attention of botanists, and caused them to look up Buckley's material. Wherry named the phlox in his honor.

This is one of the medium-tall phloxes, blooming in May and found thus far only in a few southeastern West Virginia counties and in adjoining counties of Virginia. There may be shale barrens on the slopes just above it, but it is most often found on sandy streambanks, often in mixed pines and hardwoods. Frequently it is classed as a shale barrens endemic, but this is unfortunate since it does not actually grow (so far as I know) on shale. When we moved a plant to our farm we placed it on shale, and it promptly disappeared. I believe I could do better if I were to try this again.

I have, of course, a favorite spot for this phlox. It is along the road that joins Warm Springs, Virginia, and Minnehaha Springs, West Virginia. In the latter part of May this is extraordinarily flowery country. Locusts by the thousands cover the land, and one is seldom beyond their fragrance. This is mountain land, and roadsides are crowded with azaleas, the pinxterflowers just fading but the flames in every conceivable shade at their best. Blue lupines abound in the dry woods, and on the shale slopes are creeping phlox, fire-pink, wild pink, and bird's-foot violets. Columbines grow at the base of cliffs, and on these rocks are interesting ferns, if one has the inclination to search for them.

And along the way, in many places, are fine displays of

Buckley's phlox, their stiffly held swordlike leaves a perfect foil for pink blossoms. I am glad that Samuel Botsford Buckley walked past White Sulphur Springs to find his flower there. I wish, however, that his name did not remind me of Stephen Dowling Botts, who passed away by falling down a well, a tragedy related by Emmaline Grangerford's poem and relayed to us by Huckleberry Finn.

Another plant growing beside this flowery road is one of Appalachia's "lost" ones, Fraser's sedge (*Cymophyllus fraseri*). Typical sedges, closely related to grasses, bear relatively inconspicuous flowers. Fraser's species is an exception — it has handsome yellowish-white flowers. Let us look at its somewhat complicated history in Appalachia.

Earlier in this chapter we met Mathias Kin, he of the individualistic spelling of Greenbrier. All that I know about him I have borrowed from John W. Harshbarger; he wrote at some length about botanists who have lived and worked in the Philadelphia neighborhood. This Kin, according to Harshbarger, was a character. He proudly bore the appellation of "Indian plant-hunter," conferred because he often went on expeditions dressed as an Indian, and with about the amount of baggage one of those forest hunters would carry. Kin had been sent to this country by a group of Germans who were anxious to exploit seeds and plants from the New World. He traveled extensively, often in the Appalachians, and since this was early in the nineteenth century he did not have too much competition. On one of his trips he found a plant that was new to him, and he probably had no means of knowing of its prior discovery. He sent one specimen to the Botanical Garden in Berlin, another eventually found its way to the Academy of Natural Sciences in Philadelphia. The Berlin specimen was blitzed by Allied bombers during World War II; the Philadelphia example is still available to us.

Kin had his own ways of labeling his specimens. He seems to have been polylingual; he used several languages on his sheets. Sometimes, however, these failed to satisfy him, and he made up his own words to suit his fancy. The sheet of plant material with which we are most concerned was labeled briefly and concisely "in Deigher walli in ter wilternus." That's all.

Actually, the plant that Kin sent to Berlin had already been collected by John Fraser near Morganton, North Carolina — very near, by the way, to the second-known station of Shortia. It was given many names at different times, but finally "Fraser's sedge" was agreed on, whatever scientific name it might bear.

Asa Gray saw Kin's material, just as he seems to have seen all other plants which, up to that time, had been collected in North America. He rightly interpreted Kin's jargon as applying to Tygart Valley, near the headwaters of the Monongahela River. For a long time the plant quite dropped from sight, but when it was rediscovered the upper Tygart Valley proved to be one of its best stations.

Just what is this relative of the grasses that it should have so much fuss made over it? Well, for one thing, its leaves are thick and leathery, broad and straplike, sometimes two feet in length. They might possibly suggest a lily, but they certainly don't look like a typical sedge. Before the new crops of leaves appear, often in May even at high elevations, there rises a spike of creamy-white flowers, pollen-bearing ones at the apex and female floral parts below. Any person who sees it is not likely to remain unconvinced: this is a showy wildflower.

Fraser's sedge likes the richest, moistest mountainsides. It grows in dense shade, and reaches maximum dimensions where water, from a stream or a swamp, is abundant. It barely crosses the Mason and Dixon Line into Pennsylvania; most of its stations are southward, through the Virginias and Kentucky and into the Carolinas and Tennessee. Wherever it grows Fraser's sedge is a mountain plant, one of the Appalachian endemics made the more interesting because botanists consider it very ancient, a relict species. It is growing in ancient country, all right, and could have a long lineage.

On the slopes of Gaudineer Knob, at the summit of which is the fire tower that we visited in Chapter 6, just below the spruces there is a dense northern hardwoods forest, birches predominating but maples, beech, and basswood there too. This is a garden spot for spring wildflowers before leaves have unfolded. Several small rivulets head upslope, their banks steep and moist. Along all of these are Fraser's sedge plants, some of them as large as any I have seen. The sedge's light blossoms are open when hobblebush has its showy white flowers, and just as these are fading painted trilliums and pink lady's-slippers are in full display. And, by the way, from the tower on Gaudineer's peak one can almost, if not quite, look down into Tygart Valley.

Lest it be thought that only plants have been lost in Appalachia, we might turn for a time to the other kingdom of living things. For example, we might consider a "lost" frog. Around 1889 Edward Drinker Cope collected a new treefrog, his notation reading in part, "taken in west Pennsylvania, near the Kiskiminatas (sic) River." Eventually the animal became known as the mountain chorus frog (*Pseudacris brachyphona*), but it was to remain virtually unknown for forty years — another living thing lost in the Appalachians.

During the summer of 1931, Albert H. Wright was teaching and collecting in West Virginia. Near Beckley he was shown a treefrog that he did not recognize, and the next evening he heard the calling of a frog he could not identify. His party succeeded in capturing one of the animals; he immediately suspected that it might be Cope's mountain chorus frog. P. Cecil Bibbee, a teacher in a nearby college, showed him specimens of the animal taken in spring, and Wright's surmise proved to be correct: it was the long lost *Pseudacris*.

This discovery launched a reappraisal of frog populations among herpetologists in the Appalachian area. N. Bayard Green, then a teacher at Elkins, West Virginia, discovered to his amazement that mountain chorus frogs were abundant in his territory. He had simply been overlooking their voices, blended in as they usually were with those of spring peepers. Neil Richmond, then at Fairmont, West Virginia, was skeptical; he could not believe that a strange frog voice would be overlooked. Making something of a game of it, Green came to visit him, and they found five stations for the frog within a few minutes.

The voice of the mountain chorus frog is quite distinctive once it is learned and listened for. I remember driving one evening through the Unicoi Mountains in southeastern Tennessee. We had been listening to choruses of another treefrog. Suddenly from a ditch along the road we heard the calling of a mountain chorus frog. We collected the animal, which was, I believe, the first Tennessee specimen. As was to be expected, it proved common in the mountain area, once local biologists had learned to look for it. This frog is a true endemic of the unglaciated Appalachians. As we shall see, there are a number of endemic salamanders, members of the other branch of the Amphibia, but the mountain chorus frog is the only one of the "leapers" so restricted.

Thus far we have been concerned with plants, and an animal, which have been discovered, lost, then rediscovered. There are others with less definite histories; a few plants which were found once or twice, then not seen again, and some that have simply been reported, with no collection to support their existence.

There is a temptation to wander away from the Appalachians at this point, in order to mention the famous Franklinia tree (*Franklinia alatamaha*). This ornamental, now widely cultivated, was found in the wild along Georgia's Altamaha River late in the eighteenth century, was seen once again in its original locality, and after that, for 170 years, completely disappeared. Fortunately, it was saved for posterity by John Bartram; it is a member of that restricted group of native woody plants which bloom in August and September. Its story has been told many times. The Altamaha is not an Appalachian river, so we cannot claim Franklinia. One of its relatives in the tea family, mountain camellia (*Stewartia ovata*), does occur in the southern Appalachians, at least in their lower reaches.

Some plants are in process of becoming lost. In the West Virginia mountains there is a colony of transplanted Swiss centered around a community which is quite appropriately named Helvetia. These Swiss brought many things to their new home — their costumes, their dances, their skill in making fine cheese, and the plants from their home gardens. For some reason or other these exotic plants, for a time at least, did wonderfully well in their new setting. Foxgloves of two species, purple-flowered (*Digitalis purpurea*) and creamy-white (*D. lanata*), spread throughout the countryside, appearing in locations twenty-five or thirty miles from Helvetia. Two famous Old World members of the pea family, Scotch broom (*Cytisus scoparius*) and gorse (*Ulex europaeus*), also became established locally. Japanese spirea (*Spiraea japonica*) became a roadside weed throughout the region, the shrubs so abundant that nurserymen hauled away truckloads of the plants.

These, of course, were not natural members of the Appalachian plant community. They were established for a time; some have been lost and others are disappearing. No person, to my knowledge at least, has seen either Scotch broom or gorse in the wild for many years, although the broom has been established from another planting about twenty-five miles away. The foxgloves once grew abundantly in mountain pastures, associating with patches of hay-scented fern, which local inhabitants call "ferron." Now they are scarce in some places, completely gone from others. Japanese spirea has persisted, perhaps not so abundantly as formerly. It may be that in time all will be "lost" plants, so far as this section of Appalachia is concerned.

There is still a will-o'-the-wisp among mountain plants, an unknown of which I have been told many times, always with just enough circumstantial evidence to make the accounts enticing. These stories concern a *yellow* rhododendron, supposed to exist in the Allegheny Mountains country along the Virginia–West Virginia border. When chestnut blight first began to afflict this most important of our forest trees, West Virginia, along with neighboring states, attempted to control it by quarantine and removal of diseased trees. One day a timber scout, so employed, a sober man with much experience in the woods, asked me if I had ever seen yellow rhododendron. I assumed that he was referring to flame azalea, but he was insistent that this wasn't so. He said that in wild country, either in Bath County, Virginia, or Pocahontas County, West Virginia, he had found a patch of rhododendron in bloom, its leaves obviously evergreen, and its blossoms much like "big laurel" (rosebay rhododendron) except that they were bright yellow.

Somewhat later, a trout fisherman who had been trying a stream that flows down from the Alleghenies in Pocahontas County told me he had seen a rhododendron bush, a big one, whose leaves didn't look like those of ordinary rhododendron. Again I made an assumption — this time that the man had found an out-of-range plant of Catawba rhododendron. I asked him if he could show me the plant, and he agreed to do so. Several of us went to the area and left our car in the barnyard at a mountain home. We noticed that someone there had planted an unusually fine collection of ferns and wildflowers about the house, and we stopped to talk with the woman of the house. We found her uneducated but highly intelligent, interested in everything out of doors.

On some inspiration one of our group asked her if she had ever seen yellow "laurel." She said emphatically that she had, that her grandson had brought her a large bouquet of it just the past spring. Again we questioned her about azaleas. She was scornful of the suggestion, said she knew all about "honeysuckles," all the kinds there were — pink, yellow, and white. This, she said, was a big laurel, with thick, evergreen leaves. Then, in dead earnest, she said, "I tell you, Mr. Brooks, those flowers were *yellow, yellow* as a cow punkin."

Although it was past the blooming season for rhododendrons, we went to search for the strange plant that the fisherman had described. And we found it, a big clump, obviously a rhododendron but with leaves very different from those of any plant in this group that we had ever seen. They had unusually long petioles, and the leaves were narrow at the base and slender even at the tips — distinctive in every way.

The plant appeared vigorous, was seven or eight feet tall, and showed no signs of disease. There were no clusters of old seeds on it, nor were there blossom buds for next year. Sometime or other the plant had seeded — we found two smaller plants nearby, one of which we transplanted to our farm. We collected specimens, sterile of course, and sent them to herbariums; the Gray Herbarium at Harvard, the New York Botanical Garden, and the herbarium at West Virginia University were three. Notations came back. Most of them simply stated "Rhododendron, species unknown." One read, "Species unknown, doubtfully rhododendron."

That is about the end of the story. I have been back to see the plant, but I have never found it in bloom. The last time I visited the area it was vigorous, but there were no signs of any new plants. The small specimen we took to the farm lived twenty years, without doing much growing in that time. One botanist to whom I showed the foliage suggested that it might be a sterile mutant. Maybe so. I still would like to know how those two young plants got there.

There are rhododendrons in Asia which bear yellow blossoms, usually pale and not in any way suggesting a "cow punkin." The story of a yellow-flowered one in Appalachia may be a myth — all the weight of probability would indicate that it is. But this is big country and old country. It holds other relicts, some of them rare and highly restricted. There just might be a plant so completely lost that it hasn't yet been found.

17. Lungless Salamanders

IT TOOK some doing to get the vertebrates out of water. Tradition was against it, a tradition that had been a good many millions of years developing. Strictly speaking, fish were the only backboned creatures, and all of them lived in water. Despite some variants, most of them took their oxygen from water that had, at best, only about seven parts per million of the dissolved gas. They were poorly prepared for life in a gassy medium which includes about 20 percent of pure oxygen. Fortunately for mankind, some of the fish had developed a happy combination of parts — lungs and fleshy fins. These seem to have turned the trick, and life in the air was launched.

There isn't any evidence that protoamphibians chose to live in the air; rather, it was a matter of survival. When droughts came, creatures with lungs and fleshy fins had a chance to scramble through the mud to another water hole; those that lacked such structures never made it. This is guesswork, obviously, but the facts we have support the theory, and it may have happened that way. Even today most amphibians live in moist places, breathe through gills for a part of their life, and get back to water when it is time for them to reproduce their kind.

Sometime in their development (and they have had ample time; three hundred million years or so), the amphibians took two divergent paths. One, the more highly specialized of the two, led to the "jumpers," frogs and toads as we know them. The other, more conservative, path led to the salamanders, creatures with tails, if we translate the Latin of their Order name. Assume that you are willing to learn something about salamanders; the Appalachian Mountain system is the place to do it, the best one there is.

Salamanders occur throughout the length of the Appalachians. Even in the Gaspé there are at least five species, more than in all of Great Britain. Southwestward the number of species builds up, slowly at first, then much more rapidly after we pass the line of farthest glacial advance. Unglaciated Appalachia is the salamander hunter's paradise, a happy land where even today new species and races turn up with surprising frequency. Zoologists don't take such things lightly. The ornithologist or mammalogist has little chance to discover an authentic new North American species; the herpetologist may just make it.

A major cause for the diverse and complex salamander population in the Appalachians derives from topography — the manner in which ridges and isolated peaks are separated by deep valleys. There are, of course, some long, more or less continuous ranges, the Blue Ridge and the Alleghenies being prime examples. Particularly toward the south, however, there are numerous smaller mountain masses isolated by valleys several thousand feet lower than their summits. During the millions of years that these mountains have been above water and without glacial ice, they have served as laboratories for the production of new races and species.

Consider the situation of an animal that finds shelter and reproduces its kind in decaying spruce logs. Spruce occurs on virtually all the higher Appalachian peaks as far south as the Great Smokies. During Pleistocene glaciation, we can assume, spruce forests were much more widespread, occurring at lower elevations. Under such conditions dispersal of an animal dependent on spruce was easy. With warming climate and receding ice, spruce forests could persist only on the higher peaks and ridges. Below the spruces were forests of other types, and these were not suited to the special requirements of a dweller in spruce logs. The animal's movements were now definitely restricted. If he was situated on a long continuous elevated ridge, he might still have considerable freedom of movement, but if he had been caught on an isolated peak he was there to stay until the climate changed, or until his race came to its end.

A roll call of some of the isolated mountain masses and solitary peaks in southern Appalachia is enough to stir a biologist's imagination. Who really knows what may live in the Balsams, the Nantahalas, the Snowbirds, and the Unicois? Such outstanding peaks as Grandfather Mountain in North Carolina and the Mount Rogers–White Top complex in Virginia have been rather thoroughly explored, but there are many that haven't been. And herein lies the real source of excitement; almost every one of these well-studied mountain masses has yielded its own endemic species or race of salamanders. No one doubts that there are discoveries yet to be made.

Most characteristic of Appalachian salamanders are members

of a family known in scientific circles as the Plethodontidae. Never mind the classical derivations; we'll call them the lung-less salamanders. These beasts have got themselves out on a limb. As adults they have neither gills nor lungs, but must breathe through their skin and the lining of their mouth. To absorb oxygen their skin must be moist, hence they are restricted to damp situations. From the evolutionary standpoint, it doesn't look as though the lungless salamanders have anywhere to go. They have overspecialized.

As is usual among systematic zoologists, authorities cannot agree as to which salamander forms are full species and which should be relegated to the less select category of races. One recent author recognizes as valid 79 North American species and races of lungless salamanders, about four times as many forms as are known from any other family. On one point, however, there is no disagreement; Appalachia is the place to go to for studying this particular family. The author who recog-nizes 79 forms lists almost exactly half of them, 38 species and races, as occurring in the Appalachians. This won't be strictly accurate when you read these figures; new forms have been, and will be, discovered and described.

It seems highly probable that the Family Plethodontidae had its origin in the Appalachians, perhaps the only major vertebrate group of which this is true. Certainly there are more species and races here, and greater numbers in the populations, than in any other part of the world. In fact, the Great Smoky Mountains National Park claims, with justification, the most varied and abundant salamander fauna to be found anywhere.

I don't know how to impart it, but there is a strange fascina-tion, a growing excitement in putting on old clothes, taking a collecting bag and a flashlight, and going mucking through a stream or wet woods on a rainy night to look for salamanders. Try it sometime with a devoted herpetologist, and you'll see what I mean. I am certain that I have watched Graham Netting convert at least twenty-five skeptics into willing amateurs, a few of them into competent professionals. He has the kind of enthusiasm that rubs off. I suppose that if I had to classify myself zoologically I would put down "ornithologist"; but I know this, when I dream (literally) of finding some beast new to science it's always a salamander.

The beginning collector who chooses to work along a stream (or even in a wet roadside ditch) is likely to make an early acquaintance of an unimpressive animal which the systematists call dusky salamander (*Desmognathus fuscus*). Perhaps he learned to call it a "water-lizard" as a boy. Certainly, if he is a bass fisherman, he will have heard it called "spring-lizard." Just about anywhere he may be in eastern North America there will be a race of dusky salamander present.

This salamander is a most unsatisfactory subject for study. Individuals vary widely in coloration, and there is no sure-fire set of identification characters. Most individuals will be a shade of gray or muddy brown, but some are reddish, some partly yellow, and some almost black. Usually there is a dorsal stripe lighter in color than the remainder of the body. Generally speaking, this dorsal stripe has scalloped edges — also a help. The average length of adults is between three and four inches, but, to keep confusion throughout, occasional examples reach five inches or more.

I remember giving a practical examination to graduate students in which I used twenty salamanders collected in the area. Only one student got them all right, and she was possibly the least interested member of the class. But she had stumbled onto a piece of herpetological wisdom. Every specimen I showed her which wasn't plainly something else she called a dusky, and she was 100 percent correct. Perhaps this is a good working formula: learn to identify all the others in the community, and if your specimen doesn't fit any of them it is a dusky or a new species.

As soon as the collector leaves stream margins and begins to turn over logs and rocks in drier woods, the chances are that he will find another widely distributed species, the red-backed salamander (*Plethodon cinereus*). This is a more attractive animal. Characteristically there is a foxy-red dorsal stripe that contrasts with the dark pigment of other exposed portions. The belly (hard to see on a wiggling animal) is a pepper-and-salt mixture of dark and light spots. All this makes for relatively easy identification, but there is a catch in it: some individuals have solidly dark backs, without a trace of red pigment; others are intermediate between the two common types. Salamanders don't make it simple for you. Red-backed salamanders occupy the entire Appalachian area, and much territory besides. Dusky salamanders are not found quite so far north, but their range is vast nevertheless. I have no idea which is the more abundant species. I suspect that these two are the most numerous land vertebrates in Appalachia.

About now some practical soul will concede (grudgingly, perhaps) that although hunting for salamanders may have its points he would like to know what the little beasts are good for anyway. The three witches in *Macbeth* used "eye of newt" in their brew, but their activities are not apt to be widely copied today. Man hasn't made much use of salamanders — and that may be the reason these amphibians are still with us.

If humans find few direct uses for these amphibians, the same cannot be said for lower flesh-eating animals. A single salamander is small, hardly a good bite for a raccoon, weasel, or fox, let alone a bear. But to look at the dimensions of a single individual is to miss the point: salamanders occur in very large populations, they are easily found and captured, especially at night, and they are active throughout warmer portions of the year. A large carnivore may occasionally make an important kill, but the diminutive salamanders are a dependable bread-and-butter source of food, available and abundant. After deep-burning forest fires have destroyed the salamander population, there undoubtedly will be few fur-bearing mammals in the region.

The beginner who doesn't become discouraged at the dull colors and unimpressive appearance of dusky and red-backed salamanders is rewarded by some pleasant discoveries. A stout-bodied red salamander (*Pseudotriton*) coral- or salmon-colored, overmarked with black spots, is a showy creature. Green salamanders (*Aneides*) actually have apple-green areas on their bodies, these contrasting nicely with the dark gray surrounding them. Bronze flecks on a Cheat Mountain salamander glow like bits of gold under a head lamp's beam, and in the same light red cheeks of Jordan's salamander have the fire of rubies.

My recurring dream of finding a new salamander hasn't yet become a reality, but I was present when one was discovered and shared vicariously in the experience. Some years ago groups centering around Oglebay Park, Wheeling, West Virginia, began to go on camping expeditions to various sections of the mid-Appalachians. Largely made up of amateurs, these groups carried on field work with such dedication that they soon attracted the interest of professionals. Throughout the years such people as Graham Netting, George Miksch Sutton, Edward C. Raney, Roger Tory Peterson, and many others have camped and worked with them. In recent years the Brooks Bird Club Forays, under the tireless leadership of the Conrads — Chuck, Mary Kay, Caroline, and Dorothy — have become famous occasions for collecting, photography, exploration, and meeting naturalist friends.

Oglebay groups have been attracted to the Cheat Mountain country and have made a number of expeditions to this wild portion of Appalachia. On one we visited Barton Knob, collecting what we could find in the dense mosses and under decaying spruce logs on top of the mountain. Presently Leonard Llewellyn walked over to Graham Netting, handed him a small squirming salamander, and asked, "Graham, what's this?"

For a long time Netting looked at its chocolate-brown color, slaty belly, and, above all, the many tiny gold flecks that covered back and sides. Finally he shook his head, almost in disbelief. "I don't know," he said. "I never saw anything like it in my life."

Search as we might on this and other days, we could find no more. The lone specimen went to the Carnegie Museum with a notation — "*Plethodon,* species unknown." Later in the summer one of my enthusiastic students helped me collect two more specimens, and that same season N. Bayard Green and Ned Richmond found a small series on another part of the Cheat range. This was enough to work on; presently Green described it as *Plethodon nettingi* sp. nov., the Cheat Mountain salamander.

Many herpetological discoveries in the Appalachians have followed a curiously similar pattern. There is the initial discovery; then hard work turns up a few additional specimens that museums drool over. Someone in literature is practically certain to refer to it as the "rare and little-known —— salamander." Then some lucky collector finds himself in the right spot at the right time, and there is the new creature in abundance. It may still be local, but it is certainly no longer rare.

Thus it was with the Cheat Mountain salamander. In succeeding seasons many collectors worked the Cheat area, most of them enjoying the hospitality of Traveler's Repose, a haven for field scientists maintained by Mr. and Mrs. Brown Beard. Amazing numbers of zoological specimens have been made up on the Beards' back porch. All the herpetological collectors had similar experiences. When they worked in mature spruce stands the salamander was absent or excessively rare. When they collected in stands of seedling or sapling sizes, however, the animals were abundant. It was just a matter of discovering the right niche for the species. Presently we had extended its known distribution along about forty-five miles of the Cheat summits.

Just west of the Cheat range is the Gauley range, and to the east are Middle Mountain and Allegheny Backbone. All have high peaks and stands of spruce. In none of them, notwithstanding, has the Cheat Mountain salamander been found. This is not due to lack of searching. Apparently this particular salamander is restricted to high Cheat.

Herpetological exploration in the Appalachians has had its adventures, mishaps, even tragedies. In 1930, Worth Hamilton Weller, a high school student from Cincinnati, visited that paradise of field naturalists, Grandfather Mountain, so frequently mentioned in this book. Young Weller was by no means the first collector in the area, but he came with one advantage — he didn't know when and where to stop as he climbed.

The fire that swept Grandfather's slopes had quite effectively destroyed ground-dwelling animals. Such comparatively slow-moving creatures as the salamanders have reoccupied the burned areas sparsely, if at all. Collectors who climbed the mountain shared a common experience: at first the fauna was rich and varied, then as the burn line was reached there was nothing. After a few hundred feet of such frustration, most gave up the ascent.

Young Weller, however, scrambled on to the top, and near the summit he found the unburned spruce-fir area that was described in Chapter 7. As he turned over logs and stones he found a strange gold-spotted plethodon, then more of them, until he had a series — small, but sufficient for his purpose. His salamander proved to be one unknown to science, and appropriately it was given his name, *Plethodon welleri*.

The following year he led a party of collectors to the area, and on one of the peak's steep cliffs he lost his balance, fell, and was killed.

On a recent trip to Grandfather, Ruth and I talked and thought about Worth Weller as we used the ladders that he didn't have available. We searched for his salamander too, and under a bit of decaying spruce almost at the burn line we found one.

Biologists set great store by type localities for species and to specimens from these localities. Type specimens are the master yardstick, the original meter-bar, by which standards are fixed and maintained. They enable the collector to return to first causes. A sort of Grand Tour of lungless salamander type localities in Appalachia may be made simply by traveling the Blue Ridge Parkway, with a few short side trips. The first stop would be at Peaks of Otter, Virginia (an intriguing name for a scenic area). Here is one of the puzzling dark brown, gold-flecked plethodons which doesn't seem to fit too well with any other known population. At present it is classed as a race of the ravine salamander (*P. richmondi*); sooner or later, perhaps, all these gold-flecked or spotted plethodons of the southern Appalachians will be combined in one super-species.

Grandfather Mountain would have to be the next stop. This is, of course, herpetological holy ground. Emmett R. Dunn, who was patron saint to the entire Family Plethodontidae, collected here and came to regard the area as one of his greatest favorites in all North America. Traveling out along the old Yonahlossee Road, he stopped one night in what seemed a likely spot, began his search, and suddenly glimpsed a big salamander that showed white below a chestnut-red backstripe. When he succeeded in making a capture, he knew that he had an entirely new species. It was named the Yonahlossee salamander (*P. yonahlossee*), and collectors still visit Grandfather to look for it in its type locality. It is one of the largest and handsomest of the plethodons.

Weller's find has already been noted. Grandfather is the type locality to still a third of the lungless group, the aptly if unesthetically named northern shovel-nosed salamander (*Leurognathus marmoratus marmoratus*). No other Appalachian peak, so far as I know, has yielded the first specimens of three salamander species.

In the "Four Peaks South" chapter we have already visited Mount Mitchell, just off the Parkway. And, as we have seen, it has been the discovery area for a good number of plants and animals. One of these, the Blue Ridge mountain salamander (*Desmognathus ochrophaeus carolinensis*, if you want a mouth-filling technical name) , has been assigned a first home on Mount Mitchell, although the purists would point out that Mitchell is not a part of the Blue Ridge.

Sunburst, North Carolina, would lay no claim to being a metropolitan center, but this Balsams Mountains community is the type locality for two salamanders: the widely distributed (in southern Appalachia) Metcalf's (*Plethodon jordani metcalfi*) and the black-chinned red salamander (*Pseudotriton ruber schencki*). At nearby Waynesville, the southern shovel-nosed salamander (*Leurognathus marmoratus intermedius*) was first found. The Davis farm, a short distance from Waynesville, has probably been visited and tramped over by herpetologists as much as has any southern Appalachian tract.

The red-cheeked salamander (*Plethodon jordani jordani*) is a Great Smoky Mountains specialty, a species to be looked for by every visitor with the slightest interest in cold-blooded vertebrates. It is medium-sized for a plethodon (four to five inches) and has a blue-black body and cheek patches that are usually cherry-red. Fortunately it is abundant at higher elevations and may be easily observed. Once more a reminder: don't collect it in the park.

One dampish night I was walking along the Appalachian Trail north of Newfound Gap. I had a head lamp and every so often I turned it on to see what might be moving. As I played it over a claybank through which the Trail was cut, sparkling ruby reflections came back to me. It took me a startled moment to determine that these reflections came from the cheek patches of the red-cheeked salamander, an amazing number of which were emerging from burrows in the clay. A single square yard might hold a hundred or more of these burrows.

There was nothing about such burrowing in literature dealing with red-cheeked salamanders, and I had heard of no con-

firming observation. Checking with Art Stupka, I found that
he hadn't heard of this either, so we went back to visit the area
the next night. Fortunately there was a good performance. The
glow of those ruby patches under artificial light is worth seeing.

The road from Newfound Gap to the Clingmans Dome area
climbs for a while, and just as it reaches an elevation of a mile
above the sea it passes through Indian Gap. The old road that
once passed across the mountains and through the gap has left
few traces; there are trails here, and along these are ski runs, that
may be the most southern in eastern North America. I remember an Easter season during which students from the University
of Tennessee found great sport there.

The relevance of Indian Gap to this account, however, lies
in the fact that it is the type locality for the red-cheeked salamander. As if that were not enough to endear it, it is also the
type locality for another handsome species, a race of the mountain spring salamander (*Gyrinophilus danielsi*). Just downhill
on the Tennessee slope is the source of one tributary of Little
Pigeon River. The salamander is aptly named; it does seem to
"love" the springs, and it may be found (as it originally was) in
the cold waters of the rivulet. Coral-red or bright vermilion in
color, this creature is a fit companion for the red-cheeked species
which has become almost a trademark of the region.

And, by the way, that name Indian Gap has somehow got into
herpetological literature as Indian Pass. In the local view this
is city-slicker affectation not in keeping with local terminology.
Indian Gap it is; most of the passes are in the West.

No highway leads to the top of Mount Le Conte, the fine peak
dominating the skyline at Gatlinburg. You may ride horseback
to the summit, or you may hike over several trails. If you are a
zoologist you may want to see the area from which Willis King
collected the first examples of pygmy salamander (*Desmognathus wrighti*), tiniest of the lungless group. A good average
adult would be one and one-half inches long, a two-inch speci-

men would be a giant. It lives under mossy floors that cover the earth under high mountain forests. Luckily for the observer, it usually carries a set of true identification marks, a row of brown chevron-shaped bars running the length of the back.

If the Blue Ridge Parkway extended south into the Nantahalas and the complex of other ranges toward the Georgia border, we could add other type localities to the list. But we have looked at a fair cross section of Appalachia's lungless species, and there is always the possibility that the reader is not a connoisseur of salamanders. Even though this may be true, there is one other worthy of special attention. At Virginia's far extremity, where Cumberland Gap was a passageway for Daniel Boone's Wilderness Road, there is a country of low but very steep mountains, mixed forests, sandstone ledges, and narrow, deep-cut valleys. Someone (Boone, perhaps) called this land the "Roughs" of Virginia. The term is appropriate.

Lee County was for a good many years the place for seeing green salamanders (*Aneides aeneus*), especially prized because this is the only genuinely green member of our eastern salamander fauna. Someone discovered that they could be found on wet sandstone cliffs, and in shallow caves that abound in the region. The old story repeats itself. People began to look in similar situations elsewhere, and from West Virginia to Alabama they found green salamanders, often in abundance, in crevices and on faces of sandstone ledges. In recent years, Pennsylvania and Mississippi have been added at the range's extremities. I felt somewhat foolish when outside collectors discovered it in numbers right on my home ground. That's an old story too. The visitor so often sees things the resident has overlooked — a good reason for welcoming visitors.

One rainy June night four of us were collecting green salamanders in southern West Virginia. Conditions were just right and the animals were out in numbers. Presently one of our party discovered a pair of the salamanders engaged in courtship and mating. We all quickly gathered round; at that time nothing on the mating of green salamanders had been published, and we were practically writing our note right there.

Suddenly a car stopped near us, and in a moment we were in a bright spotlight. From the car came two state troopers, suspicion evident in every movement. Here we were, four wet and bedraggled men, out well after midnight, gazing at the face of a cliff.

"What's going on here?" one of the officers wanted to know.

It was no time for a lie, and besides none of us could think of a convincing one. The truth had to be told. I said, "We are watching a pair of green lizards mating. Have you ever seen them?"

He walked over to us, turned his flashlight for a moment on the clasping salamander pair, and then looked at us, still with suspicion and bewilderment on his face.

"Yeah, I've seen them," he said. "Often."

Not all Appalachian salamanders are lungless. There are the newts whose land-dwelling subadults are often abundant on forest floors after a heavy rain. These efts (a name dear to the makers of crossword puzzles) are bright vermilion, strikingly colorful as they move over brown leaves or green moss. Newts have lungs, as do a number of other handsome species.

I am always afraid, however, that someone not favorably disposed toward salamanders in the first instance will see a hellbender — waterdog, grampus, call it what you will. Scientists have named it *Cryptobranchus alleganiensis;* it is our largest salamander, and it is surely one of the world's ugliest creatures. Dull muddy brown in color, with skin folds that seem just some leftover pieces, hellbenders are the "devil's walking parodies" of all other salamanders.

If waters are not heavily polluted, hellbenders are abundant, amazingly so sometimes, in streams that flow down Appalachian slopes toward the Mississippi. They are nocturnal, and how so many large animals can remain concealed on a stream bottom during the day is a mystery. Somehow they do it; when night-time comes they are there.

These thick-bodied, flabby creatures regularly attain lengths of twenty inches, sometimes more. By a curious turn of fortune, Netting and I were present when the record-holder, a grotesque female measuring just more than twenty-nine inches, was brought to Art Stupka at park headquarters outside Gatlinburg. A boy fisherman caught it in the Little Pigeon River, and I have marveled that he saved it. Many persons believe (wrongly, of course) that these creatures are deadly poisonous; many a fisherman cuts his line rather than release one.

This outsize monstrosity is atypical; most salamanders, after all, are inconspicuous. Whether they are large or small, we humans would do well to look at them with interest and re-spect. They did vital work in smoothing the way for air-breathing vertebrates; without them we might not have been here in our present form. So all honor to our ancestors, how-ever humble and remote they may be.

18. Hawk Flight

"COMING IN at eleven o'clock — high."

That might be the warning of a gunner-observer on a bombing plane; it might also be the alert of a sharp-eyed hawk watcher on some Appalachian ridge. As bird observers have proliferated and spread their quests, it has become apparent that migrating hawks, particularly in autumn, congregate — by ancient custom perhaps — at certain places and in certain flight lanes. Hawk watching has become an exciting fall pastime; its devotees are constantly searching out new observation posts, new pathways of flight. One good day afield may turn the beginner into a lifelong hawk enthusiast.

Years ago it was discovered that on specific fall days many hawks appeared at Cape May, New Jersey, flying low over the village, circling the lighthouse a time or two as though to get their bearings, then, if wind and weather were favorable, taking off across Delaware Bay in the general direction of Cape Henlopen. Such flights begin in September and often extend into November. Sharpshins are usually most abundant, at least early in the season, but there are days when many other individuals of a number of species are in passage.

Two points at the ends of Lake Superior, Whitefish to the east and Minnesota to the west, have become famous places for hawk observation. Point Pelee, Canada's southernmost tip, together with the chain of islands stretching across Lake Erie to the Ohio mainland, is fabulous for hawk flights, as well as for mass migrations of other birds. The Canadians also have favored spots on the north shore of Lake Erie from which they often count hawks in such numbers as to leave us in awe — 75,000 in a single day, according to W. W. H. (Bill) Gunn.

It may be that misdirected sportsmen were the first to discover that large hawk flights occur along specific Appalachian ridges. They discovered Hawk Mountain, in Pennsylvania, they flocked there to slaughter low-flying hawks, and their killing led, indirectly but surely, to a protective policy for all hawks which is now in legal force over much of eastern North America. Mrs. Rosalie Edge and her crusading companions saved Hawk Mountain; Maurice Broun and his staff have changed it from slaughter area to sanctuary, one of Pennsylvania's finest outdoor attractions.

To present the flavor of a hawk day along the Appalachian ridges, I cannot do better than describe a recent one spent with Robert C. Conn of Bound Brook, New Jersey. The date was September 20, a clear, cool day with brisk northwest winds. We began our observing at Rothrock Fire Tower, a lookout that sits at the top of Allegheny Backbone on Maryland's highest point. As we left our car at the foot of the tower, a broad-winged hawk flew past, following the ridge, which here has a northeast-southwest orientation. It was 9:30 A.M., Daylight Saving Time, and we watched continuously until 4:30 P.M. Wind at the summit of the tower was entirely too strong and cold for comfort. We stopped on a landing at intermediate height, elevated enough to give us unobstructed views along both slopes of the knifelike ridge — which here is a secondary Continental Divide that separates waters flowing eastward through the Potomac to Chesapeake Bay from those moving westward through the Cheat, Monongahela, Ohio, and eventually through the Mississippi to the Gulf of Mexico.

Clouds in the morning were high, mostly cirrus, but as the day progressed cumulus banks appeared, and the hawks characteristically took full advantage of the thermals beneath these cloud masses. As they reached one of these columns of rising air, they would begin to circle, working upward until at times we could see them only through our glasses. Then, as the highest bird reached a wind current moving in the desired direction, he would take off, gliding with arrow-straight flight to the southwest. Soon all the others in the funnel reached the same current and followed him in an extended line. The hawks had gained great height without much work; now they would move southward on a supporting current. They had solved a good many problems in aerodynamics.

This day was somewhat unusual in that the hawks were aloft early — just how early we had no means of knowing. Most of the time during the next two and one-half hours there were hawks in sight, usually somewhat to the right of the crest as we faced northward. Most birds were high when we spotted them; some we could see only by looking almost straight up, a neck-straining exercise at best. Even so, we felt that we were missing the more elevated birds of passage, conceivably more than we were seeing.

Often during the day lone birds passed over; usually there were less than a dozen in a group, and our largest flock (seen in early afternoon) had fifty birds. Broadwings were several times as numerous as all other hawk species combined, although we did see a few redtails, red-shoulders, Cooper's, sharpshins, and one sparrow hawk. A high point of the day was the passage, singly or in pairs, of six pigeon hawks, an unusual number of these speedy little blue-gray falcons.

By noon we had frozen out on the tower, so we made a quick ten-mile jump to another Allegheny Backbone lookout point in Tucker County, West Virginia. Here we had some protection from the weather, could use our car as a warming place if necessary, and presumably could see the same flight as would pass Rothrock Fire Tower a few miles away. A drawback of the second location lay in the circumstance that we could see only one side of the ridge; if there were migrants on the other slope, we missed them. There was a comparatively dull period between twelve and one o'clock, but movement was fairly brisk during much of the afternoon, and, as noted, we had our largest flock about 1:30. When we left the observation point at 4:30 we had seen no hawks during the preceding thirty minutes. The day's flight may not have been over — I have seen good movements later in the afternoon — but we had to be on our way.

And our totals for the day? By comparison with some more favored spots they are not impressive. During seven hours afield we listed 205 hawks, an average number, perhaps, for the season and the location. Even so, it was a larger number of these fine birds than I customarily see (except while hawk watching) in an entire year.

During the short periods when no hawks were in sight, we watched the migrating warblers, in fair movement on September 20 but not nearly so numerous as they would be a week later. Most bird students, it seems, think of wood warblers as exclusively nocturnal in their migration flights. Observers along the seashore or along a mountain ridge know better, of course; there are often heavy diurnal flights of these birds, especially noticeable when they are following ridge crests. From one Allegheny summit, George Hall and Wayne Davis once counted 1403 passing warblers in a three-hour period. Almost any late-September day will bring hundreds of the birds.

On the day of our visit Conn pointed out that warblers were crossing the ridge, flying directly into the wind just as they would do in coming in from sea to land along a New Jersey beach. When breezes are less fresh, however, songbird migrants often follow the crests just as hawks do.

Wood warblers are not the only diurnal migrants among song birds. Rose-breasted grosbeaks are sometimes conspicuous, fifty or more passing in a single morning. Red-breasted nuthatches move southward in small groups, stopping for a time to feed, then making long flights. Blue jays are constantly on the move, but groups can be seen trending southward in what is apparently a migration movement. Observers sometimes get hints of things to come in the early appearance of evening grosbeaks on the ridges, often several weeks before they appear in the lowlands.

Nearly every hawk trip brings its extra dividends, some of them more or less expected, some not. On the trip discussed above, the extra was provided by a raven, first heard, then seen as it flew low along the highway, dodging upward as it passed us but soon returning to its habitual fifty feet, searching endlessly for anything killed along the road. Ravens are resident in the mountains, but it is always a pleasure to see them, particularly when they are indulging in aerial maneuvers.

On another trip there were early cloud banks that rose above our lookout point about ten o'clock. This is always a favorable situation: many birds move just below such clouds, and this morning was exceptional in the number that did. There were hundreds of warblers, a good many grosbeaks, and what seemed to be a movement of cuckoos. The surprise came when a group of common snipe flew over, strange birds to see on a 3000-foot mountain.

One year we went late, in early November, hoping to find a movement of the larger buteos — redtails, red-shoulders, and perhaps a roughleg. The hawk flight was disappointingly small, but we saw a number of flocks of Canada geese, their V's following the ridge as exactly as do the hawks. On yet another November trip there were few hawks, but along the road that leads to Rothrock Fire Tower there were flocks of pine grosbeaks, more of these northern visitors than I have seen elsewhere so far south. Rarely do we draw a blank on these heights; there is nearly always something worth seeing.

Maurice Broun, and others, have given more detailed descriptions of these Appalachian hawk flights than I can possibly offer here. Most of us watch hawks two or three times per season, usually on weekends. Broun and his associates are on Hawk Mountain every day, and they really know what is passing. There are, however, some general observations that need to be made.

First of all, where to go? In the central Appalachian region, hawk watchers have had poor luck on the most western Allegheny ridges. Through Pennsylvania, Maryland, and West Virginia, the crests of Chestnut Ridge and Laurel Ridge have yielded very low hawk counts. The first reasonably good ridge, so far as our experience goes, is the Allegheny Backbone, which would include Mount Davis, Pennsylvania's highest point, Rothrock Tower in Maryland, and on south to Peters Mountain on the Virginia–West Virginia line.

Just east of the Allegheny Backbone is the steep escarpment of Allegheny Front, an eastward-facing slope that has good hawk flights on some days. The Wheeling section of the Brooks Bird Club observes each fall at Bear Rocks, on the Roaring Plains, an area described in Chapter 13, "Mountain Heaths."

They make good counts from this overlook, as do Charleston members of the same organization on their visits to Peters Mountain. Counts of several hundred during the day are regular; occasionally the numbers reach a thousand birds or more.

Eastward from Allegheny Front are the long parallel ridges that make up the Ridge and Valley Province. Elevations are not great, but slopes are steep and crests are often knife-edged. Lifting air currents seem to develop well in such situations; all these ridges may have good hawk flights.

Lloyd Poland and Clark Miller have had good luck on North Mountain, due west of the Shenandoah Valley. Farther south there have been some high counts in the Abingdon, Virginia, region.

The Kittatinny Ridge, with Hawk Mountain, Pennsylvania, as its best-known feature, sees fine hawk flights. For some reason birds often move along these slopes at elevations below the ridge crests; it is therefore possible to look down on them. Visitors to Hawk Mountain are pleased because the birds are close in, easy to observe and readily counted. Another source of excitement is the human visitors; sooner or later, all field ornithologists in the East find their way there. That fellow with the glasses just may be the author of the manuals you may have been using.

In the unglaciated Appalachians, southward movements of hawks begin in early September. Migration is usually light during the early two weeks, then it begins to pick up, and greatest flights of broadwings occur between the 15th and the 30th. Almost any day in this period (if observation is possible at all) may yield good counts. After September, flights are more scattered and uncertain. Red-shoulders and redtails, as well as Cooper's and sharpshins, are moving through, but they may be widely dispersed. Under some weather conditions, however, they concentrate along narrow flight pathways, and the observer outdoors at such a fortunate time will have an exciting day. Flights occur all through October, and into early November — after that they are about over in the Appalachians.

Autumn winds are usually from the southwest or northwest, balmy if from the former, and cool and biting if from the latter. To the hawks it doesn't seem to matter too much — rising air currents along the western flanks of the ridges are to their liking, and on almost any day, at some height they can find currents to bear them southward. In warm "bluebird" weather they tend to disperse rather widely, making observation more difficult. On days of cool, strong winds, however, they follow remarkably narrow flight paths along the ridges. Hundreds of birds may funnel through this narrow air channel; an observer a mile away might see no hawks at all during a day's watching.

When clouds are low the birds fly under them, even if this is below ridge summits. An ideal time to be on an observation point is just as cloud banks are lifting, particularly if this comes at ten or eleven in the morning. Hawks will move just under cloud masses, and for a time they may pass remarkably close to the observer. As clouds rise, so do the birds; presently they may be so high as to be almost beyond vision. One then sees the birds — if he sees them at all — by looking straight up.

So far as my experience goes, flights seldom begin early in the morning. Birds may be feeding or resting during the hours just after sunrise; they are seldom on the wing. On some days, assuredly, they are waiting for those natural elevators, the thermals, to form; on others they may await a rising breeze. To watch for early stragglers, I have reached a good many lookout stations at dawn, but I have seen few hawks before nine o'clock. Sometime between nine and ten, if this is to be a day that sees the usual pattern of flight, a single broadwing, or perhaps a pair, comes into view, often with such suddenness that you wonder where these birds have been. There may still be a lull, but by ten or half-past the hawks are usually on the move, if they are going to move at all. Largest groups of the day often pass between eleven and noon, then a slow period may follow, only to have the flight pick up between one and two. By three o'clock the major movement may be over, but it's not safe to count on this — there sometimes are birds passing just before dusk. I have never discovered the signs by which I might predict the day's flight pattern; the only way to be sure is to be out during all daylight hours.

Broadwings, handsome hawks with alternating dark and light bands on their tails, make up the bulk of September's flights. Other raptors that pass constitute the salad course and dessert of the day's meals. Along most Allegheny ridges there are resident pairs of red-shouldered hawks; these may fly about in almost any direction, circling a fire tower, crossing the ridge, flying counter to the major movement. Often at this season the birds will be calling, their cries closely imitated by blue jays.

If cleared lands are nearby, there may also be a few redtails. These large buteos drift through in small numbers until their movements pick up in October. Even a high-soaring bird will usually turn to allow a glimpse of his fox-red tail. Rarely, there are birds in color phases that become more common westward — individuals with abnormal amounts of light or dark plumage.

At Cape May, and other sea- and lakeside hawk concentration points, the accipiters are often abundant — notably the sharpshins. If there are ever major flights of these short-winged hawks in the Appalachians, I have not been fortunate enough to see them. During a day when a few hundred broadwings pass by, there will often be five or ten accipiters, Cooper's usually outnumbering the sharpshins. I have never been lucky enough to spot a goshawk on a hawk watching trip, although Hawk Mountain observers have seen them on many occasions.

Marsh hawks — harriers — hunt their food low to the ground and over open country; only occasionally are they to be seen from the ridges. A good day may bring five or six ospreys, their large size and contrasting colors making them conspicuous when they are among other hawks.

Falcons usually pass at tree- or tower-level, flying so fast as to be in sight for only a few moments. Sparrow hawks are not numerous, three or four being the most I have seen on any one day. As already noted, pigeon hawks are somewhat more common. The bonus day is one on which peregrines are flying. Like the other falcons, they frequently sweep through at tree-top level; I have looked down on them from Rothrock Tower. Sometimes they are moved to take a pass at a buteo overhead. When this happens, it is revealing to see the speed at which they gain altitude, and the extraordinary grace and flexibility of their flight as they stoop at a larger and clumsier hawk.

Everyone who goes hawk watching wants to see eagles, and, sooner or later, everyone is rewarded. During some seasons I see none at all. At other times occasionally a single bird passes by. On my best day of record I saw two from the observation spot on Backbone Mountain. A good day on Chesapeake Bay or in the Bulls Island region might yield more eagles than I have seen in twenty seasons of Appalachian hawk flights; it really doesn't matter, since eagles create their own excitement in the viewers, and since seeing one from a tower or a mountaintop is still an event.

I have no doubt that there are persons who, seeing a dark-bodied eagle a quarter-mile away, can say with certainty (and accuracy) that the bird is a golden eagle or an immature bald eagle. I have watched, with great respect, the skills that come with sharp eyes, long experience, and, most important of all perhaps, a flair for bird identification. I cannot number myself among these favored ones; if an eagle is a long distance away and shows none of the conspicuous markings of the bald species, I simply call it an eagle, and have to be satisfied with that. Both species occur, and I have seen both under circumstances that allowed me to be sure of my identifications. There is excitement and satisfaction in the appearance of an adult bald eagle, its snowy head and tail being unmistakable advertisements.

A mile or so northward along the ridge your glass catches an approaching bird, and you sense that it is more nobly proportioned than were the hawks that you have been watching. Presently there is a flash of white, and you are reasonably sure. The electrifying call "Eagle!" brings everyone in the party to the tower's highest platform. As the bird approaches, its contour — huge head, massive body, broad wings — is sharply outlined. Then it passes along the ridge just below you, and you look down on the pure white in its plumage. A little while more, and it is gone. Years may pass before you see another one under similar circumstances.

Golden eagles, nowadays at least, are much rarer in migration than are their white-headed relatives. This wasn't always so — thirty or forty years ago there were golden eagles at all seasons in the southern Appalachians. It is extraordinarily difficult to pin down actual nestings, but there were young birds, some of which must have been reared locally. Northfork Mountain, in Pendleton County, West Virginia, was a famous place for these birds; another was the Devil's Backbone, in Highland County, Virginia. I have seen as many as seven golden eagles in the air at one time from Northfork, and few trips to the area were without eagle observations.

What was happening to them, however, was all too apparent when the visitor dropped into local post offices, filling stations, hotel lobbies, or even private homes. There were mounted golden eagles in these public and private places. One post office had nine mounted birds, and felt righteous in the possession. This is sheep country. Local herders are fully convinced that golden eagles are implacable enemies of lambs. They become just as determined in their efforts to wipe out eagle populations, and they have had almost complete success. Today the sight of a single golden eagle in the mountains is an event.

During the Depression years, much of central and southern Appalachia suffered from a curse that went under the name of "vermin campaigns." By definition, a "varmint" was any animal, cold- or warm-blooded, which might conceivably kill anything that man wanted to kill. Local sportsmen's groups, often with full encouragement from state conservation departments, organized these campaigns, drawing up lists of "varmints," each one carrying a number of credit points for the killer. Everything that anyone had ever heard of or could imagine as a predator was included. Lists included kingfishers, hellbenders, virtually all carnivorous mammals, and of course all owls, hawks, and eagles. A golden eagle was a prize, and carried a lot of points. Goshawks were also given special attention; an amazing number of broadwings, redtails, and even sparrow hawks became "goshawks" to the judges. One year the grand prize of such a statewide campaign was a four-year scholarship to college. A young man in Nicholas County, West Virginia, was the successful contestant. He won because of his meritorious accomplishments in destroying eleven nests of "goshawks," with all their young. It is more than slightly ironic that there is not an authenticated record of goshawks ever having nested in West Virginia.

Unemployed men and boys (sometimes women and girls too) were encouraged to go afield, particularly in spring, to hunt and destroy "varmints." Many of them killed anything they found; animals on which they could receive points were shown to local "judges" of such contests. There was special incentive to find and destroy hawks' and owls' nests, since points were awarded on each animal killed and displayed. After thirty years, our populations of these "vermin" have not recovered.

A special word needs to be spoken to those who may know of, or may discover, a peregrine's nest. Keep such a find strictly to yourself — even your best friends may be practicing, or aspiring, falconers. Falconry is without doubt a noble and fascinating sport. If we had good populations of falcons, I would be all for it. But unfortunately, nests of "noble" falcons are becoming scarce (or non-existent) in the East; the few remaining simply can't stand pressure from falconers. Falconry enthusiasts are often young and active persons, with a real zest for outdoor things. They are not dismayed at scaling cliffs — the necessary rope work is a challenge. They will drive almost anywhere, and explore endlessly, once they hear of a peregrine falcon's nest. I don't think I am being selfish when I hope that some nests will escape their attentions. I, too, like to see peregrines.

In the mid-Atlantic states the same secrecy should be maintained as to nesting ravens. These giants among passerine birds are becoming scarce in many places, so much so that they typify the wilderness to city dwellers with bird interests. A young raven is a treasure for a children's museum, or even for a backyard menagerie.

One of the things that add a fillip of interest to the campus on which I teach is the presence of one or two nesting pairs of ravens within ten miles of the University. To the misfortune of these birds, one nest is rather well known and accessible. For many years it was visited each spring by a former resident of this area who drove from another state in order to remove one or more of the young birds. It wasn't that he needed them; they were interesting pets, and if he didn't want them some of the neighbors' children might. Ravens are persistent birds. They tried for a good many years, but they finally abandoned this one site. I trust they have hidden well their new location.

Returning to hawk flights — most of what I have so far written applies to fall movements of these birds. This, I suppose, is because fall flights are predictable. If you are in the right place on almost any late-September day you will see some birds. Spring flights occur also, but if they have a fixed pattern or course we haven't learned much about them in the unglaciated Appalachians. Those who are out every spring day (the Hawk Mountain people, for example) see northward-moving hawks, but not in such numbers as in autumn. Most of us wait years to see a spring hawk flight.

My best day was April 20, and the location was Deep Creek Lake in western Maryland. My son Fred and some of his companions, all veteran fall hawk watchers, were with me on one of those days when everything seems to happen. There were rafts of coots and other water birds on the lake. On a smaller nearby impoundment we watched an adult male European widgeon at close range, a new bird for some of us. There were shovelers also, handsome ducks that we don't often find in the mountains. Watching from an exposed snag was an osprey.

Toward noon we began to see buteo hawks moving northeast along a ridge above the lake. Most of them were redtails or red-shoulders; few if any broadwings were among them. Presently a flock of twenty-five or more circled and towered, then took off in the same arrow-like pattern that is followed by autumn birds, the direction reversed but the behavior identical. We saw between forty and fifty birds, no great number, but more than I have found on any other spring day. This is a matter that deserves more attention; hawks do concentrate in spring where there are northward-pointing spits of land or chains of islands (in western Lake Erie, for illustration); they must follow favorable flight pathways to reach such concentration areas. Perhaps they may move so high in order to escape observation, most times at least.

A valuable by-product of hawk watching is found in the additional attention that a good area may receive at other seasons from field workers. Once you have followed hawk flights there, you realize that there are other interesting possibilities.

Operation Recovery, the systematic capture and banding of migrant birds through the use of Japanese mist nets, has been most developed along the Atlantic Coast, but Appalachian hawk watchers have recently joined the activity, and with good results. An area that has received considerable attention is a Forest Service campground at Red Creek Spring, on West Virginia's Roaring Plains. I am certain that the site was selected because observers had been visiting nearby Bear Rocks on hawk-counting expeditions. These nets, their fibers so fine as to be almost invisible, are placed low to the ground against backgrounds of dense vegetation into which birds might be expected to dart for cover. Results are sometimes amazing; through these captures we have learned that inconspicuous species — yellow-bellied flycatchers, Philadelphia vireos, and Connecticut warblers as examples — are passing through in good numbers, although they usually escape the attention of bird students who have only eyes and glasses to assist them. During times of active migration, two or more workers will have their hands full in releasing and banding birds captured by a battery of five or six nets.

Familiarity with the area because of hawk counts may also have led the Brooks Bird Club to hold its 1960 Summer Foray in Tucker County, West Virginia. One result of this study expedition was the discovery of an occupied nest of black-billed magpies. The nest, found by Robert K. Burns and others, was on the Roscoe Beall farm, in Canaan Valley, Tucker County, West Virginia. It held five eggs, one of which was collected for scientific reasons. Previous to this discovery, the most easterly known nest of this species was in Manitoba, about four hundred miles north of Winnipeg. Mr. Beall states that magpies have been in Canaan Valley for a number of years, and that he has found their nests on other occasions. We have no record of the release of any captive birds in this mountain area. How they came there is anyone's guess. In the light of this, and other such occurrences, it may be understandable that those of us who work in the Appalachians come to believe that just about anything is possible.

During autumns for the past several years I have been taking groups of boys, usually friends of Fred's, on such hawk counts as my schedule, and theirs, would allow. This has many advantages; the boys climb up and down a fire tower with considerable more speed than I can display, and they can certainly see farther and better than I am able to. As the seasons have passed, I have followed their careers.

Bill Berthy is blessed with the sharpest pair of eyes that I have seen at work in the field. He gazes, without benefit of binocular, for a long time into the northern sky, then he says, "Broadwings coming in about twelve-thirty — sixteen, seventeen, eighteen of them." After a time, with my glasses, I pick them out. They are broadwings, and there are eighteen of them. Those eyes will be an asset to field biology. Bill has been working with the Wildlife Division of the West Virginia Department of Natural Resources.

Charlie Thomas is with the Bureau of Land Management in Oregon. Bob Netro works for the Forest Service in Montana. Larry Schwab is studying medicine, but he has an abiding interest in things outdoors.

I make no claim that hawking expeditions are solely responsible for the vocational interests of these young men. I believe, however, that the hawks have helped. An autumn day spent on some Appalachian peak is not to be taken lightly.

19. The Wood Warblers

"Swainson's warblers?"

Those two words, with the question mark which follows them, were published in a hand-printed local bird journal in 1939. The writer of the note (who was also the editor of the journal) was William C. Legg; his locality was Mount Lookout, Nicholas County, West Virginia, a wooded section of the Allegheny Plateau. In the brief account that appeared under the heading, Legg stated that he had seen and heard birds which he believed to be Swainson's warblers in several situations near Mount Lookout, and that the birds were summer residents.

Legg's publication set off a chain of events which led to a complete re-evaluation of the position and habits of Swainson's warbler, added an interesting species to the Appalachians' list of known breeding birds, and brought the little Mount Lookout community (and Bill Legg) to the attention of field workers throughout North America. Legg is gone, but the visitors still come, drawn by the expectation of seeing this elusive warbler.

Swainson's warbler (*Limnothlypis swainsonii*) was discovered by John Bachman in 1832 near Charleston, South Carolina. It was not recorded again for about fifty years, then observations began to appear in print, all of them from the warmer parts of the Atlantic and Gulf of Mexico coastal plains. No summer residents were found except in this region, so the idea became fixed that this species was restricted to coastal swamps and tangles in the South, almost always with cane holding a prominent place in the flora. The manuals, all of them, said the birds were so restricted; very well, let it stand. No one, it seems, bothered to look elsewhere.

I have vivid recollections of a June day in 1924 when P. Cecil Bibbee, then collecting birds for the museum of West Virginia University, came in one evening full of excitement and unbelief. He told me that he had collected a male Swainson's warbler near Morgantown, in the Cheat section near the Pennsylvania border. He had the bird, which proved to be in breeding condition. It is preserved, but so strong were our fixations that nothing was said about it. The record wasn't published until eight years later.

Fred M. Jones, a competent field worker in mountainous southwestern Virginia, found Swainson's warblers near Bristol, and in 1932 discovered a nest with eggs. There followed an experience distressing first for him, then later for some of the other persons involved. Mr. Jones reported his find to Virginia ornithologists, who were completely skeptical. He then submitted his find to some of America's most eminent ornithologists; they all agreed that he had sent them the nest and eggs of Swainson's warbler, but they told him quite frankly that they couldn't believe in its discovery in southwestern Virginia. He submitted an account of his find to our most respected journal of ornithology; its editor politely refused to have anything to do with it.

The moral would seem to be that one should never try to publish anything that runs counter to views expressed in accepted literature.

A few years later, Alexander Wetmore collected a Swainson's warbler in hilly Lincoln County, West Virginia, not far from the area of Jones's finds. I think this shook him up a bit — he won't mind (since he tells the story on himself) my revealing here that he was one of the ornithologists to whom Jones had submitted his nest.

It would appear that these discoveries, obscure and scattered as they were, should have been enough to alert bird students to the possibility of a breeding population of these warblers in the Appalachians. But not so — the fixation was too strong. It took Legg's finds and the chain of events which followed them to bring the situation into focus. Now we know at least a portion of the truth: there are breeding Swainson's warblers in the mountains and hill country from West Virginia and eastern Ohio southward to upland Georgia and South Carolina. We know it, but I have a suspicion that some traditionalists would still prefer not to admit it.

It seems appropriate at this point to give further attention to Bill Legg. Before his untimely death, he met, guided, and assisted a good segment of Appalachian field biologists. His contributions, both to zoology and to botany, were not minor ones. He had little formal education, but he tramped his native hills by night and by day, at all seasons and in any weather. Short of stature, and with a mountain slouch in his gait, he covered ground entirely too fast for most of us who tried to hike with him, but we still found it worth while to try keeping up. Where Bill Legg was, discoveries were likely to follow.

Somehow or other he had acquired an ancient Washington hand printing press. When he learned that a group of youthful bird enthusiasts were anxious to start their own journal, he volunteered to print it for them. These youngsters were scattered everywhere, their mutual tie being readership of one of the boys' magazines. They sent Bill Legg their copy, and he printed it in *Field Ornithology*, a rarity today among bird journals. Some of the articles were good (Don Eckelberry was one of the boys involved) ; some were pretty terrible. Legg did not try to be selective — everything that came to him was grist for the mill. *Field Ornithology* did not long survive, but it lived long enough to give us a great deal of information about the mountain Swainson's population.

One day, after we had been observing Swainson's warblers along Malinda Creek, Legg told me that he had seen at close range a singing warbler that he identified as Bachman's. He had been so right about Swainson's — I have wondered ever since if we shall discover some day that the other Carolina Low Country warbler specialty also has an Appalachian population.

Legg did not restrict his publishing activities to bird material; he wrote and published a booklet on American holly which is a collector's item, in the best sense of the term. It contains a great deal of first-class horticultural information, and it is written in terms and language that were Bill Legg's own. One of his sentences will give the flavor better than I could possibly describe it. He writes, "Dr. Tryon of West Virginia University is experimenting on methods of rooting holly cuttings as well as other men."

To take up once more the story with which the chapter began: very soon after the appearance of Legg's note, William A. Lunk and I went to Mount Lookout to see what we could find. We located the birds, at least four singing males, along the highway before we reached Legg's home. The next day Legg took us to a forested stream, its dense understory consisting chiefly of American holly, rosebay rhododendron, mountain laurel, and Canada hemlock. It was a far call from southern canebrakes, but in a mile and a half we found thirteen singing males which seemed to be on territory. One was collected in the interests of science.

We found these birds in every suitable habitat throughout the region. Where there was a dense understory along a stream, we could count on Swainson's. A few days later, George Sutton arrived to share the experience. He, too, took specimens. Legg had found nests, but none the year of our visits. We searched, and so did Sutton, but without success. The following year Legg discovered two occupied nests. Elevations at their locations were above 1600 feet. There were hooded, Kentucky, parula, worm-eating, black-throated green, even Blackburnian warblers in the neighborhood. Some of these would have been at home on the coastal plains, some certainly would not have been.

During the years that immediately followed Legg's finds, bird students flocked to his area, learned to recognize the species by its song, and returned to investigate their home territories. It wasn't long until these searches produced results. Within a couple of years, we knew of Swainson's warblers in fourteen West Virginia counties, and their discovery in eastern Ohio followed shortly. Presently they were found in Cades Cove, in the Great Smokies.

The most remarkable of West Virginia's centers for this bird (so it seems to me, at any rate) is near the state's capital, Charleston. I may be wrong, but I think West Virginia's Charleston can produce more of the birds than can the other Charleston, where the species was first discovered. Just east of the capitol grounds, and across the Kanawha River, the Chesapeake & Ohio Railroad skirts a series of low wooded hills. Streams, often temporary, cut ravines through these hills, and the bird student who traverses almost any of these ravines may expect to find Swainson's warblers. They arrive in late April, they nest here, and they remain until early autumn.

The forest cover is largely a mixture of scrub pine and central hardwoods — oak predominating. Moisture is sufficient to produce a fairly dense understory, grape tangles abounding and spicebush common where moisture reaches the surface. The warblers nest in such tangles, often well uphill from any water. It would be difficult to imagine a region of less conformity to the canebrake stereotype that once was used to limit this species.

Charleston bird students are properly appreciative of the unusual situation at their doorsteps, and they have devoted much of their attention to this species. During a single season Eleanor Sims found and studied eleven Swainson's nests, and she and Russell DeGarmo wrote at length about these observations. John and Polly Handlan have introduced many visitors to their first examples of this bird, and Charles O. Handley has given much of his time to them. When Bill Gunn wished to record Swainson's songs he came to Charleston, and was guided by the Handlans. Visitors are still coming, and seem likely to continue. There are many bird students who have yet to add Swainson's warbler to their life lists.

It may seem that a disproportionate part of this chapter has been devoted to one species. True, the species is interesting, especially so in its relationships with the Appalachians. But there are many other warblers that should not be neglected. I have chosen to treat this species at length because it illustrates so well an important point, namely, that warblers in the Appalachians often behave in ways that would seem strange to persons who know them in other portions of their ranges. Birds in unglaciated Appalachia really are different. Therein lies a great deal of their fascination.

Consider some of the reasons why this should be true. As we

have seen, the Cumberland and southern portions of the Alleghany Plateaus preserved a Tertiary forest which appears to have been little modified during the glacial period. We may suppose that if plant life was not greatly affected by ice fronts a comparatively short distance away, neither were the birds. Warbler species of the southern states (those Legg found as companion species of Swainson's, plus others such as the prothonotary, yellow-throated, yellow-breasted chat, Louisiana waterthrush) found suitable homes in such a forest and at its edges, even though glaciers may have been only a hundred miles or so removed. If the term be allowed, the austral component of wood warblers was preserved intact in unglaciated Appalachia.

Now, if you will, think of the problems that confronted warblers nesting northward when ice sheets began their slow advance. Each season their breeding grounds were more restricted, even if by only a little. Each year these northerners were pushed, willy-nilly, closer to the homes of their more southern relatives. Finally, the conifer dwellers from half a continent were faced with three possibilities: they could nest in coniferous forests (then doubtless more extensive) of the southern Appalachians, they could adapt themselves to new situations and find new niches in predominantly deciduous woodlands, or they could perish. There may have been species, as there certainly were individuals, in the last category; we have abundant evidence that some species survived by means of the other two choices.

In the spruce-fir forests of the Southern Highlands, it seems fitting and proper to find nesting Canada, black-throated blue, black-throated green, Blackburnian, and magnolia warblers as far south as Tennessee. It is not too surprising that these species, plus Nashville and mourning warblers and northern waterthrushes, occur in the West Virginia mountains. Coniferous forests, even so far to the south, are scarcely to be distinguished from those in New England and northward. Northern warblers should be at home there, and they are.

It is in the predominantly deciduous forests just below spruce-fir that things become unsystematic. In the northern hardwoods — birch, beech, maple — and in the cove hardwoods even farther downslope, ecology is really confusing. Here, if I may be permitted a good-natured observation, is where my ecologist friends from the American midlands find their pet systems, each with its horrendous neo-Greek terminology, going out the window. The country and its biota refuse to conform; it is simpler to ignore them, as has been done in a good number of learned volumes. Speaking as one with an avowed Appalachian prejudice, I happen to think that this neglect is unfortunate, an easy way out, but more than a bit unscientific. I have tried, and shall continue to do so, to describe things in the mountains as they are. If they don't fit handily into a system, it is not the fault of the plants and animals that dwell there.

Unglaciated Appalachia is an extensive area, as large as all New England. When New England, and much of the other land to the north, was a refrigerator, deadly to most living things, the mountain ridges beyond the ice sheets were offering sanctuary to plants and animals of land, water, and air. Some of them demonstrated their plasticity — their biologic abilities, if you please — by taking on new characteristics, adapting to new conditions, reproducing their kind under strange situations, and surviving to reoccupy the land as ice retreated. There is abundant evidence that some of the behavior patterns, those once forced on many species, have persisted and are still being followed. If they seem strange, they may be all the more instructive. One thing is certain, unglaciated Appalachia is the place to look for such aberrant behavior.

Take as an example the black-throated green warblers. They nest in coniferous forests well to the north, and they follow the spruce-fir down to the Great Smokies and beyond. There is

Big families in the hills forced younger sons to settle in poor and remote surroundings. "Uncle Frank" Randall has had to work to keep alive.

Mountain People and Crafts. Outlanders are slow and re-
luctant to part with cherished myths, and none has been more persistent than
the old canard about mountain "characters" with their feuds, their moonshine, their language, and their "quaintness." Southern highlanders have
been isolated in the past, but they are people like their neighbors, except for
the fact that many of them have become more observant of the world in
which they dwell. Descended from pioneer hunters, these hill people have
learned to depend upon their own skills, and to use what is at hand. Only
yesterday whittling, weaving, basketry, and pottery-making were necessities.
Today they are becoming folk arts, valued by native and visitor alike.

This picture and the preceding one show classic features of southern Appalachian cabins — square logs for the walls, a clay-chinked outside chimney of fieldstone, the whole roofed with white oak clapboards. As families grew, extra rooms were added, and a porch became a social center for family and visitors.

Among mountaineers, dogs are not pampered pets but, rather, working members of the community. They learn to drive cattle, to herd sheep, to tree coons and possums, and to warn of intruding bears (or humans) visiting the pigpen. This hunter hopes that his hounds will not stray beyond the sound of his dog horn.

Wood for every purpose is abundant in Appalachia. The tradition of woodworking, from whittling and carving to the fashioning of necessities and luxuries, is a fundamental part of hill culture. Chairs are fashioned according to old rules: use cured wood for the rungs and green wood for the posts so that natural shrinkage as the posts dry will lock the rungs in place.

Craftsmen and artists in ceramics came early to Appalachia, some of them trained in the workshops of Josiah Wedgwood. Using local clays for the most part, they shaped and fired crocks, churns, vats, bottles, pitchers, and other articles of utility. As mattes, washes, and glazes came into use, pottery became art, and so it is today.

The mountain fiddler, although frowned on by the more deeply religious, gave young people an excuse for kicking up their heels at square dances. Fiddles and other stringed instruments were often fashioned of local wood by local artisans. Devoted women teachers, such as this one with the banjo, brought new ideas and new life to remote communities.

Opposite: Blankets of wool were too expensive for many mountain people, so they came to depend for warmth on cotton-filled quilts. Variety in the patches and patterns of these challenged women quilters, and the more artistic among them acquired local reputations. A quilting party was a social event, with visiting and jollity a welcome relief from isolation.

New understanding of the land and its needs has come to mountain people, as this farm, broken for contour-strip crops and contour furrows in pasture-land, demonstrates. Clearing and plowing of progressively steeper lands is no longer the pattern; it was backbreaking and it was wasteful, so trees are growing where once there were hillside cornfields. This is more than a picture, it is also a promise. There is to be a future, and the soil and water to support it are to be held in place. The land will be occupied by those who have found their deepest satisfactions among the hills.

also a resident race in cypress swamps along the coastal plain. This species is, it would appear, an obligate of the conifers, and most manuals so describe it. In so doing, they completely ignore a situation, common from southern Pennsylvania down through Maryland, West Virginia, and Virginia, and into Tennessee and North Carolina. Here in deciduous forests, often with no conifers at all, black-throated green warblers are common, sometimes abundant breeders. A situation ten or twelve miles from my campus is typical. On a dry, second-growth ridge, the commonest forest tree is black cherry, with black locust also abundant and chestnut oak fairly so. This is sterile land, with a sparse understory. I know of no native conifers close by, although there are some small ones in a plantation distant a half mile or so. In this unpromising forest, the five- or six-note call of black-throated greens is the most characteristic warbler song in summer. No other warbler appears to be half so abundant. During glacial times, perhaps, there were just too many black-throated greens for the available conifers. Some of them had to move to new quarters, and their descendants still occupy the neighborhood.

A look at parula warblers may also be instructive. This species has a large population in southern forests and another one in northern conifers. The two used to be considered racially distinct, but not so much attention is paid such matters nowadays. In any event, no one was ever able to determine the race to which should be ascribed birds nesting in West Virginia, western Maryland, and southwestern Pennsylvania. Individuals in this region didn't fit.

Down south the parulas build their nests in Spanish moss, that picturesque, if atypical member of the pineapple family. In northern forests the birds use superficially similar, if wholly unrelated, usnea moss. The botanical irony that Spanish moss is a flowering plant and usnea moss a lichen may be ignored here; what is disturbing is that neither of these plants occurs in large areas of the mid-Appalachians. Theoretically, with no acceptable places to nest, the birds should be absent. But they are not; parulas occur in forests of different types, at low elevations and high, and under a wide variety of circumstances. They nest in hemlock and spruce trees, even in dense clusters of white oak or sycamore leaves. Those of my ornithological friends who have been willing to admit this truth have done so in pain and sorrow; others have simply chosen to remain silent, ignoring the whole matter.

Once again, we may guess that birds in the northern population got pushed southward until they began to meet the competition of residents beyond the ice walls. There wasn't room for all in the Spanish moss country, some had to remain farther north, and, in so doing, to find new nesting sites. If hemlock trees are available, parulas build their nests in dense masses of needles toward ends of twigs. If no conifers are nearby (and in this region of dominant hardwoods such situations are frequent), the birds will build in thick bunches of white oak or sycamore leaves or in the "witches' brooms" of hackberry.

Wood warblers demonstrated their adaptability in the period following the death (by blight) of chestnut forests. In some Appalachian areas chestnut made up from a quarter to a half of all tree stems in the forest. When blight struck, mature trees died, but from their roots sprang dense clumps of sprouts. Into this cover moved low-nesting warblers, particularly black-throated blues and Canadas, species that normally choose evergreen vegetation in which to build. The situation was, of course, a temporary one; chestnut sprouting is now sparser, and other plants have moved in to compete for space once held by chestnuts. Nevertheless, for a few years these birds gave convincing evidence of their ability to survive under suddenly changing conditions.

If further evidence is needed to show that warblers in the Appalachians behave in ways that would seem strange in other parts of the country, we might consider the northern water-thrushes. Their name alone would suggest their affinity for water — stream margins, lakesides, swampy tangles — and in such places they build their nests throughout most of the species' range. In Chapter 6 it was noted that these birds are common around Gaudineer Knob, in West Virginia's Cheat range. Some elaboration of this seems desirable.

As young spruces have grown up around Gaudineer's summit, closing the forest crown and providing a moist forest floor for mosses, ferns, and other shade-dwelling plants, northern water-thrushes have moved in to become common, one of the more abundant warblers at present. There are no springs, seeps, or swampy areas. Nearest streams are half a mile downslope, and most of these are temporary. These birds are nesting in a habitat radically different from ones they usually choose — just why we cannot guess, since there are plenty of streams a short distance below and since these are certainly not overpopulated by breeding waterthrushes. All the observer can do is record this departure from the norm — and wonder about it.

In wooded hills just back from the Ohio River, blue-winged warblers nest, advertising their presence by their two-part buzzing calls. They are locally abundant; I have heard five or six singing males as I stood at the edge of a mature oak stand. A few miles to the east, blue-wings practically disappear, their places in brushy openings being taken by golden-wings. In the zone of overlap, where one species is rare and the other common, we have the classic situation for hybridization.

Those puzzling and much sought hybrids, Brewster's and Lawrence's warblers, occur in this area of overlap, greatly to the satisfaction of bird students who go there to look for them. Bill Lunk probably has done more work on them than has anyone else; in areas forty or fifty miles from the Ohio he has found Brewster's (or forms that approach it — there are wide variations) more common than either golden-wing or blue-wing.

Lawrence's, the recessive member in this cross, is much rarer, although Russell West and others have found it in the hills back from Wheeling.

I wish there might be something new to write about Sutton's warbler. A good many bird students must have looked with longing at the color plates of this enigma, yearning to see it in life. A few have reported such observations, often with a great deal of corroborative evidence. The fact remains, however, there are still only two known specimens of *Dendroica potomac,* one male and one female, and these are safely deposited in the museum of the University of Michigan. If you have the proper credentials you may see them there, and you may find them just as much objects of wonderment as have others of us.

One evening in early June 1939, Karl W. Haller stopped at our home, and with an air of complete disbelief told us that he had collected two warblers, a male and a female, both adults and both in breeding condition, which did not fit any known species. He had the specimens with him, and we spent a long time examining them. Superficially they resembled yellow-throated warblers, although they lacked some important characteristics of that species. In the middle of their backs was an area of suffused olive-green, such as is found in parula warblers. To add to the confusion, the male was singing a song that seemed typical for parulas but was doubling it at each utterance.

Haller had been collecting with J. Lloyd Poland, student of the birds of West Virginia's Eastern Panhandle. About twelve miles south of Martinsburg, in a region of scrub pine and second-growth oaks, they heard this double-parula song, and they collected the male bird. Two days later, in an entirely different habitat, a female was collected. The locality was in riverbottom forest along the Potomac River, about eighteen miles from the area of the male's collection.

I would like to know how many ornithologists saw these two warbler specimens during the next few weeks. The list, I am certain, would include many of the elect among bird systematists. At one great museum the bird was hailed as an authentic species new to science, an event that was duly chronicled in the editorial section of the Sunday *New York Times*. It is fair to say that others were not convinced — some held from the start that these specimens were hybrids, probably with yellow-throated warbler and parula warbler as end-members.

Haller wished to honor his teacher and mentor, so the new bird was called Sutton's warbler. George Sutton painted it, his work being reproduced in *The Cardinal*, journal of the Audubon Society of the Sewickley Valley (western Pennsylvania). Sutton's plate accompanied Haller's original description of the bird. Bayard Christy thus had the honor of presenting this first description and account in the journal he edited.

In addition to the hybrid theory of origin of these birds, there were two other possibilities under discussion. One suggested that these were members of a relict population, survivors of some ancient and all but extinct species. In this connection, Kirtland's warbler was of course very much in mind; if a relict population of one warbler could nest in only ten counties in Michigan, why might there not be another such occurrence in West Virginia? The second suggestion, never very strongly urged, was that these new birds might represent an emerging species, genuine novae produced by some mutation. Presumably evolution is not static: if such a thing had occurred in past times, there seemed no reason to suppose that the process might not repeat itself.

If a new wood warbler was to be found within sixty miles of Washington, bird students were determined to find it and to learn more about it. They swarmed to the area for a while, but with the advent of World War II in 1941, the quest tapered off and all but ceased. Most active field workers were otherwise engaged.

In May 1942, Bayard Christy and the writer visited the region, going as nearly as we could to the exact spots where Haller and Poland had found their two birds. On the second day of our search we found a male and observed it at close range for a good many minutes. I cannot forget the expression on Bayard Christy's face as he saw the bird, as he checked each significant point of identification, and as he established to his own complete satisfaction that this was an authentic Sutton's warbler. It was a moment of fulfillment — one of the things, I am convinced, which made bright the last days of his life. We were planning a return trip for further studies when he passed quietly away. I shall not know a finer gentleman.

Through all the years since these events many have searched, and a few are strong in their belief that they have seen additional Sutton's warblers. With these sight records I have no quarrel. After all, Christy and I asked others to believe that we had seen a bird in the flesh. It will be a great satisfaction to many of us, however, when some day the bird is rediscovered, its status made clear, and additional specimens taken so that we may know what it really is.

Bird students nowadays are in general agreement that the hybrid theory seems the best one to account for Haller's two specimens. One difficulty that seemed a real one at the time has disappeared. When Sutton's warbler was first found, and for many years thereafter, no yellow-throated warblers had been found within a good many miles of the Eastern Panhandle region. Recently, thanks to the energies of the Brooks Bird Club, these birds have been discovered nearby; there could have been individuals present to mate with parulas had the occasion arisen. It still tortures the laws of chance that two such crossings might have occurred eighteen miles apart, and that a pair of collectors should be lucky enough to find an example from each crossing. For want of any other explanation, this must be accepted as the most likely one. Did someone suggest that Appalachia holds no further challenges?

Like the botanists who were attracted to Appalachian ridges and peaks, nineteenth-century ornithologists did much exploring and collecting in the eastern mountain country. Both Audubon and Wilson made journeys down the Ohio River and collected in the plateau country back from its banks. They make few references to warblers; their attention was on larger and showier birds. Both noted and collected Carolina paroquets. Ohio Valley bird students would give something to see wild parrots today.

During his student days at Harvard, William E. D. Scott spent a summer with his classmate, William Seymour Edwards, in Kanawha County, West Virginia. Young Edwards was the son of W. H. Edwards, whose beautifully illustrated volumes on American butterflies occupy a place in the literature of Lepidoptera comparable to that of Audubon's bird works. The atmosphere must have been stimulating. Scott and Edwards collected birds, among them West Virginia's first specimen of the inland race of yellow-throated warbler.

Other New Englanders of ornithological fame reached West Virginia in 1874. During the summer of that year, William Brewster, Ruthven Deane, and Ernest Ingersoll camped in Ritchie County, West Virginia, and gave particular attention to the warblers they found there. Among their studies the one on the cerulean warbler has long been a classic in the literature dealing with this species. As New Englanders, they also found hooded and worm-eating warblers unfamiliar and fascinating.

Dr. William C. Rives, of Washington, D.C., was the first visiting bird student to discuss the red spruce belt on high Allegheny summits and assess some of its ornithological possibilities. He found summering mourning warblers at the edges of this forest, and wrote of them in 1898. Since that time their known range has not been extended much southward.

By the turn of the century, Appalachia began to develop its own resident bird observers, and in the years since 1900 these have proliferated mightily. I think it is fair to say that abounding warbler populations, both as residents and as migrants, have stimulated much of this interest. I shall raise once more a question already suggested. Where else besides Gaudineer can a bird student expect to find twenty-two species of breeding warblers on a single mountain?*

A spring wave of migrating warblers can be a wonderfully exciting thing for bird students, particularly if they are afield in the folded ridge country east of the Allegheny Backbone. For some reason these bright-plumaged birds move in greater numbers on slopes and in valleys eastward; west of the main Alleghenies their passage is more diffused. I have had some rewarding mornings with the warblers along the old Chesapeake & Potomac Canal, between Harpers Ferry and Cumberland. In the willows, sycamores, elms, and oaks along that storied waterway, it seemed that all the warbler species in eastern North America might be found. As they flashed by, I thought it little wonder that Latin Americans sometimes confuse the warblers and the butterflies, calling them all *mariposas.*

Wood warblers hold high rank in the select group of Appalachian specialties. In this they join with Appalachian spleenworts, shale barrens endemics, mountain heaths, broad-leaved trees, and lungless salamanders. For them, as for other living things, I hope that no spring will ever be silent.

* Listed in A.O.U. *Check-List* order, the following wood warblers have been found nesting on Gaudineer Knob, Randolph-Pocahontas Counties, West Virginia: black-and-white, worm-eating, golden-winged, Nashville, parula, yellow, magnolia, black-throated blue, black-throated green, Blackburnian, chestnut-sided, prairie, ovenbird, northern waterthrush, Louisiana waterthrush, Kentucky, mourning, yellowthroat, yellow-breasted chat, hooded, Canada, American redstart. From foot to crest, the altitudinal range is something more than 2000 feet.

20. Not by Bread Alone

IN THE PRECEDING CHAPTERS we have been concerned primarily with places, topographic features, and plants and animals that adorn the landscape. In these last chapters we shall deal more closely with people — the ways in which they have adapted to mountains, the uses they have found for woodland products, and the graces they have created through crafts and artistic skills. These too are a part of Appalachia, and we would be remiss if we neglected the area's human heritage.

A stereotype as to mountain people — their homes, customs, limitations — was created many years ago, and it still restricts the thinking of too many outlanders. This is a queer situation.

The mountain people have changed, adapting their lives to an expanding world; only the outsiders, with their insistence on "quaintness," have maintained their frozen concepts. Most mountaineers are sophisticated enough to be wryly amused when they find that visitors are unable to break away from the stereotype — mountain people must be lazy, must have a drawl, must use a language that is a caricature of Elizabethan English, must be feudists, and must have moonshine stills up every hollow. Such pictures are so grotesque as to be merely funny. Residents of the hills do not see themselves in such a framework, so they feel sorry for the writer or the cartoonist who betrays his ignorance.

Those who would know the people of southern Appalachia as they were forty or fifty years ago are referred to Horace Kephart's *Our Southern Highlanders,* a book that seems to me to be the best of its kind. Kephart knew his people; he lived with them, shared their activities, and brought a keen and appreciative mind to his writing. He told the truth, good or bad, and he never condescended or patronized. As a result of his integrity, he could go back to live in the mountains after his book appeared. That hasn't been true of all who wrote about the Southern Highlands.

Kephart had another inestimable advantage — he lived with mountaineers before and during their time of great transition. Factors in this change might be listed in order: the rural free delivery of mail, the mail-order catalogue, the Model-T Ford, the improvement of roads, the radio, and the television screen. Remote human habitations are just about gone; mountain people order the same clothes, hear the same news, and watch the same TV programs as do city dwellers. There yet are wild places in plenty, but the people who once tried to settle them have moved away. Although hermit souls exist here and there, they seem as strange to their mountain neighbors as to an outlander.

Some of those who have visited the mountains and have developed an admiration for old ways of living are now doing their best to impose another idea upon us — that a priceless ancient heritage is being lost, that new generations will neither know nor value the ways of their forefathers. In part this is true; old ways always disappear as easier (if not better) ones appear. There have been losses, and there will be more. My thesis in these last chapters is, however, that much that was good in old skills, old crafts, and old points of view remains and is likely to continue for our enjoyment. There are still artists and artisans among mountaineers. Outsiders who have time and patience to seek them out will have a rich reward.

In a forested country, pioneers are always hunters. It could not be otherwise. No cereal crops or vegetables can be planted until the forest is cleared, and the introduction of domestic livestock must await production of grain and other foodstuffs. While all this is being accomplished, a painfully slow job when done with the hand tools of our ancestors, wild game and other forest products must keep the settler and his family alive. If soils are fertile, and if the land is suited to husbandry, hunting, fishing, and gathering of forest products become avocations rather than necessities. The prairie farmer could put aside his rifle for moments of relaxation; the mountaineer had to live by his, so he kept it with him and practiced its use. As a hunter he gained a knowledge, a very pragmatic one, of wild animals and their ways. If he had skill enough to call up a wild turkey or stalk a deer, his family ate. Those who couldn't do these things depended on their neighbors or went hungry.

I have never ceased to be amazed at the wildlife wisdom amassed by such unlettered woodsmen as Harvey Cromer and Frank Houtchens, both of whom have appeared previously in this book. Knowing about living things was their way of life. Finding game undoubtedly stirred the hunter in them, but it was also an esthetic experience, something to be remembered and savored. When any strange animal appeared, or when a familiar one displayed some new trait or behavior pattern, the fact was duly noted and filed for future reference. It has interested me to note how many of my mammalogical and ornithological acquaintances have come from woodland backgrounds. They began as hunters, and somewhere in their development they became field scientists. I think they enjoy hunting and fishing all the more because they appreciate the animals they are pursuing.

All this is by way of saying that mountain people have retained their zest for the chase in all its forms. Down on the Blue Ridge Parkway is an area called Foxhunter's Paradise. Here the hunters gathered of nights, put their hounds on a hot fox trail, built a fire on a commanding knoll, and spent the hours admiring the baying of their dogs. Each canine voice was familiar, and long experience enabled human listeners to follow the chase, to tell when hounds were confused or were in close pursuit. Of course no foxes were ever caught; the hunters would be mortally offended at anyone who destroyed one. The chase, not the kill, was an end and an enjoyment.

Most hunting, obviously, has a different purpose. Meat is good, it is available, and the hunter who can secure it gains stature in his own eyes and in those of his fellows. Gradually the idea is spreading: if land is well managed there will be game, and most years there will be a surplus for the hunter to take. So long as we preserve our forests we can count on having woodland wildlife.

It is deeply gratifying, if a bit surprising, that big game animals which dwelled in Appalachia when European settlers arrived have survived so well. Many, of course, are on greatly reduced ranges, but few species have been lost, and some are even extending their occupied territory. The twentieth century has been much kinder to wild things than was the nineteenth.

Most restricted, and most northern, of Appalachian big game animals is the woodland caribou. A wilderness species, it once reached northern Maine and in 1964 was reintroduced on Mount Katahdin. Today it persists in the Gaspé's Shickshocks and in the low mountains of western Newfoundland. Somewhat more extensive was the range of America's largest deer, the moose. Wherever the wilderness lingers in northern New England, Quebec, New Brunswick, and Newfoundland, moose do surprisingly well. Once they ranged as far south as Massachusetts, but they do not tolerate settled regions.

In early times another large deer, the wapiti, or American elk, must have ranged practically throughout Appalachia. From one end of the mountain system to the other there are Elk Mountains, Elk Creeks and Rivers, Elk Licks, Elk Counties, and other nomenclatural evidences of the animal and the impression it created. For many pioneer families the killing of an elk was a godsend, something for which to give humble thanks. Elk are huge; they provide several hundred pounds of acceptable meat, some to eat fresh and more to be smoked and otherwise preserved. If an elk was bagged there would be protein in the diet during cold months.

Eastern elk disappeared more than a hundred years ago, unable to compete as farm and grazing lands were cleared. They lived on in western mountains, and few could have guessed that they would ever re-establish a population in eastern United States. But they have. Virginia now shelters several elk herds, and during some recent years there has been a limited, but highly successful, open hunting season on these animals.

Almost all eastern states have tried reintroducing elk, particularly since national parks and forests in the West have a surplus they are glad to distribute. At times New Hampshire, Pennsylvania, and West Virginia have had elk under confinement, herds that multiplied and usually succeeded in eating themselves out of a suitable range. When these animals are closely confined, they eat about anything they can reach, and a browse line on timber can be seen many years after the elk have gone. The usual story is that fences eventually break down, the animals disperse, and they soon disappear.

Virginia's experience has been somewhat different. Western elk have been brought back to the Old Dominion on a number of occasions, and in certain mountainous counties the animals, completely free to roam as they will, have established sizable herds. Game biologists estimate that there are two hundred or more in the state today.

In Giles County just south and east of the Narrows, a spectacular notch carved by the New River as it cuts through the Alleghenies, is a wooded mountain that for some reason bears the name Angel's Rest. This is the location of one of Virginia's more successful elk herds and a spot much prized by hunters, since they are permitted, in restricted numbers, to try their hand at big game hunting in this heavily wooded region. A few are successful, and the lure of a trophy head brings applications for many times as many licenses as can be granted. It is difficult to see why this area is better suited to elk than are a thousand others in the southern Appalachians. There are larger and wilder tracts of woodland; vegetation is not conspicuously distinctive, and soils seem much as in many other mountain regions. But Angel's Rest must have something the elk need. In any event, they stay there, they grow to great size, and they multiply. No place in eastern North America except Virginia has an open hunting season on this big deer.

Another big game species, the American bison, once occurred in the Appalachians. This is attested to by the many appearances of "Buffalo" in place names. Although we may never know their boundaries and exact relationships, there were two races of these wild cattle. Pennsylvania's woodlands had an eastern race, said to be a very dark color and to lack the hump of the plains animals. The last example of this eastern race disappeared about 1800. It seems unlikely that we shall ever know much more about it than we do now. Individuals of the plains bison wandered through Appalachian woodlands from western New

York to Georgia. Ranges of the two races must have overlapped; whether or not they were mutually compatible we shall never know. So strong is a buffalo tradition in the land today that legend still holds to the story which credits buffalo with having found the easiest grades and lowest gaps, establishing routes followed by transmontane highways today. This is an article of faith of those who dwell along the old Northwestern Turnpike, Route 50 of present times.

Many public and private menageries have plains bison today, but there are no unenclosed herds in eastern North America, nor does it seem probable that any will be established. Elk keep pretty much to the woods and so are welcomed; but buffalo are grazers — potential enemies to farm crops.

Restoration of white-tailed deer as abundant game animals throughout much of the East is a biological triumph — due in large measure to man's harvesting of the forest, but with considerable credit earned by wildlife biologists. Heavy virgin forests poorly supported deer herds; these animals thrive on woody vegetation such as sprouts, twigs, and other new growth with tender bark. When forest land is harvested, or when fire sweeps over it, sprouting is a result, and deer are likely to abound for a few years. As new forests reach pole or young-timber stages, the deer's natural food becomes scarce and the animals thin out. Some have moved to settled country, living in wooded areas that intersperse with farmlands. Warnings of deer crossings along the New York Thruway near large cities continue to startle me.

Mountain hunters, to whom venison once may have meant life or death, recognized the scarcity of deer in heavy woodlands, so they brought woodsmen's crafts and skills to the hunt. Much hunting was based on a knowledge of salt springs and the knowledge that deer must sooner or later visit one of these. Ruminant animals cannot digest their rough food without salt to renew the potency of their digestive juices.

The location of a saltlick was a carefully treasured secret. In some areas — the valleys of certain Ohio River tributaries are examples — natural salt seeps and springs were common; this was good deer country, and the hunters knew it. Where nature did not provide salt (and this was true over vast areas), man must do so if he hoped to harvest much venison. Large-bitted augers were used to make openings in logs that had naturally fallen or had been cut for the purpose. These openings were filled with salt, the supply renewed as deer were attracted. Usually a man-made deer lick was placed near water; deer able to satisfy both salt hunger and thirst tended to linger in the vicinity. It is interesting to note the number of times one finds "Lick" in Appalachian place names.

Salting of cattle and sheep in mountain country today has largely removed the need for natural licks. Wise hunters, those who live in the community and are familiar with its features, study the movements of deer, learning where the animals cross through gaps, where they find shelter at night, and where they go in early morning to feed. Mountaineers do not lack venison, if they happen to like this meat. It remains true, nevertheless, that big woods seldom shelter a good deer herd. Deer are scarce in the Great Smokies.

One other large animal with even-toed hoofs has a place in Appalachia — the domestic pig gone wild, or the larger and fiercer European wild boar. Razor-back hogs are a part of pioneer tradition, particularly in the southlands. Settlers who liked pork and wanted a surer meat supply than could be harvested from wild game brought in hogs, used their own methods of ear-notching as a demonstration of ownership (the parallel of cattle branding), and turned the animals into the forest to feed on grubs, snakes, and berries during the summer, then on acorns, beechnuts, and chestnuts as these mast species ripened. Domestic pigs under such conditions were domestic no longer. They became slim-bodied, long-legged rangy animals, just about as wild as any other forest creature. Since there wasn't much of a fat deposit along the backbone, the term "razorback" was appropriate. An old sow with a litter of pigs was formidable, but otherwise the animals avoided man when they could.

After autumn's nuts had flavored the meat, and when cool nights made butchering and meat preservation practicable, the community's men and boys united in a razorback hunt. Ownership of harvested animals was determined by their earmarks. Then there were busy times around the settlers' cabins. Women cut portions of the meat and children turned sausage mills. Fat, what there was of it, was heated and the lard tried out. From this process the residue was carefully preserved, since it would furnish the basis for "cracklin'" bread. Usually it was a man's job to select the hams, shoulders, and sides of bacon for curing and to prepare the brine according to a recipe that called for exact amounts of salt, brown sugar, and saltpeter, and after a time to smoke the meat as a final preservative process. Dried hickory was a favorite wood; each piece of meat had to be hung so as to receive its full complement of smoke. It was a fragrant process, and it still is. The Appalachian method of curing ham and bacon is not a lost process — it is very much alive. There are enough people who know and appreciate good mountain ham and have proper scorn for the synthetic meats that have been needled with preservatives and painted with pyrogallic acid in lieu of genuine smoking to ensure a continuing demand for the genuine article.

City dwellers are often surprised to learn that wild hogs are still numerous in southern woodlands, more plentiful adjacent to swampy lands but present in Appalachian areas as well. One game biologist has estimated that the Southland may have two million or more of these animals, some of them hunted and harvested just as they were in earlier times. Razorbacks and their numerous descendants are with us yet.

The long-tusked European wild boar, a prized and respected

game animal throughout much of Eurasia, is a very different animal. It has been introduced in Appalachia by sportsmen's groups, always under confinement at first, then as fences decay becoming a free-roaming creature of the forest. The Blue Mountain Game Preserve in New Hampshire had some of these animals, but the most successful introduction was made in the Unicoi Mountains, on the Tennessee–North Carolina border. As with Virginia's elk, there is a legal hunting season on these animals and it is unique in eastern North America.

Tellico Plains in southeastern Tennessee is headquarters for the wild boar country. It is at the edge of the Cherokee National Forest; leading eastward are Forest Service roads that reach the summits of the Unicois and continue on to the Joyce Kilmer Memorial Forest and the Snowbird Mountains in North Carolina. This is a vast mountain area, little explored by biologists and holding tremendous possibilities. Most wild boar hunting is on the Tennessee side. Would-be hunters register, await the luck of the draw, and, if chosen, pay their license and guide fees. During some years at least, hunting continues until the season's quota has been taken. The drove is small, and any year's harvest must be strictly limited. Those who have experienced this hunting will argue that the wild boar is the most dangerous feral animal in the East, and possibly in the forty-eight contiguous states. In the Rockies, grizzly bears are showing some signs of getting mean once more, and certainly one of these would be more formidable, but an adult boar, its teeth long and sharp, is dangerous enough. These animals hide in rhododendron thickets, wait a close approach by hunters, and sometimes charge without warning. Most hunters like to work with dogs; these are usually ahead, and will draw the charge. It is a costly system for canines.

With Graham Netting, Bill Lunk, Harry Sturm, and some of my forestry students I have collected in the Unicois and eastward into North Carolina. I must confess that we never went too far from our cars, and that we spotted handy trees as we went through the woods. I never yet have seen a boar in the wild, and I presume the chances of my doing so are small. Nevertheless, they are in your mind when you are in that country; and I am quite well satisfied not to meet a 200-pounder when he is annoyed about something. So that visitors may see animals in the flesh, the Tellico Plains Ranger Station of the Forest Service sometimes keeps one or more in confinement. They are not handsome, and they look as mean as they are reputed to act.

Under wilderness conditions, native hoofed animals had two natural enemies, the timber wolf and the panther. They were effective in keeping populations of browsing and grazing animals under control. Both have largely disappeared in Appalachia. Whether either or both will ever reoccupy former ranges is debatable.

I remember Thompson Seton throwing back his head, giving a long and wonderfully realistic wolf howl, and then expressing the belief that as surely as white-tailed deer increased and spread in eastern North America just so surely would the gray wolves return to prey on them. This hasn't happened yet, but I would lay no bets that it won't. Wolves are highly adaptable animals; they have survived in such ancient and thickly populated lands as Spain and Portugal. Who will say that they cannot learn to live once more in our eastern mountains?

There are wolves in Canada just north of Appalachian ranges; perhaps a few may survive in the Shickshocks. Until early years of this century there were wolves in central Appalachia. One was killed in Randolph County, West Virginia, in 1905, and another in Tazewell County, Virginia, in 1910. Perhaps it is too much to expect that any animal could survive what man would surely do were these great dogs to reappear in the East. But stranger things have happened. Many species which fifty years ago seemed doomed have made surprising recoveries. So long as a population exists somewhere there is a chance for expansion of range.

The great cats might be mountain lions, cougars, or pumas in other parts of the land, but in Appalachia they were panthers to the educated and "painters" to less-lettered mountaineers. They too, in innumerable places, have left their name on the land and its features. A hunter who encountered a "painter" never forgot it, nor did he intend that anyone else should.

In a previous chapter I have mentioned my puzzlement as to what to do with Harvey Cromer's and others' recent panther accounts here in the East. In New Brunswick the animals have reappeared after a very long absence. There are reports from the Berkshires in Massachusetts that seem substantial. On the basis of tracks found (casts of them were preserved), mammalogists from the United States National Museum reported panthers in Pocahontas County, West Virginia, in 1936. A West Virginia state geologist and a highly reputable professor of botany at West Virginia University have told of seeing panthers in that state in recent years. Harvey Cromer's accounts have been described. During the summer of 1962, a party of forestry students working in the Monongahela National Forest saw a big brownish cat, its body solid-colored and its tail long. The cat was at close range, so everyone had a good view.

All this seems overwhelming. Yet why are none of these animals trapped, shot, or treed by hunters? Why have none of the state's wildlife biologists seen one, or any convincing evidence of one? I have talked to lion hunters on the North Rim of the Grand Canyon, and they say that these cats tree readily, once dogs are on their trail. The same portion of the Appalachians which is purported to shelter panthers is also black bear country. It is intensively hunted each season by experienced men with good dogs. Why do none of these packs ever chase and tree a panther? I have no answers to any of these questions. The whole matter is just another Appalachian mystery. One thing is sure, however. There are plenty of mountain hunters who believe that the big cats are there.

This leaves the black bear among eastern big game species. Bears have shown remarkable ability to survive under adverse conditions — they occur in virtually all the Appalachian states and provinces. Despite the pressure of hunting and the implacable enmity of sheep raisers, they still occupy the forests, pay visits to settled lands, and make occasional appearances in towns and cities. Black bears, it would appear, are biologically sound.

Wolves, panthers, and buffalos are only traditions to most mountain people; caribou and moose are limited in range, unknown save in the North; elk and wild boars are specialties of small regions; bears, however, are all but universal in the mountains, known to everyone, familiar to many, almost like old friends to a few. Unless a person has domesticated animals which he believes are being attacked, bears inspire no animosity. It is interesting to watch people as they see one. Most adults smile and most children laugh.

A perennial favorite among mountain stories has some variant on the theme of the hunters who thought they had a coon treed, only to discover that their supposed victim was a mad black bear. In such a situation "Granpappy" Comer, who was crippled up with "rheumatiz" but had begged to be carried along on the coon hunt, made a miraculous recovery and came into the cabin "ahead of the dogs." Riley Wilson, and after him John Handlan, used to tell this story. People came for miles to hear it.

Save for the hunters who go out looking for bears, few people are lucky enough to see one in the wild. An exception, of course, must be made for park bears — in the Smokies in the East, in Yellowstone and other parks in the West. Great Smokies bears are something of a nuisance to park personnel, but a major public attraction for all that. It is amazing to see crowds gather when a bear appears to feed on food scraps at the Newfound Gap parking area. Should the ursine visitors be a female with cubs, the excitement is even higher. Amateur photographers seek points of vantage, and if no one prevents them may form a circle around the feeding bears. This the animals will not tolerate. They must see an open escape route, so they break out, and if someone is in the way he may get thoroughly mauled. Such incidents give park naturalists high blood pressure.

In years that furnish a good crop of wild fruits and nuts (the sweet mountain blackberries are particularly important), bears keep mostly to park lands, where they sense that they are protected. Should the blackberries fail, bears are hungry and they visit the settlements outside park boundaries. Pigs, chickens, sheep, and even a calf or two will suffer from these forays; their owners are infuriated with the bears but take out their anger on park employees, who are easier to locate. Park rangers watch the annual blackberry prospects with considerable interest.

Among eastern mountaineers who no longer have to hunt to eat, the pursuit of big game is a spice to everyday activities, valued because it is so limited. Small game seasons are much more extended; the enthusiastic hunter finds his "bread-and-butter" sport provided by squirrels, grouse, and, in more open country, rabbits and quail. Out of small game season, he hunts woodchucks. There is a winter trapping season for those so inclined, and for hunters who are also fishermen, there is outdoor sport in the mountains throughout the year. The proportion of mountain people — men and women, boys and girls — who are ardent in these activities is amazing. Nearly everyone participates; it is evident that pioneer tradition is still a force in the land.

Hunters in my own state (and, I suspect, in hilly country that surrounds West Virginia) have made the gray squirrel the Number One game animal. According to conservation officers, more people buy licenses to hunt squirrels than for the quest of any other game. When American chestnuts still clothed the hills at all elevations, this was understandable. Chestnuts were abundant and never failing, the principal food of game. Now this food is gone, or practically so, but the tradition dies hard. Squirrel hunters in vast numbers take to the woods on opening day, and the man who "gets his limit" is respected and envied by his fellows. There is another lingering tradition in some sections — squirrels must be hunted with rifles, and the man who takes a shotgun into the woods for that purpose is low-caste.

Spruce grouse are found in Appalachia from New England northward, but they are elusive birds, seen, if at all, by hunters in wild areas. For the most part, they are too scarce to give the hunter much excitement. The more familiar ruffed grouse is a very different bird — one widespread in wooded sections, holding his own or even spreading; a fine, gamy bird and a challenge to the hunter. Again Appalachian people have developed their own terminology for a species. European ancestors of pioneer settlers may have sung about a partridge in a pear tree; southern mountaineers with an Anglo-Saxon tendency to leave out letters where possible took the word and made it "patridge." They will tolerate a visitor's calling the birds grouse, but if he puts the extra r in the old name they know it is affectation, and the user will draw suspicious looks.

I was with a field class from the University of Virginia's Mountain Lake Biological Station when we looked down the road and saw a mountain woman approaching. Before we met, a grouse ran across the road between us. We stopped to talk with her, knowing quite well that she was highly aware of wildlife around her despite her probable lack of schooling. One of the students started a conversation which went as follows.

"Mrs. B____, did you see that bird that went across the road?"

"That patridge — yes, I seen it."

"Do you ever eat them?"

"Yes."

"How do you cook them?"

"Bile 'em with cabbage."

Occupying a special niche between small and big game is the wild turkey, a bird that has maintained the respect, interest, and almost the affection of hunters from colonial days down to present times. Appalachia has a fine stock of these woodland fowl. Their feathers are tipped with rich bronze, which shows the pure eastern wild strain unmixed with domestic turkey blood. Few hunting trophies are more highly prized — the hunter who gets a gobbler or a well-fleshed hen feels that his season has been a success. The ability to call up turkeys in the wild is a valued woodcraft skill; hunters will practice for hours and years to perfect their technique. Some do their mimicry with their own vocal cords, others prefer a mechanical caller. One type of these mechanical devices uses a certain part of a raccoon's skeleton, the bone being drawn across a membrane which vibrates in a realistic manner. No matter about the method — the successful turkey-caller is an assured member of mountain aristocracy.

One of the biological treasures of high Allegheny ridges in West Virginia and Virginia is a small but persistent population of varying hares (snowshoe rabbits, in hunters' parlance). This forest mammal, whose summer pelage is rich brown and white and whose winter coat is immaculate white, reaches the southernmost fringe of its range in the Virginias, where it is the only mammal that regularly changes its garments to suit the seasons.

There are some peculiarities of this peripheral population. First of all, it is disjunct; between it and the next varying hares to the north there is a gap of perhaps two hundred miles. Furthermore, the gap has existed as long as we have records. There are no old hunters' accounts of these mammals in southern Pennsylvania.

Biologists both in North America and in Europe have given

a great deal of attention to the rhythmic fluctuations in populations of these hares. Every ten or eleven years, numbers of the animals reach a crest; then there follows a spectacular drop, at the bottom of which populations are only a tiny fraction of those in peak years. This is not the place to discuss possible causes of such cyclic population changes, nor to detail the disputes that have raged around certain phases of the cycles. The main pattern is fairly clear. In parts of the hare's range, at least, there is such a cyclic fluctuation, and it reaches its peaks every tenth or eleventh year.

Varying hares in the Virginias, even when they are at maximum numbers, never approach population densities achieved northward, nor do they show any signs of suffering from food shortages. They eat a great variety of plants, and none of these, except possibly a favorite — the mountain bush cranberry — ever appear overbrowsed. And, to repeat, this is a population widely removed from other animals of its kind.

Here is the crux of the matter. During some thirty-five years the hares in the West Virginia mountains have been under close study. They have been observed and counted by all methods commonly used to assess numbers of the species. And, despite their isolation, year by year they have followed the same population curves and been subject to the same fluctuations as have populations studied in New York, Maine, and eastern Canada. What forces, cosmic or terrestrial, are influencing these few hares in the Virginias so that they follow the patterns of their distant fellows? Here is a great mystery; the more I think of it, the more it intrigues me. We know so little, and there is so much to learn.

There are so many more animals too, game and nongame. The ancient pattern of beaver work may still be seen on the land; thousands of mountain habitations are built on silted-in beaver dams, the engineering of these mammals having provided a bit of level land for house and garden. The return of the beaver to Appalachian communities, even far southward, is a triumph of wildlife management.

Some of the mammals whose home is in the northern conifer-ous forest, and whose presence in southern Appalachia is due to that precious tongue of spruce-fir forest that reaches down the ranges, have been mentioned — the big gray flying squirrel, the water shrew, and the voles, for example, but there are many more, just as there are some which come up from warmer southern lands. Appalachia's mammals are wonderfully varied and of diverse origins.

I have dwelled on the game species, however, because they contribute most directly to a way of life in the mountains. If my emphasis on species that are hunted has left the impression that mountaineers appreciate game only as it stirs an itching in their trigger fingers, I am truly sorry. There is an esthetic side to wildlife, and mountain people sense it deeply. On Sundays and at other times when they cannot or do not care to hunt, they go to the woods to see and enjoy the living things around them.

21. Hill Culture
and Appalachian Crafts

A GOOD MANY PEOPLE who have moved to the cities to become urbanites, suburbanites, or exurbanites retain stirring
memories of a time when they were closer to the land. At least
they like to recall the crisp flavor of newly cracked hickorynuts
and black walnuts, the taste of corn cakes baked from fresh
water-ground meal, the scent of a balsam fir cut especially for
the family Christmas tree. They may romanticize the texture
and aroma of an apple variety that never appears in city stores,
or they may look back with nostalgia to an early spring sugaring-
off party in some center of maple production.

Such things are often recalled as experiences of the distant past never to be recovered, gone from the American scene. This is a pity. Appalachian people still savor wild fruits and nuts and still enrich their lives through rural experiences. Every good activity of less-complicated country living is in practice today. The major difference is that what was once done of necessity is now done for pleasure. Mountaineers no longer have to do these things, but they cherish them in their traditions.

During the years of the Great Depression, many things were rediscovered and re-evaluated. In an effort to find additional sources of income, more and more people looked to the traditional crafts of hill people, to those fringe-benefit products of the forest, to the graces of rural life when that life can be freed of drudgery and hopelessness. They revived useful but forgotten work for human hands, making use of neglected products of the land.

Workers in the agricultural extension services, rural sociologists, teachers in the settlement schools in remote communities, the Society of Friends, even some of the foundations — all had important parts in the re-evaluation program. Some inspired person attached a name to these activities, a name that persisted even when jobs became more plentiful and incomes better distributed. The term is "hill culture," meaningful and stirring to the imagination when used in the proper context. Hill culture embraces the traditional pioneer crafts — basketry, woodcarving, weaving, and pottery. It includes the finding and harvesting of wild fruits, nut kernels, and other foodstuffs. It takes in the collecting and marketing of Christmas greens, wild bittersweet, ginseng, evergreen ferns and galax leaves, partridge berries decoratively arranged in glass bowls, all the diverse things, in fact, which add variety and zest to the rural scene.

When I was a boy living on a hill farm we had no nearby source of Christmas trees. We could, I suppose, have bought one in the county town a dozen miles distant, but no one thought of such a possibility. So my father, and as soon as I was old enough I too, hiked through December woods to the ravines of Laurel Fork, three miles away, where there was a natural stand of hemlock trees. We stopped to ask permission of the owner, which was always freely given, and then selected and cut a heavy-branched young hemlock, shouldered it, and carried it home. Thus was the tradition preserved.

When we moved to a university campus in a small city this family experience seemed worth continuing. We couldn't cut a tree locally — there weren't too many places where this would have been possible, and I have a prejudice against indiscriminate cutting of trees on the lands of others. So we began to look farther afield. About sixty miles from our community is Canaan Valley, an area whose many attractions have already been introduced. Lying between two high Allegheny ridges, the valley is a natural refrigerator, its peaty soil and sphagnum swamps perfect places for the growth of northern balsam fir. Among American Christmas trees this is the *ne plus ultra*. Properly grown, it is more shapely, denser, more fragrant, and longer-lasting than any other conifer. We knew that if we could bring home a Canaan Valley balsam, we would have the best.

The next step was to establish friendly relations with some valley landowner. A sack of Christmas candy for the children was a good introductory note, and we made it clear that we expected to pay a fair price for our tree. We were cordially received.

While Fred was younger, we often took ax and saw and went into the swamp to bring out our own tree. In later years our host has found it to his advantage to have some balsams growing near his house, so we select the tree, he cuts and wraps it for us, and we bring it home amid fragrance and with satisfaction. Often before we leave, our host points out a fine young tree that will be ready next year and promises to save it for us. He always remembers, so we have a continuity to our program. We have done this thing for twenty years, and I expect that we shall continue it. To us it is an integral part of the Christmas season.

An excursion such as this in December is almost certain to hold more rewards than are provided by the main accomplishment. Sometimes the weather has been very cold, so every spruce twig and needle on Allegheny Backbone and Canaan Mountain will be coated in diamond-shining ice crystals — a palace for a mountain king. If highways are snow-covered and have been cindered, evening grosbeaks and pine siskins are likely to be feeding along the way, seeking the grit necessary for digestion. Blackwater Falls, its canyon a mass of ice, is nearby, and we often take the side drive.

Throughout the land today there are Christmas tree farms. Most trees used in our cities are local products. Some of these tree farms are large commercial enterprises but others are smaller, with time for the individual who may wish to select and cut his own tree. In some of the national forests (and they spread along the Appalachians from New Hampshire to Georgia) there are announced times when rangers will show the visitor to stands of young spruce or balsam, permitting him to cut a tree that might otherwise be removed in thinning operations.

There are many possibilities throughout the year for family holidays of this nature. For instance, travelers along the Blue Ridge Parkway in early June probably will see many family groups and individuals harvesting the wild strawberries which grow abundantly along some sections of the right-of-way. Most of these pickers are local inhabitants, but the visitor with some curiosity is pretty sure to stop for a sample of this crop. During any good season there will be hundreds or thousands of gallons of berries picked. The National Park Service makes no objection; the crop is there, it should be harvested, and it promotes goodwill on the part of the pickers.

Those who have not previously tasted freshly picked wild

strawberries are likely to face a pleasant surprise. Many wild berries are sweeter and more flavorsome than commercial varieties. Here is further proof that many fruits are best when they have just been harvested and have had a minimum of handling and transportation. There is pleasing variety in the taste, color, size, and texture of wild berries. One well-marked form has small fruits closely resembling the famous *fraises des bois* of France. They are wonderfully delicate and sweet; occasional berries have no trace of red coloration, the flesh being pure white and the small seeds yellow.

No matter what their size, it seems to me that strawberries have just so much flavor. The enlargement of fruit is due to additional water, and the result is a dilution of sugar content and flavor. I suspect that this impression holds some flaws, but the fact remains that nearly everyone who tastes them finds wild berries sweeter and better than commercial varieties.

It is perhaps unnecessary to say so, but wild berries in park and forest areas are not held and distributed under any cartel system. Family groups from towns and cities who might like to make a day of it and enjoy having something tangible from the day's fun are welcome. If public areas of this kind are too distant, there are wild strawberries, many of them unharvested, on rural lands everywhere in the East. Picking may be arranged for a small fee or "on the shares," and those wild-berry preserves taste just as good in town as in the country.

As with wild strawberries, so is it with mountain blackberries. Along forest roads, in old fields, or where fire has run over the land, blackberries flourish, in so many forms and varieties that Liberty Hyde Bailey ran out of friends for whom to name them. There is strong local tradition for harvesting this crop. Blackberries, preserved as canned fruit, jelly, jam, or even in wines and cordials, constituted a staple among rural foods, particularly before the days of frozen foods and accessible stores. Hill people are still uncomfortable if there are unharvested blackberries about. Ordinarily they will take the family and do something about it.

Blackberries of the lowlands and many of those of higher elevations are different plants in some particulars. Lowland species are generally thorny, the canes cruelly armed with sharp prickles. Penetrating the center of a lowland blackberry thicket can be costly to flesh and clothing. And if one is well within such a prickly stand and then encounters a colony of mad hornets, wasps, yellowjackets, or bumblebees (not an improbable situation), the results can be interesting. Upland blackberries are, generally speaking, much less formidable plants. Their spines are shorter and much weaker; they will scratch exposed flesh but will scarcely penetrate thick clothing. A picker who holds up his arms can pass through a thicket with little or no damage. The fruits borne on mountain canes are characteristically more slender, longer, somewhat sweeter, and less juicy than are lowland berries. They also have a spicy taste, which comes through in jam and preserves. Whether or not they are better is a matter of opinion, but they are assuredly different.

Along mountain roads, especially in some of the national forests, any August weekend will see dozens of parked cars and trucks and pickers busy at the harvest. There is time for visiting and good-natured banter, and everyone seems to be having a pleasant time. No member of the group is under pressure to fill a certain number of pails; the work and the workers are relaxed. If bears, foxes, turkeys, and small birds get some of the fruit, that is all right — there will be enough for everyone, and in two or three more days there will be a new picking.

For some reason, the harvesting of blueberries ("huckleberries" in the Southern Highlands) is more of a business and is more intensive. Wild strawberries and blackberries are seldom sold, bluberries frequently are. A busy family can pick more than they and their neighbors can use at any one time; therefore it is good sense to market some of them.

The "Huckleberry Plains" at the crest of West Virginia's high Alleghenies have been mentioned in previous chapters. During a period of six or seven weeks, from July to September, this region is visited by thousands of persons, all bent on filling their pails with the small blue fruits. Different species ripen at different times, so the season is a protracted one. There are many acres closely grown with blueberry bushes; they appeared after lumbering and fire, and their numbers and area are gradually contracting as the forest reasserts itself. In a few more years the blueberry hunters will have to look elsewhere. Meanwhile, they are using the resource to the full, always mindful of the fact that this is pretty good country for rattlesnakes. The timid stay out, but experienced pickers use a club to stir the bushes in front of them, listen for the warning buzz, and if it isn't forthcoming, go right ahead with their work.

The Appalachian country has native species of edible nuts which in abundance and variety make the area a productive one. Several of them contribute to the community wealth, and can qualify under the hill culture program. Others are more limited in use, being harvested principally for personal satisfaction and enjoyment. American chestnuts were once a source of revenue for farm families. The crop was seasonal, covering a few weeks in autumn. Chestnuts were eaten fresh, some were roasted and others boiled, and the surplus was sold or bartered — five cents a pound cash, six cents in trade. Chestnuts did not store well; they dried up quickly and became hard to chew. But the principal objection to keeping these nuts into the winter was their tendency to get wormy.

There are two long-snouted weevils that lay their eggs in chestnuts, both pestiferous insects. The eggs of one hatch before or just about the time chestnut burs are opening and the nuts dropping. Heavy-bodied larvae eat their way out of the shells at this time, leaving the nuts worthless to man but valuable to bobwhite quail, since these birds enjoy both insects and nuts.

When you gathered chestnuts you threw out the ones obviously wormy and hastened to sell your crop before further evil days came. Eggs of the second species hatch and become succulent larvae somewhat later, so that gatherers and local merchants who handle the nuts would race to dispose of them before their condition was too obvious.

My father once collected a measured bushel of chestnuts, all of which had unbroken shells when he assembled them. He hung them in burlap sacks above sheet metal that trapped the worms as they dropped out. In a period of five weeks he collected 3600 worms from his bushel of nuts. This may explain why the chestnut season in cities was a short one.

Chestnuts at best are rough food, good enough for ordinary occasions, but nothing special. The dessert nuts, a treat at any time, are black walnuts, hickorynuts, and, particularly northward, white walnuts, locally called "butternuts." No nuts anywhere are richer in flavor — none have more use around the home. Every hill family, in past days at least, liked to have a good supply in storage, with a view to cracking them around the fireplace on long winter evenings.

Black walnuts grow naturally throughout central and southern Appalachia, and they may be successfully planted somewhat farther north. The nuts aside, black walnut is a plant of many uses. It is high-crowned, and makes a large and attractive tree. It is, of course, one of America's valued cabinet woods. Even in poor surroundings, the tree has an innate capacity to enrich the soil through which its roots penetrate: the grassy court under a black walnut is often covered with Kentucky bluegrass in contrast to surrounding vegetation in which broomsedge, poverty grass, and blackberries predominate.

In size, flavor, richness, and crackability, black walnuts vary widely. Some trees bear nuts that are almost valueless to humans and best left to the squirrels that are willing to struggle with them. But when good nuts are borne on vigorous, disease-resistant trees, the nurserymen have a strain worth naming and perpetuating. A walnut variety named Thomas has been popular in the eastern United States for many years, and deservedly so. The Ohio variety is easier to crack, but the tree is not so vigorous in growth. There are many more, and there will be new and improved strains. With these horticultural refinements, the average landowner, or the person who goes afield to hull a mess of walnuts, will not be much concerned. Walnuts are walnuts, and if one stumbles onto a good tree, he is in luck.

Until sources of internal combustion or electric power came to the farm, walnut hulling and cracking were hand jobs. On a warm Saturday, the children in a family were equipped with small wooden clubs, one end rounded for easier holding, the other left square. Piles of walnuts, still in their sticky hulls, were assembled, the hullers went to work with their clubs, used their fingers as supplementary tools, and, by hard and staining but fragrant toil, finally produced a pile of nuts in the shell. These were destined to be spread out and dried for winter consumption. A school child who didn't have walnut stain on his fingers would have been an autumn curiosity.

Cracking was more exacting work. In their aproned laps women held a family flatiron, turned upside down. It took a hammer to break hard shells, and the skill lay in striking a nut so that it would produce the largest possible kernels. Metal darning needles were used to pry out recalcitrant pieces. Often enough, the children stood around begging for the largest and plumpest kernels, so, until bedtime, the job did not progress very fast.

All that is changed, of course; at least, nearly all. When the Model T reached the hills, many an owner discovered to his delight that walnuts could be spread on a rocky piece of road or on a shed floor, the car driven over them, and the hulling accomplished with saving in time and fingers. Some who were

more mechanical took power off a jacked-up wheel, devised
drums with abrasive sides, and hulled their walnuts in whole-
sale lots. Improved home crackers also reached the market, and
presently large and cleverly designed machines replaced the
housewife's skill. Many people still do hand cracking for fun
and a few for profit, but most modern homes don't even own a
flatiron.

Native hickories are of many kinds, some bearing small bitter
fruits eaten by squirrels, a few producing high-quality flavorsome kernels. We always knew where the shellbark trees were.
Pignuts, mockernuts, and bitternuts were lightly valued, except by squirrel hunters, but a shellbark was a precious piece of
property. If it happened to produce tasty kernels in thin shells,
then our cup of joy was full.

Shellbarks grow from Quebec southward, abundantly on
many Appalachian slopes. These trees produce a sweet sap, its
flavor different but as rich as that which flows from sugar maple
though in a much reduced measure. Run your moistened fingers
over the top of a freshly exposed hickory stump or the butt end
of a log, then taste the residue, and you will see what I mean.
Dried hickory faggots are sovereign for imparting flavor to
country hams.

Butternuts reach their best development somewhat farther
north than do black walnuts. Blended into maple sugar, they
add flavor to a confection that is popular in New England.
These nuts do not crack well, and it is difficult to extract kernels in large pieces. Storage is also a problem, since the abundant natural oils of the nuts become strong rather quickly.
Freshly harvested and cracked, however, no native nuts are so
flavorsome.

Hickorynuts of fine quality are machine-cracked in Appalachian communities today, the store that sells walnut kernels
often having these as well. For the city dweller who is possessed of a nostalgia the local nut shop doesn't relieve, now

may be the time to suggest sources of information as to native nuts and other country products. All the states have Land Grant Universities, and all have divisions of agricultural extension. In this connection, a few have specialists in hill culture, with benefits that the term implies.

These agricultural extension specialists do a great deal of traveling, and they are persons who appreciate the good things the land produces. They know, and they will inform you, where there are stores that will ship nut kernels, pure maple products, and similar delights. If there is a local source of water-ground cornmeal or buckwheat flour, they will know about it. They have information about producers of fine farm hams and bacon. They may be able to tell you where you can get fresh-cut Christmas greens. These, in other words, are useful people with very specialized knowledge. It is time, I think, that more city people learned of the services they can offer.

I used to suppose that special admiration for water-ground cornmeal was due to a nostalgia, a sort of mystique, with which many people surround traditional country products prepared in ancient ways. A country miller friend tells me I am wrong about this — that water-ground products are different, and, to his way of thinking, better. He explains that mill buhrs powered by steam or electricity turn rapidly on each other, and in the process heat the grains, changing somewhat the flavor of the germs within the seeds. Water-powered buhrs move much more slowly; consequently, there is no excessive heat, and the flour or meal emerges with the natural taste of the whole grain.

Many areas have their own hill culture specialties, not too important, perhaps, in the regional economy, but locally significant. One is mistletoe. Mistletoe is common in southern Appalachia, the green masses adorning twigs and smaller branches of a good many cove trees and being particularly in evidence after leaves have fallen from host plants. Waxy yellow-white fruits ripen in fall and persist into winter, some of them eaten by birds which distribute the seeds. There is a constant market for mistletoe; it can be turned into cash.

There is, however, a difficulty in harvesting it. Mistletoe usually grows near the tips of branches on mature trees. For some perverse reason it is seldom within easy reach of the ground. Climbing to it is out of the question — limbs will not support so much weight — so the mistletoe collector is thrown back on his own ingenuity. This sounds like fiction but happens to be fact. A traditional harvesting procedure is to shoot off the bunches, using a .22-caliber rifle to cut the supporting twigs of the host plant. Some of those who hunt gray squirrels with rifles keep their shooting eye in shape by collecting mistletoe.

A prime purpose of this book has been to depict the varied environments of Appalachia, and to tell something of the communities of living things that are at home there. I have tried to show the intimate relationships between people and their plant and animal associates. And throughout all the chapters I have borne in mind a definition which to me seems meaningful and satisfying: "Conservation is man's attempt to live in harmony with his surroundings."

It is in this context that I would call your closer attention to crafts and arts that have been molded to the Appalachian scene. These have made use of products at hand and they have followed patterns and used motifs suggested by things around them. They have met local needs, and a few of them have expressed the best things that mountain life may hold. They are as much a part of Appalachia as are the forests, ferns, heaths, or the wood warblers.

It was only yesterday that people from the Old World arrived to take up residence in the Appalachians; the complex of races we call American Indians had come long before. At times, in hill and valley, these races had settled down to become planters of maize, had made pottery for their cooking needs, and had developed textile skills. Effigy and burial mounds have preserved remnants of their culture, tributes to the energy and aspirations of Adena, Hopewell, and Forest peoples.

Europeans arrived in the Appalachian country at a low point in Indian civilization. Skills and crafts of earlier periods had largely disappeared; resident humanity lived a nomadic life, with few of the graces that develop among more sedentary peoples. The white men found no spinning and weaving, little pottery, and only a few centers of basketmaking. One can only think with envy of the rich culture the Spanish explorers encountered in the Southwest.

Perhaps they preserved earlier skills, or perhaps they learned from white settlers. In any event, there are two major centers of Indian basketry in the Appalachians today. Curiously, they are near the extremities of Appalachia, one in the Shickshock foothills on the Gaspé and the other in the Great Smokies of North Carolina. There is also a smaller one in Maine where Indians produce some baskets.

Micmac Indians dwell along Chaleur Bay on the south shore of the Gaspé Peninsula. They are a flourishing tribe — as numerous, perhaps, as they ever were. The waters of their land are rich in fish life, so the Micmacs have become users of this resource. To carry their catches they have developed baskets — useful, strong, and very handsome. Typically the wood in these baskets is black ash, a common tree in swampy areas of Shickshock foothills. To prepare this wood for separation of basket splints, blocks are soaked in freshwater for two weeks or so, and in this condition the growth layers may be parted. In earlier times, women and girls of the tribe used their teeth in the process, so consistently in some cases that teeth were worn to the gums. A less taxing method in use today involves pounding ash logs until the splints can be separated.

Micmac baskets are exceptionally strong and well made. Handles are attached with a weave that leaves a diamond pattern, practically a trademark of these workers. No color is applied on baskets the Indians themselves use, but many are now made for the tourist trade, and some of these are dyed in pleasing shades.

Cherokee Indians on their Qualla Reservation in North Carolina have become major producers of handicraft articles, some of them revivals of ancient skills, others learned in their modern schools. On their own lands, or nearby, they find an abundance of basketry materials, and they manufacture fine baskets of many types, sizes, and shapes. Native honeysuckle vines are easy to weave, and make loose, light baskets. Those made from white oak splints are in the southern Appalachian tradition and closely resemble the work of white craftsmen. The most characteristic, and most varied, Cherokee baskets are woven from splints of the tough bark of small cane, a common native grass.

European settlers who came to the Atlantic seaboard of America brought with them ancient traditions and skills in basketry. They found the native plants of the New World similar to those with which they were accustomed to work, so basketry became an early endeavor, and it has persisted. Allen Eaton, in his volumes on native handicrafts, suggests that the Appalachians may hold the richest and most varied basketry handicraft in the world today.

It must have been a natural step from the weaving of baskets to the weaving of cloth. Long before Europeans came, American Indians were growing cotton, spinning it into thread by some means, and using upright looms, perhaps much like those found among Navahos and Hopis today. On these they were producing cotton fabrics. As we have seen, mound builders in the Allegheny Plateau had such cloth.

Like many other crafts, weaving was practically a lost art among eastern Indians when white settlers arrived. Some tribes, notably the Cherokees, have relearned it, but most Appalachian home weaving is a European skill, built on European tradition but modified by the different conditions of the New World. It has progressed from necessity to avocation, from craft to art. We now have Appalachian weavers — many of them — working in wools, linen, and cotton and producing everything from bedspreads to scarves and table linens.

Weaving among the Cherokees is a recent but flourishing activity. These Indians have good teachers, and they mark their products with the maker's name. They have selected an individualistic design for their fabrics, a pattern of curved lines which they call "The Road to Soco." When asked the meaning of this, workers probably will reply, "If you had ever been over the old road to Soco, you would know the reason for the name." Visitors to Soco will soon have an easier route: the Blue Ridge Parkway extension from Asheville to the Great Smokies passes through Soco Gap.

Wrought iron is another Cherokee craft, of recent development but flourishing. In this they are following the lead of white settlers in Appalachia, who early discovered the low-grade iron ores there and built crude but effective stone furnaces for the recovery of the metal. There have been many workers in iron and other metals — at Berea College, at Burnsville, North Carolina, at Penland, and at Arthurdale, West Virginia. In this field, Lees-McCrae College at Banner Elk, North Carolina, is outstanding. Work here began under the direction of Daniel Boone, descendant of a famous ancestor, and students of the college have developed it into an art. There are, of course, many metalworkers who make crafted articles in New England and Pennsylvania. Many of these centers began as blacksmith shops where the owner had extra skill and imagination.

Archeologists are not in agreement as to which developed first — basketry or pottery. American Indians were using native clays, hand-shaping them into fine shapes and firing their utensils many centuries before white settlers reached these shores. There are shards to be found at virtually every ancient town site which has been investigated. Pottery made by eastern Indians was usually undecorated, in contrast to the imaginative coloring and design that distinguished pottery made by some tribes in the Southwest. Pottery in the Appalachians is therefore an ancient craft, but little was being shaped (and that was of poor quality) when European settlers arrived. The ceramic arts as we have them today were developed along Old World lines and traditions. No Indian tribe used the potter's wheel; its use by white artisans is practically universal.

The making and use of stoneware containers came early to America — preservation of meats, milk, and other products demanded such vessels. Here and there were finer clays, brighter and smoother glaze materials, and the workers with imagination to use them. Pottery making became ceramic art in such hands. Beautiful ceramics have been and are being made throughout the Appalachians, with significant centers in New England, West Virginia, Kentucky, North Carolina, and Tennessee. Most are shaped from local clays, although certain artists work in materials not found in Appalachia.

The traveler interested in ceramics is more apt to become aware of local products in areas where craft centers and outlets are maintained. The League of New Hampshire Arts and Crafts, with ten centers, is outstanding. In the southern Appalachians, the Southern Highlands Handicraft Guild has many productive members and well-placed outlets to market their products, among which fine pottery is to be found. In display of wares the Southern Highlands rival the pueblo country of the Southwest.

A sharp pocketknife is an essential tool for mountain people, and when imagination and skill are combined surprisingly artistic results may be obtained by whittling. The whittler does all his work with a knife; his strokes are visible and his products are usually left unfinished. When he uses more elaborate cutting tools he becomes a carver. There are artisans of both kinds in the Appalachians. Perhaps because their mountain lands make fewer demands on their time, the people of the Southern Highlands have developed as notable whittlers. Wood for every purpose is abundant, and the universal pocketknife is so handy a tool for fashioning articles to make life easier or more attractive. Early houses were made of wood, almost without hardware; furniture, often rough but usually substantial, was wooden; so were table utensils, milk pails, churns, hand-fashioned rifle-stocks, even the children's toys.

Since the southern Blue Ridge is composed of igneous rock it holds gemstones, which are mostly of the semiprecious varieties. Occasionally a few more valuable gemstones are found. Lapidaries in several North Carolina communities collect or buy these heat-created crystals, polish them, and sell them, usually unset.

There are, of course, many other crafts and crafted objects in the long sweep of the Appalachians. My intent has been to emphasize those that are indigenous to the land, make use of native materials, or reproduce native objects. Such crafts, with the people who produce them, are, I think, an important part of Appalachia, a facet of the region which must not be overlooked. To develop this theme a little further: there are mountain craftsmen and there are craftsmen in the mountains. It is with the first that I have been primarily concerned. In recent years a number of skilled and sophisticated artists in the craft field have come to the mountains, found living there congenial, and have opened studios. They have added, and will add, breadth to the region's handicrafts, and their new skills and ideas will undoubtedly stimulate craft workers who are native to the scene. In time they may grow closer to the land, its products, and its people. As they do this, they will become mountaineers, true sons and daughters of Appalachia.

22. A Few Words More

THE HILLS are our symbol of eternity. There they stand, the
evidence of things seen, as nearly everlasting and unchangeable
as anything man may know. One who has dwelled within them
senses that they are beyond the horizon, even when he is in the
level lands. For this reassurance, all hill people will be duly
thankful. Unless he is witness to man's contrived destruction,
it is not given to any one person to see that the hills are mutable.
Natural processes are too slow — one lifetime cannot note or
follow them. The time scale of our human experience gives

us no basis for understanding geologic ages. They are as incomprehensible as are astronomic distances.

Cambrian sediments which make up some of Appalachia's ridges hold the fossil evidence of living things that had their little day 500 million years ago. In the sweep of time these sediments became rock and were elevated by forces of the Appalachian Revolution. Creatures of the water became fossils of the land, set in place to remain above the sea throughout all the ages since the mountains were folded. Perhaps we can tell the story in human terms. Most of us have some familiarity with a football gridiron, where 300 feet separate the two goal lines. To this let us add 200 feet, and in our expanse we shall let each of the 500 feet represent a million years. This is the span of life exposed in parts of the Ridge and Valley Province. It becomes significant as we place human experience within the framework. The written history of mankind will be encompassed by the last tenth of an inch in the five-hundredth foot, and there will still be room to spare. In such perspective, it is no wonder that the hills appear eternal.

And yet, of course, they are not. Neither topography nor life can be static. The Appalachians have been elevated, then baseleveled, then raised again. How many times this has occurred only the geologists are qualified to guess. One thing is certain — the horizon of today will differ from that of the last and the next geologic epoch. So too with living things. Only yesterday there were woolly mammoths and giant mastodons roaming Appalachian hills. The Ice Age brought muskoxen to West Virginia, and their skeletal remains can yet be found. Long before were the fernlike forests that became coal. There must also have been giant reptiles to feed on this opulent vegetation. Separate the layers of shale in still older rocks and there are the fossils of sea creatures. At the top of some of Appalachia's highest peaks these testimonials to change abound. Life of water and life of land are joined; so too are organic and inorganic matter.

For those with skill to read, the rocks tell the story of the past, not yet fully revealed but unfolding as understanding eyes scan the pages.

Few portions of the earth compare with Appalachia in revelation of long and continuous geologic and biologic records. Here has been a master experiment station — with space and time for trial and error — for the cosmic sifting of forms that have their day and pass and for those that are to endure until man may glimpse them. The shortness of man's domicile in the Appalachians and the changes he has brought about in this brief span are both astounding. In two centuries ax and plow have accounted for erosion which nature might well have spread throughout millennia. In the worst of these alterations, mountains have been denuded and their underlying strata disturbed. Other transformations have been less destructive, although it is indisputable that man modifies what he touches.

But Appalachia is a huge land, broad enough to hold and maintain areas that have been little or not at all changed. Everywhere — on the cleared and the tilled slopes, in burned areas, even in the desolation of strip mining — are the evidences of healing. Vegetation in this land of abundant rainfall quickly renews itself, and sets in motion the process of soil rebuilding. Furthermore, much of man's work has been wisely done. There are the parks and forests, the planted stands of trees, the roads, trails, and campsites which invite the presence of those who can enjoy and preserve unspoiled country. Appalachia has many friends, and gains new ones year by year. These will hold the land in trust, making certain that scenic, scientific, and human values have a future.

Alpine gardens still bring the subarctic to northern mountain summits. Spruces and firs, reminiscent of Canada, stretch their range to include North Carolina and Tennessee. White stars of cinquefoil adorn Appalachian balds, and somehow the snow buntings find these remote openings when winter brings tundra weather southward.

Appalachia is a birthplace of rivers, some flowing down to the Atlantic Coastal Plain, others passing through American midlands on their course to the Gulf of Mexico. Borne on the outflowing waters are seeds of plants, those of ancient lineage having been sheltered on the summits when inundations from the sea or advancing glacial ice made islands of their sanctuaries. River valleys are natural travel routes, most of the movement downward, but occasionally allowing passage of lowland species to higher country.

Men, too, have followed the streams from mountain heights to coastal plain and prairie. Some have found their new homes congenial; others have remained transplanted mountaineers, strangers in a strange land. As with the plants, there is a reverse human movement; people from the lowlands have discovered highland values in which they wish to share. Most who make such choices bring the vitality of new ideas and new appreciations to the ancient setting of the hills.

In some manner, a mountain country places its mark on those who dwell within its shadows. Scots carry with them a Highland pride of birth and place, even though they may wander thousands of miles from heather-covered moors. Natives of Switzerland see the Alps, although these peaks are far below the horizon. And thus it is with those nurtured in Appalachia — they leave, but they look back, remembering pleasant things. The land has claimed them, and its ties will not be severed.

Index

Index

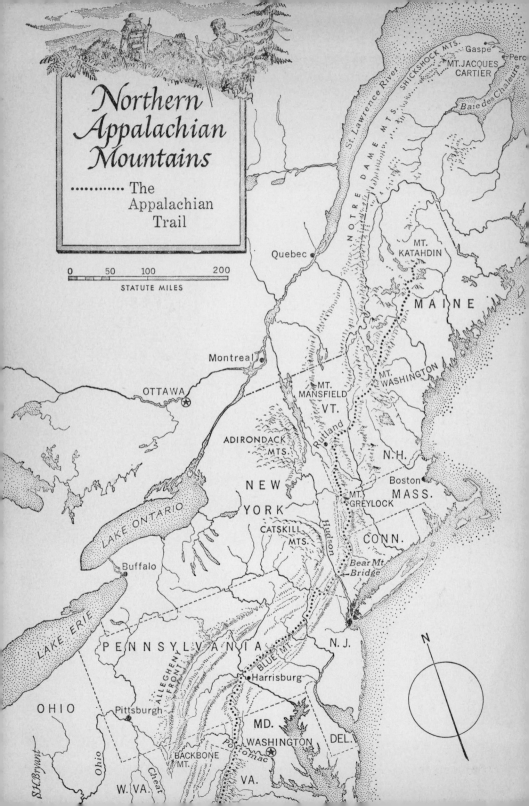

Northern Appalachian Mountains

········· The Appalachian Trail

0   50   100   200
STATUTE MILES

Gaspe
Perce
MT. JACQUES CARTIER
Baie des Chaleurs
SHICKSHOCK MTS.
St. Lawrence River
NOTRE DAME MTS.
Quebec
MT. KATAHDIN
MAINE
Montreal
OTTAWA
MT. MANSFIELD
VT.
MT. WASHINGTON
Rutland
N.H.
ADIRONDACK MTS.
NEW YORK
Boston
MT. GREYLOCK
MASS.
CATSKILL MTS.
Hudson
CONN.
LAKE ONTARIO
Buffalo
Bear Mt. Bridge
LAKE ERIE
PENNSYLVANIA
BLUE MT.
N.J.
ALLEGHENY FRONT
Harrisburg
OHIO
Pittsburgh
MD.
WASHINGTON
DEL.
Ohio
Cheat
BACKBONE MT.
Potomac
W. VA.
VA.
N

S.H.Bryant